Discursive
LEADERSHIP

To the memory of Albert and Agnes Theus

Discursive
LEADERSHIP
In Conversation With Leadership Psychology

Gail T. Fairhurst
University of Cincinnati

SAGE Publications
Los Angeles • London • New Delhi • Singapore

For information:

Sage Publications, Inc.
2455 Teller Road
Thousand Oaks, California 91320
E-mail: order@sagepub.com

Sage Publications Ltd.
1 Oliver's Yard
55 City Road
London EC1Y 1SP
United Kingdom

Sage Publications India Pvt. Ltd.
B-42, Panchsheel Enclave
Post Box 4109
New Delhi 110 017 India

Printed in the United States of America

Library of Congress Cataloging-in-Publication Data

Fairhurst, Gail Theus
Discursive leadership : in conversation with leadership psychology / Gail Fairhurst.
    p. cm.
Includes bibliographical references and index.
ISBN-13: 978-1-4129-0424-7 (cloth)
ISBN-13: 978-1-4129-0425-4 (pbk.)
    1. Leadership. I. Title.

HM1261.F35 2007
303.3′4—dc22   2006027189

This book is printed on acid-free paper.

07   08   09   10   10   9   8   7   6   5   4   3   2   1

Acquisitions Editor:	Todd R. Armstrong
Editorial Assistant:	Sarah K. Quesenberry
Production Editor:	Libby Larson
Copy Editor:	Teresa Herlinger
Typesetter:	C&M Digitals (P) Ltd.
Proofreader:	Word Wise Webb
Indexer:	Molly Hall
Cover Designer:	Bryan Fishman

Contents

Preface   vii

Chapter 1. Two Traditions   1
    Defining Leadership   4
    Defining Discourse   6
    The Case for Discursive Leadership   8
    The Path Forward   17

Chapter 2. Sequence and Temporal Form   23
    Act, Interact, Double Interact   25
    Turn Taking, Adjacency Pairs   29
    Narrative Schemas, Episodes   32
    Scripts   38
    Script Formulations   41
    A Backward Glance—Final Thoughts   44

Chapter 3. Membership Categorization   49
    Membership Categorization Defined   50
    Categories and Organizational Coordination   52
    Categories and Organizational Role/Identity   54
    Categories, Sensemaking, and Meaning Management   56
    Categories and Social Structuring   62
    Categories in Task Structuring   66
    A Backward Glance—Final Thoughts   71

Chapter 4. Disciplinary Power   75
    A Primer on Foucault   76
    Discipline and Surveillance in
        Performance Management Technologies   83
    Performance Management Governmentality   90
    A Backward Glance—Final Thoughts   92

Chapter 5. Self-Identities, Interpretative Repertoires   97
>The 'Self' in Leadership Psychology and Discursive Leadership   97
>Interpretative Repertoires and Subject Positioning   109
>A Backward Glance—Final Thoughts   114

Chapter 6. Narrative Logics   119
>Leader–Member Exchange Theory   119
>The Narrative Basis of LMX   121
>A Backward Glance—Final Thoughts   137

Chapter 7. Material Mediations   141
>Materialist Critiques of Discourse Analysis   143
>Actor-Network Theory   144
>Rudy Giuliani and September 11, 2001   150
>A Backward Glance—Final Thoughts   162

Chapter 8. Praxis and More Conversation   167
>Discursive Leadership and Praxis   167
>Discursive Leadership and Leadership Psychology   174
>Leadership Psychologists   175
>Discursive Scholars   183
>Conclusion   189

Appendixes   191
>Appendix A1: Conversation Analysis   191
>Appendix A2: Interaction Analysis   193
>Appendix A3: Speech Act Schematics   194
>Appendix A4: Discursive Psychology   195
>Appendix A5: Foucauldian Analyses   196
>Appendix A6: Critical Discourse Analysis   197
>Appendix A7: Narrative Analyses   198
>Appendix B: Transcript of Police Rescue   199

References   203

Index   229

About the Author   243

Preface

This much I know about leadership: *It is a topic for the ages.* Discussions of leadership date back to Plato and the early Greeks, but also Chinese and Egyptian societies. It was a topic during the Renaissance with Machiavelli's *The Prince,* which survives as a reference today. Proceeding onward through the turn of the twentieth century, it emerged in 'great man' theories, marking the start of serious scholarship that continues to the present. Such scholarship now joins a business press eager to dispense sage advice to hungry leaders. What is it about leadership that sustains this kind of interest? Bass (1981) asserted that leadership is a universal human phenomenon, the templates for which are supplied by parenthood. If true, it should be no surprise that we find leadership in a host of society's collectives—business and governmental organizations to be sure, but also remote African villages, sports teams, and Girl Scout troops.

Few agree on a definition. Leadership scholars are famous for their inability to agree on a definition of leadership, leading some analysts to remark that there are as many definitions as there are leadership scholars (Bass, 1981; Fiedler, 1971; Rost, 1991). However, there are good reasons for this inconsistency. Leadership occurs amidst a tremendous amount of situational variability, and it has that elusive 'eye of the beholder' quality. Some will make sense of complex conditions by arriving at an attribution of leadership that others would vehemently contest (think George W. Bush, the 43rd president of the United States, and his handling of the war in Iraq). Yet, Meindl (1995) suggests that our attributions are romanticized in this regard because too often we see leadership as *the* cause of organizational success or failure when a more complex explanation is in order. Even so, one person's leadership is another's tyranny or ineptitude.

Organizational leadership was once the sole province of men. While the concept of leadership has been around for some time, the serious study of leadership is about 100 years old. As mentioned, it began with the turn of the twentieth century 'great man' school of thought, which led social scientists to look for those characteristics and traits (such as intelligence, dominance, height, and so forth) that differentiated leaders from non-leaders. Organizational leadership was considered the sole province of men until women began to enter the workforce in large numbers in the 1970s in other than low power positions (Kanter, 1977). Since then, gender differences in leadership have ranked among the hot topics in both the academic and business press as well as in countless discussions at watercoolers and boardrooms in organizations worldwide (Buzzanell, 2000; Collinson, 1988; Kanter, 1977; Reardon, 1995).

Leadership psychologists have supplied important foundational work in leadership studies.[1] Their early trait theories gave way to the study of leader behavior styles, famously captured in the Ohio State leadership studies, which examined initiating structure and consideration as two dimensions of leader behavior (Stogdill & Coons, 1957). Contingency theories followed, such as Fiedler's (1971) emphasizing leader–member relations, task structure, and a leader's position power as determinants of the type of leader effectiveness. Leader–member exchange (LMX) theory subsequently adopted an exclusive relational focus, where high versus low quality leader–member relationships differed in terms of the resources exchanged and outcomes delivered (Dansereau, Graen, & Haga, 1975; Graen & Scandura, 1987). At about the same time, neo-charismatic leadership theories arrived on the scene, emphasizing leaders' charisma, vision, and the ability to inspire followers well beyond the terms of their employment contract (Bass, 1985; Conger, 1989; Shamir, House, & Arthur, 1993). Also, the information-processing school of leadership began to study implicit leadership theories and the role of cognition in the enactment and attribution of leadership behavior (Hanges, Lord, & Dickson, 2000; Lord & Maher, 1991). LMX, neo-charisma, and implicit leadership theories continue to this day, as authentic leadership (Gardner, Avolio, Luthans, May, & Walumbwa, 2005), spiritual leadership (Reave, 2005), and leadership in team-based organizations (Day, Gronn, & Salas, 2006) assume the newcomer roles.

As good scientists, leadership psychologists have challenged their own theories, methods, and findings over time (House & Aditya, 1997; Lowe & Gardner, 2000). Interestingly, much of the criticism points to the socially constructed nature of leadership (Calder, 1977; Lord & Brown, 2004; Meindl, 1995), a perspective that, if taken seriously, has the potential to both challenge and complement leadership psychology at a foundational level.

I do not mean to imply that psychologists are uninterested or unwilling to pursue a socially constructed view of leadership, nor do I wish to diminish their contributions to this topic in any way. I only wish to observe that their concerns for the individual and psychological rather consistently outweigh their concerns for the social and cultural. I argue that both sets of concerns must be entertained in equal strengths in order to understand a socially constructed world. Thankfully, a body of theory and research directly applicable to the social, linguistic, and cultural aspects of leadership has been accumulating. I call this work *discursive leadership* because of its focus on organizational discourse, both as language use in social interaction and the view of Discourse made popular by Michel Foucault. In his view, Discourse is a system of thought and a way of talking about a subject that together supplies the necessary linguistic resources for communicating actors. Foucault's work is typical of the burgeoning organizational discourse literature that reflects a body of constructionist theories not specifically about leadership per se, but with great potential to illuminate it in ways that we have not yet seen. That potential motivates the writing of this book, which is less a literature review and more of an exploration of key discourse concepts and what they could mean for leadership. The voluminous research from leadership psychology serves as a useful point of contrast, springboard, and benchmark along the way.

There is still much to learn about leadership, especially if we surrender to its protean tendencies. As Chapter 1 makes clear, discursive leadership and leadership psychology differ on both ontological and epistemological grounds. In a nutshell, leadership psychology has been on a quest to understand the essence of leadership, whether it be found in the individual leader, the situation, or some combination thereof (Grint, 2000). By contrast, discursive leadership rejects essences because leadership is an attribution and, very likely, a contested one at that. Discourse scholars like me depart from leadership psychologists' adherence to traditional science assumptions about realist conceptions of truth and representationalist views of knowledge. Influenced by the linguistic turn in philosophy, we ask instead that both perspectives be seen as alternative ways of knowing, talking about, and justifying leadership (Deetz, 1996; Rorty, 1982).

By recognizing discursive leadership from this vantage, we have a means by which to embrace what leadership psychologists might see as the elusive, unwieldy, mutable, and maddening error variance in leadership—in short, its protean tendencies. I am certainly not claiming that discursive leadership has all of the answers to leadership's mysteries, but neither do I believe that discursive leadership is just one more approach to leadership. It represents instead a foundation for many new lines of research into leadership with potentially important implications for helping practicing leaders and others better understand how they coconstruct reality. It also represents an opportunity for new dialogue with leadership psychologists—a dialogue that I hope continues long after this book.

There are several leadership psychologists who have been gracious enough to help me begin this dialogue in Chapter 8, the book's final chapter. They include Donna Chrobot-Mason, Steve Green, Jerry Hunt, Robert Liden, and Boas Shamir. Three discursive scholars, Kevin Barge, François Cooren, and Linda Putnam, also joined in. To all of them I am grateful for the effort that they put forth under a very tight deadline. I hope that the reader finds their comments as illuminating as I did.

Some of the reviewers for this book suggested different ways in which it might be read that I found quite useful. For example, if one prefers to start out with the details supplied through language and interaction (what I call little 'd' discourse), the chapters should be read in chronological order. However, others may prefer to start with the generalities associated with a Foucauldian view of Discourse (big 'D' Discourse) as a system of thought and way of talking about a subject. In that case, I would recommend reading Chapters 4 and 5 before Chapters 2 and 3. As the book reviewers also noted, the potential readers for this book will have varying levels of familiarity with the different forms of discourse analysis. Thus, I have included a set of appendixes organized by type of discourse analysis. They are designed for quick and easy reference. Finally, except for interview discourse, the transcribed interaction in this text follows the conventions of conversation analysis (see Appendix A1). For those who do not appreciate the level of detail this provides, readers may simply skim over the detailed markings.

Those who have read all or parts of my book along the way include Carey Adams, Kevin Barge, Mary Helen Brown, Mary Ann Danielson, Jennifer Butler Ellis, David Hoffman, Fred Jablin, Robert Liden, Patricia Parker, Paaige Turner, Patricia Witherspoon, and Ted Zorn. Thank you for the time and effort that you put into reviewing my work. I especially want to thank those scholars who gave me direct feedback. They include Kevin Barge, Suzanne Boys, Lisa Fisher, Angela Garcia, Donna Chrobot-Mason, François Cooren, Rich Kiley, Linda Putnam, Edna Rogers, Marcia Schoeni, Mathew Sheep, James Taylor, and Heather Zoller. You have shaped my thinking in ways too numerous to mention.

Thanks also to Jan Svennevig and Maria Isaksson of the Norwegian School of Management BI and organizers of the 2006 Association for Business Communication European Conference in Oslo, Norway; Pam Shockley, organizer of the 2005 Aspen Conference on Organizational Communication; and Angela Garcia, director of the Workplace Studies Group at the University of Cincinnati for providing forums for the presentation and discussion of my work. Thanks also to my department head, Teresa Sabourin, for her continued support and friendship; my graduate students, Justin Combs, Zhou Fan, Stephanie Hamlett, Elizabeth Prebles, Kim Richardson, and Brian Singson for their diligent work on my behalf; and to Sadie Oliver and Priscilla Ball for all of their help and office support.

Thank you to Verne, Katie, Tom, and Kelsey, each of whom has a wonderful way of helping me to maintain perspective throughout this effort. I feel blessed every day for their love and support. To Todd Armstrong and Sarah Quesenberry at Sage, thank you for your patience and expert guidance. To Teresa Herlinger and Libby Larson, I greatly appreciated the care that you showed toward my manuscript. Finally, I have been blessed with so many wonderful colleagues, including the late Fred Jablin whose work as a leadership and communication scholar remains forever with me as a standard of excellence.

NOTE

1. Scholars from political communication (Hart, 1984, 1987; Trent, 1978; Trent & Friedenberg, 2004), political science (Burns, 1978), educational administration (Gronn, 1982, 1983), and organizational development (Kets de Vries, 1990a, 1991, 2005) among others have also made important contributions to leadership study. However, the broadest comparison appears between leadership psychology and discursive leadership. Where relevant, work from these related fields is introduced into individual chapters.

1

Two Traditions

Several years ago, Henry Mintzberg (1970, 1973, 1975) was at the center of a debate in leadership studies when he turned the spotlight on what leaders actually do and the nature of managerial work itself. Although he was certainly not the first to do this type of research,[1] his work attracted a great deal of attention because he challenged the conventional wisdom that the manager's job was to plan, organize, coordinate, and control. First introduced by French industrialist Henry Fayol in 1916, these functions became almost passé as a result of Mintzberg's behavioral observations of five chief executives (Hunt, 1991). Mintzberg (1975) argued compellingly that Fayol's functions were just folklore because managerial work is in reality too dynamic, fragmented, and unsystematic. Managers work frenetically in short bursts of time as they react to job demands and constant interruptions. From this research, Mintzberg created his well-known taxonomy of managerial roles.[2]

Applauded by many for his realism, Mintzberg certainly had his critics. Carroll and Gillen (1987) defended the classical functions and argued that Fayol's ideas would have been supported had Mintzberg asked for the reasons for the managers' observable behavior. Further, they argued that Mintzberg's observation approach was fundamentally flawed because "Managerial work is *really mental work* and the observable behaviors such as talking, reading, and writing serve as inputs and outputs to neuropsychological activities" (p. 43, emphasis added). Thus, observable behavior is not a reliable measure of what managers actually do.

On the surface, this looked like a debate over whether to characterize what managers do as abstract functions or specific behaviors. Interestingly, Carroll and Gillen (1987) found a middle ground on this issue by urging researchers to consider the unsystematic ways in which management's classic functions may be achieved—for example, how planning, organizing, coordinating, or controlling occurs through unplanned, informal, and brief conversations. However, a deeper conflict was apparent in Carroll and Gillen's apparent need to make "mental work" or "neuropsychological activities" the central and defining feature of managerial work. Observable behavior like talking, writing, and reading was then downgraded to simple inputs and outputs. Why couldn't mental work and social processes like talking both be of equal import?

One reason may have been that Mintzberg advocated a radical approach to research that was everything mainstream leadership research was not at the time. Mintzberg (1982) urged his colleagues to get rid of their constructs before they collected data, throw away their questionnaires and 7-point scales, stop pretending the world is divided into dependent and independent variables, and do away with "artificial rigor, detached rigor, rigor not for insight, but for its own sake" (p. 254). Although he allowed that he may have been overstating his recommendations a bit, he felt strongly that leadership needed to be studied simply, directly, and imaginatively, and that traditional empiricist approaches were not getting the job done. Nevertheless, his were fighting words, words that can begin paradigm wars, although Mintzberg (1982) seemed only to be calling for a methodological overhaul. However, to take Mintzberg seriously, one had to acknowledge that behavior was worthy of study in its own right. His argument had implications *both* in terms of what leadership scholars studied and how they studied it.[3]

Fast forward, if you will, to twenty-first century leadership study. At first blush, little seems to have changed—especially in the United States where a psychological lens and traditional empiricist methods still dominate (Alvesson & Sveningsson, 2003b; Conger, 1998; Knights & Willmott, 1992). However, it would be a clear mistake to suggest that the legions of leadership scholars with psychology backgrounds are unconcerned with behavior. True, their first concern is with its cognitive or social-cognitive origins and the perceptions they generate; the weight given to the mental over the behavioral in the Carroll and Gillen quote is testimony to this. However, as leaders increasingly get depicted as 'managers of meaning' (Pondy, 1978; Shotter & Cunliffe, 2003; Smircich & Morgan, 1982), the style, content, and delivery of their message or 'visions' have been the subject of scrutiny in ways that Mintzberg, circa 1970s, might have welcomed (Emrich, Brower, Feldman, & Garland, 2001; Fiol, Harris, & House, 1999; Shamir, Arthur, & House, 1994). In addition, work by Komaki (1998) and Gioia and Sims (1986) has examined the impact of leader verbal behavior on employee performance, narrative has gained a foothold in leadership studies (Conger, 1991; Gardner & Avolio, 1998; Shamir & Eilam, 2005), and qualitative leadership research in general continues to be on the rise (Alvesson & Sveningsson, 2003b; Bryman, 2004).

However, another force was afoot to answer Mintzberg's call. Spurred on by the 1960s and 1970s critiques of traditional scientific canons such as realist conceptions of truth and representational theories of knowledge, the linguistic turn in philosophy affected scholars in such disciplines as communication, sociology, psychology, and European schools of management (Alvesson & Kärreman, 2000a; Bochner, 1985; Deetz, 1992).[4] Skirmishes waged and won in the back alleys of journal publication and other scholarly venues have been producing a body of scholarship relevant to leadership that is clearly outside mainstream *leadership psychology*. Heavily oriented toward discourse and communication, I have termed this scholarship *discursive leadership*. Grint's (1997, 2000) work on the paradoxes of leadership is a good example. Through in-depth case history analyses of several political and organizational leaders, he finds that leadership is more inventive than analytic. The mainstream leadership literature often suggests the opposite because its primary lens is individual and cognitive. It is less focused on the contested nature of leadership interaction, thus it may undervalue those creative aspects that explain why leadership is more art than science. Grint also finds that reason and rationality do not carry the day as much as persuasion does, and the study of leadership is too often rooted in irony rather than truth. He sees this in the collective iden-tities upon which much leadership rests, which are not 'reflected' in empiricist data as much as they are 'forged' amidst challenge and conflict. Outcomes are far less predictable as a result, despite a literature body whose writers (particu-larly in the business press) often confidently proclaim the opposite. Thus, who may we say is better positioned to answer Mintzberg's call to study lead-ership simply, directly, and imaginatively—latter-day leadership psychologists or discursive leadership scholars like Grint? The answer may surprise: neither alone, and both in different ways.

Given the variety of organizational discourse approaches available today and the cross-paradigmatic thinking some are generating, these approaches have the potential—much like Mintzberg's work—to challenge, inform, and complement the still-dominant psychological approaches upon which so much leadership research is based. With this view in mind, two deceptively simple questions guide this book. First, what do we see, think, and talk about with a discursive lens directed toward leadership? Second, what leadership knowledge is to be gained in the interplay between a discursive lens and one that is psychological?

In posing these questions, I have no interest in debating whether discur-sive leadership or leadership psychology is the better overall lens. There is never only one conceptual or paradigmatic framework sufficient for answering all questions about leadership,[5] and I would argue that it is wrong for any per-spective to overestimate its influence at the expense of the other.[6] In making the case for discursive leadership, the substantial contributions made by lead-ership psychology to our understanding of leadership should in no way be underestimated. My bias is a discursive one, yet my intent in finding fault with leadership psychology at times is never to forsake it. Complex social phenom-ena, like leadership, have many parts that act together and define one another to form an entwined whole, although such interdependence may not be readily apparent. This orientation reflects Albert et al.'s (1986) notion of *complementary holism,* the goal of which is to provide more holistic social theory through intellectual frameworks "specifically contoured to understanding an interconnected reality" (p. 15).[7] I do not know how much holism is possible between discursive leadership and leadership psychology; I do know that such a goal is impossible without more conversation between them. As Rorty (1979) suggested, conversation across diverse theories and frameworks is "the ultimate context within which knowledge is to be understood" (p. 389). Thus, this book's purpose—to put some contours around what is discursive leadership— is aided, in part, by the possibilities for its relationship with leadership psychology. Neither discursive leadership nor leadership psychology should be seen as derivative of the other; they are simply alternative, coconstructing lenses with both strengths and shortcomings.[8] To begin this conversation then, it is necessary to map some of the contested terrain over definitions of leadership and discourse.

Defining Leadership

Any definition of leadership ultimately rests on one's ontological commitments. As such, most of the discursive approaches in this book, in varying degrees, meet the conditions of a broadly constructionist stance as outlined by Hacking (1999). Critical of the status quo, they argue for social construction precisely when leadership is taken for granted and appears inevitable. For example, consider the current interest in authentic leadership (Avolio & Gardner, 2005).[9] That there even is such a phenomenon as authentic leadership appears inevitable once you have actor or analyst claims about specific leaders' facades (for example, those of many politicians) or others' genuine or true selves (for example, those of a Gandhi, a Warren Buffet, or an Oprah Winfrey). Yet, as Chapter 5 will reveal, a discursive approach rooted in Foucault strikes down this inevitability because authenticity is equated with virtuosity by those influenced by positive psychology and, opposingly, the revelation of one's dark side by those subscribing to the traditional pathology model of psychology. These diametrically opposed conceptions of authentic leadership suggest social construction at work.

Paraphrasing Hacking (1999), a constructionist stance on leadership holds that

(1) Leadership need not have existed, or need not be at all as it is. Leadership, or leadership as it is at present, is not determined by the nature of things; it is not inevitable.

However, often a constructionist stance will go further:

(II) Leadership is quite bad as it is.

(III) We would be much better off if leadership were done away with, or at least radically transformed.

A thesis of type I that strikes down the inevitability of leadership is the common starting point for constructionist approaches. We have essentially made such a claim about authentic leadership by noting the various ways in which it may be defined. However, any given constructionist approach may or may not embrace the second and third theses. For example, Hardy and Clegg (1996) cast leadership as a mechanism of domination (type II thesis), a position held by many critical theorists who favor more democratic processes (type III thesis) (Deetz, 1995). A discursive approach that embraces critical theory (types II and III) is thus interpretive (type I), but an interpretive orientation does not presume a critical one (Deetz, 1996). The relationship is intransitive.

In various ways, discursive approaches embrace the processes of social construction and its products vis-à-vis the operation of one or more texts. Sigman (1992) captured this process orientation by observing that, "the process of communication itself . . . is consequential, and it is the 'nature' of that consequentiality that should . . . be the appropriate focus" (p. 351). Thus, discursive approaches tend to focus on *how* leadership is achieved or 'brought off' in discourse—just as Shotter (1993) portrayed managers as *practical authors,* calling attention to their everyday language use, the performative role of language, and the centrality of language to processes of organizing. Drawing from ethnomethodology, Knights and Willmott (1992) cast leadership as a *practical accomplishment* where a social order may be experienced as routine and unproblematic, but is really a precarious, reflexive accomplishment. The implications of these and other constructionist views of leadership suggest that leaders must constantly enact their relationship to their followers (Biggart & Hamilton, 1987). All must repeatedly *perform* leadership in communication and through discourse. As we will later see, conceptualizing and studying leadership in this way are often two different things.

Importantly, discursive approaches allow leadership to surface in myriad forms, whether it is street gang credibility, role-modeling heroism, or legitimate authority. Jettisoning the concept of leadership is not an option, as it has been for some 'weak leadership' approaches (Shamir, 1999) like that of self-management (Manz & Sims, 1987), or substitutes for leadership (Kerr & Jermier, 1978). As long as the concept of leadership is invoked by actors for attributions of personal potency (Calder, 1977), the concept is worthy of study. While Calder cautioned not to confuse lay constructions with scientific constructs, each can be studied without necessarily undermining the truth claims of either (Edwards, 1997; Meindl, 1993).[10]

However, if one is to accommodate the attributions and descriptions of both actors and analysts, searching for *the* definition of leadership is futile, as many scholars have already concluded (Alvesson & Sveningsson, 2003b; Barker, 1997; Rost, 1991). The definition I prefer is a rather simple one by Robinson (2001): "Leadership is exercised when ideas expressed in talk or action are recognized by others as capable of progressing tasks or problems which are important to them" (p. 93). As the ensuing chapters make clear, this definition is useful for four reasons. First, leadership is a process of influence and meaning management among actors that advances a task or goal. Second, leadership is an attribution made by followers or observers. Third, the focus is on leadership process, not leader communication alone, in contrast to heroic leadership models (Yukl, 1999). Finally, leadership as influence and meaning management need not be performed by only one individual appointed to a given role; it may shift and distribute itself among several organizational members.

Note that Robinson (2001) does not distinguish between 'leader' and 'manager' in her definition. It is a lead that I will follow unless the particular leadership literature under scrutiny makes the distinction relevant, such as in neo-charisma theories (Bryman, 1996). Note also that I am arguing for the *utility* of Robinson's definition of leadership, not its veracity.

Defining Discourse

Grant, Keenoy and Oswick (1998) observed that discourse too has been a highly contested term—over the inclusion of both written text and spoken dialogue (Gilbert & Mulkay, 1984; Sinclair & Coulthard, 1975); visual images such as art, architecture, and media images (Hodge & Kress, 1988; Kress & van Leeuwen, 1990); and reality construction processes shaped by discourse (Berger & Luckman, 1966; Foucault, 1972, 1980; Searle, 1995). Following Alvesson and Kärreman's (2000b) efforts to clarify the various meanings of discourse, I generally distinguish between two broad definitions.[11]

The term *discourse* (also known as little 'd' discourse) refers to the study of talk and text in social practices. Viewed as a local achievement, discourse embodies cultural meanings; it is a medium for social interaction where the details of language in use and interaction process are central concerns for analysts (Potter & Wetherell, 1987). However, what does it mean to study talk and text? *Talk-in-interaction* represents sociality, the processes of messaging and conversing. It is the 'doing' of organizational discourse, whereas *text* is the 'done' or material representation of discourse in spoken or recorded forms (J. R. Taylor & Van Every, 2000). Even though written documents are the simplest way to conceive of organizational texts (for example, emails and annual reports), verbal routines inscribed in organizations such as performance appraisals or job interviews also exist as texts and are reconfigured through their continued use (Derrida, 1988).[12]

By contrast, the term *Discourse* (also known as big 'D' Discourse) refers to general and enduring systems for the formation and articulation of ideas in a historically situated time (Foucault, 1972, 1980). In this view, power and knowledge relations are established in culturally standardized Discourses formed by constellations of talk patterns, ideas, logics, and assumptions that constitute objects and subjects. These Discourses not only order and naturalize the world in particular ways, but they also inform social practices by constituting "particular forms of subjectivity in which human subjects are managed and given a certain form, viewed as self-evident and rational" (Alvesson & Kärreman, 2000b, pp. 1127–1128).

Bennis and Thomas's (2002) *Geeks & Geezers: How Era, Values, and Defining Moments Shape Leaders* is a business press example of Foucault's notion of Discourse. Bennis and Thomas compare the characteristics of the Great Depression and World War II era with the era of the Internet and end of the Cold War. Their goal was to discern the ways in which the forces of history and culture shaped two generations of U.S. leaders ('geezers' and 'geeks,' respectively) and their organizations. Foucault did much the same kind of analysis, albeit with somewhat more specificity and different topics.

Discursive approaches such as sociolinguistics, ethnomethodology, conversation analysis, speech act schematics, interaction analyses, and semiotics in various ways focus on language in use and interaction process; they analyze little 'd' discourse. By contrast, critical and postmodern discourse analyses focus heavily on systems of thought; they analyze big 'D' Discourse. However, there is a third category that attempts both; it includes discursive psychology, rhetoric and literary analyses, ethnography of speaking, and Fairclough's (1995) critical discourse analysis. This book utilizes discourse analyses from each category, but makes no attempt to be exhaustive. For those unfamiliar with the discourse approaches used in this book, brief synopses of them appear in Appendixes A1–A7.[13]

The differences between discourse and Discourse notwithstanding, discursive approaches vary in at least five other ways according to K. Tracy (1995). They include (a) whether a transcript is required, and the type and level of detail a transcription should include; (b) the dominant kinds of texts used for analysis; (c) the role of interviews and other kinds of contextual information; (d) disciplinary orientations and key theoretical questions that the discourse analysis is designed to answer; and (e) the metatheoretical frame (empiricist, interpretive, critical) within which the discourse analysis is viewed as a method (p. 200). Where relevant, Appendixes A1–A7 make these differences known.

The Case for Discursive Leadership

In order to understand the contributions of discursive leadership, a fuller case must be made for its distinctiveness relative to leadership psychology. Unfortunately, any comparison risks unfairly representing all of the theories and approaches grouped under these two labels. Nevertheless, it does seem useful to try to find threads of unity within the diversity, while respecting the diversity as much as possible. This is because discursive leadership has its own ways of talking—its own language of leadership—that is different from leadership psychology. This will become evident in the following six comparisons between/among discourse and mental theater; decentered subjects/thin actors and essences; reflexive agency and untheorized/exaggerated agency; encompassing and dualistic conceptions of power and influence; textual, con-textual, and variable analytic; and communication as primary and subsidiary.

DISCOURSE VERSUS MENTAL THEATER

Reacting against Kantian philosophy and the ways it influenced contemporary psychology, the term 'mental theater' was used by Cronen (1995a) to refer to psychologists' need to "get beneath and behind experience to fret out the connections among cognitions, emotions, and behaviors" (p. 29).[14] As psychologists form and correlate the cognitive, affective, and conative variables that they believe capture experience, they must often reduce behavior to statements of intention or summary judgments of past behavior. Cronen argues that all sense of coordinated action (in its often messy, yet fine-grained detail) and any real sense of experience are thus lost in the projected play of mental operations.[15] Similarly, others suggest that when leadership is viewed as the result of variables 'inside' or 'outside' the person, the only interaction that is studied is a statistical one (Hosking & Morley, 1991; Meindl, 1993).

There is a difference between studying *actual* interactional processes where relational patterns are always codefined, and studying *reports* of such processes as if a single relational reality exists (L. E. Rogers, Millar, & Bavelas, 1985), even though both may derive from theorizing leadership as socially constructed in some fashion. Theories from leadership psychology may miss this distinction when they theorize social processes, yet measure only one party's perceptions of same. These perceptions are retrospective summarizing judgments that gloss the details of interaction over time and may give the impression that a single relational reality can be assumed and measured.[16]

Reinforcing this view, Gronn (2002) recalls the distinction between ontological, observational, and analytical units. *Ontological units* define the entity that one is studying. *Observational units* define who or what an analyst observes, while *analytical units* more specifically parcel out that which is to be deconstructed, measured, or explained. Leadership psychology focuses on the ascending series of individual-dyad-group-organization as ontological units, which Gronn (2002) argues has historically been confounded with levels of analysis and overshadowed by the dominance of *leader-centrism*—an individualist concern relative to the other units. Leadership psychologists frequently observe individuals and analyze their perceptions and summary judgments, even if the ontological unit is a leader-member dyad, group, or whole organization (Yammarino, Dionne, Chun, & Dansereau, 2005).[17] The confluence of these ontological, observational, and analytical units thus biases leadership psychologists toward the study of the individual over the social or cultural. This is in no way to discount the study of the individual or demean the fascination with mental theater (or in any way to ask psychologists not to be psychologists), only to deny the assumed isomorphic correspondence between cognitive operations and social process (Holmes & Rogers, 1995). Cronen (1995a) argues that without a clear and separate focus on social process, analysts have little recourse but to explain individuals' abilities solely in terms of hidden mechanisms and inner motors.

Discursive approaches' ontological units include subjectivity, identities, relationships, cultures and linguistic communities, organizations as macroactors, linguistic repertoires, and Discourses as stand-alone systems of thought. On the surface, this looks roughly similar to the individual-dyad-group-organization series of leadership psychology. However, discursive approaches' ontological units are often combinations of more than one 'level' because analysts argue that clear boundaries are often undecipherable (Collinson, 2006). For example, subjectivity is more about a person's image or constructed self relative to the range of conflicting Discourses that vie for control (Deetz, 1992), while the organization as a macroactor focuses on how organizations come to have voice and agency (J. R. Taylor & Cooren, 1997).

In terms of observational units, discursive approaches focus on language in use, interaction process, and/or discursive formations. Their analytical units are defined by their choice of text, of which there are all manners and varieties. As indicated below, texts can be written records, inscribed patterns, or memory traces. In the literature base for this book, texts are most often *interview discourse* as individuals' sensemaking accounts and meaning assignments are revealed in their language use, *actual dialogue* that captures language use in the back-and-forth of interaction process, or *discursive formations* that may stand alone as systems of thought or appear as dialogically grounded linguistic practices.

DECENTERED SUBJECTS/THIN ACTORS VERSUS ESSENCES

Grint (2000) asserted that in trait, situational, and contingency theories of leadership, there is an 'essence' to the leader, the context, or both that suggests one best way to lead. An essence suggests that things are what they are because that is their nature or true form, despite all appearances.[18] For Grint (2000), trait approaches emphasize the essence of individual leaders—qualities that make them leaders regardless of the context or circumstances in which they may find themselves. Situational approaches like the Ohio State Leadership Studies emphasize the essence of particular contexts, the effective handling of which requires one leadership style over possible others. Finally, contingency approaches emphasize the essence of individual and context, where individuals gauge their alignment with the context and respond accordingly, for example, when a strong leader and a crisis coincide.[19] The search for the essence of leadership derives from leadership psychologists' adherence to traditional science assumptions about realist conceptions of truth and conceiving of knowledge as representing reality (Rorty, 1982).

To reject the notion of 'essence' is to embrace a socially constructed view of leadership because "what counts as a 'situation' and what counts as the 'appropriate' way of leading in that situation are interpretive and contestable issues, not issues that can be decided by objective criteria" (Grint, 2000, p. 3). Thus, Grint and other discursive scholars problematize the variability and inconsistency in actors' accounts and analyst findings, explicate the conditions of their production, and thus try to understand how conflicting truth claims about leadership come into being and may actually coexist. These analysts expect to find the research equivalent of the fog of war in the study of social interaction. They choose a constructionist path over essentializing theory because it supplies the necessary tools to grapple with communication's unending detail and variety.[20] Included among those tools is the search for vocabularies and ways of talking that best address the purposes at hand (Bochner, 1985; Rorty, 1982).

However, in his critique of two types of discourse analysis, conversation analysis and discursive psychology, Hammersley (2003a) pointedly objected to these analysts' unwillingness to "view actors as controlled, or even as guided in their behavior, by substantive, distinctive and stable mental characteristics such as 'attitudes,' 'personalities,' 'perspectives,' or 'strategic orientations'" and their preference for treating actors as "*employing* cultural resources that are *publicly available,* and doing so in *contextually variable ways*" (p. 752, emphasis original). Hammersley thus reclaims the essentialist argument by arguing that a discursive orientation rejects anything that is unique or specific about actors in favor of what any member (of a linguistic community) could do.

Hammersley's critique raises key questions for discursive leadership scholars, namely, how should one think about behaviors that are distinctive to leadership actors across time and context? Is some essence worth hanging onto? To answer these questions, it is important to understand that leadership psychology traditionally relies on a Western conception of human beings as unitary, coherent, and autonomous individuals, whose 'selves' are separable from society (Holstein & Gubrium, 2000). Essentializing thus appears to be a natural way of making sense of leaders' complex inner lives as well as the contexts in which they operate. For most forms of discursive leadership, society and the individual are inseparable (Giddens, 1979). In postmodern thought, for example, the self is neither fixed nor essentialized for this very reason. Instead, *subjectivity* emerges as a historical product of sociocultural forces embedded within a specific context (Foucault, 1979, 1983). Such a focus often examines the discursive, gendered, multiple, and conflicting nature of subjectivities in this regard (Ashcraft & Mumby, 2004).

However, neither conversation analysis nor discursive psychology goes so far as to portray actors as decentered subjects. Yet Hammersley (2003) still finds their model of the human actor to be rather "thin" compared to the actor with a strong inner motor. In his rejoinder to Hammersley, Potter (2003) argues that "a certain kind of thinness," best characterized as lacking "a predefined model of the human actor," is necessary in order to focus on social practices, the constitutive role of language, and the contributions of the cultural (p. 78–79). Interestingly, both Hammersley and Potter legitimate both actor orientations, although Potter flatly rejects Hammersley's suggestion that discursive approaches be viewed less in paradigmatic terms and more as methodologies. Indeed, few discourse scholars would stand for any minimization of their commitments to theory. However, Deetz (1996) offers a more accommodating solution, one that I prefer. That is, paradigmatic differences should not be seen

> as alternative routes to truth, but as specific (D)iscourses which, if freed from their claims of universality and/or completion, could provide important moments in the larger dialogue about organizational life. The test . . . is not whether they provide a better map, but whether they provide an interesting way to talk about what is happening in research programs. (p. 193)

Deetz's poststructuralist solution finds further grounding in Rorty's (1979) notion of 'conversation,' where the "focus shifts from the relation between human beings and the objects of their inquiry to the relation between alternative standards of justification" (p. 389–390).[21] Discursive leadership and leadership psychology are thus usefully conceived as complementary Discourses or alternative ways of talking and knowing about leadership.

ENCOMPASSING VERSUS DUALISTIC
CONCEPTIONS OF POWER AND INFLUENCE

The Western conception of an autonomous self adopted by leadership psychology and the self that is inseparable from society embraced by discursive scholars also implies different ways in which to view power and influence. Collinson (2006) observes that traditional conceptions of power in leadership psychology treat it as a negative and repressive property exercised in a top-down manner. Influence is thus treated independently, most often as embodying the very definition of leadership (Antonakis, Cianciolo & Sternberg, 2004; Rost, 1991; Yukl, 2002). To be more precise, leadership is understood as a "positive process of disproportionate social influence" (Collinson, 2006, pp. 181–182). Indeed, by today's common standards, shaped heavily by leadership psychology, leadership fails when a leader must resort to his or her authority to gain compliance. Such a view also explains our admiration for charismatic and transformational leaders who excel at the influence game by winning the voluntary cooperation of followers, at times under extraordinary circumstances. In order to explain forced versus voluntary compliance, leadership psychology treats power and influence as dual notions.

Many discursive approaches would not restrict their study of leadership to positive and disproportionate influence. Their views on the inseparability of self and society derive from a view of power that is much more encompassing, one that integrates various forms of power and influence and conceives of them in both positive and negative terms. Such a view draws heavily from Foucault (1990, 1995), who argues for the cultural and historical contingency of subjectivity along with its Discursive roots in power and knowledge systems. For Foucault, all power is local, relational, and embedded in specific technologies governed by Discourses with the power to discipline. As we will see in Chapters 4 and 5, such technologies are usually aided by systems of surveillance that turn individuals into knowable and calculable objects (Miller & Rose, 1990). With this kind of apparatus, we are able to see the individualizing effects of power, especially as individuals come to discipline themselves around that which a Discourse deems 'normal.' Power stays close on the heels of resistance here, traveling its same routes in order to overcome. Finally, when multiple Discourses are considered, the positive, productive, and creative aspects of power reveal themselves especially as individuals forge their identities (Collinson, 2006). Thus, discursive scholars find that more encompassing views of power and influence are necessary to explain the inseparability of self and society.

REFLEXIVE AGENCY VERSUS UNTHEORIZED/EXAGGERATED AGENCY

Leadership is often viewed as a force for change (Bennis & Nanus, 1985; Hickman, 1990; Kotter, 1990), making it nearly synonymous with the terms 'agency' or 'action.' However, agency per se is an infrequent topic in leadership psychology, which has led critics to make two seemingly contradictory observations about this literature body. First, Hosking (1988) argues that leaders are too often untheorized as agents, which results in an odd disconnect between leadership research and the rest of the field. Bryman (1996) puts it more bluntly: "Leadership theory and research have been remarkably and surprisingly uncoupled from the more general field in which they are located" (p. 289). Hosking (1988) argues that, while the skills of leadership are the skills of organizing, leadership psychologists have been too caught up in assuming the organization has an entitative status—neither questioning how the organization got to be an entity in the first place, nor how it maintains itself as an entity. When researchers ignore the processes of organizing, Hosking notes "a sharp divide between person and organization such that the agent, responsible for the latter, is left untheorized as an agent" (pp. 149–150). Consequently, leadership appears epiphenomenal.

Second, Gronn (2000) makes the case for exaggerated agency by noting that the individualism and leader-centrism of leadership psychology results in a rather unsophisticated leader-follower dualism in which "leaders are superior to followers, followers depend on leaders, and leadership consists in doing something to, for, and on behalf of others" (p. 319). According to Gronn (2000), this "belief in the power of one" results in an exaggerated sense of agency because of an undertheorized view of task performance and accomplishment (p. 319). Indeed, Robinson (2001) too portrayed leadership psychology as floating ethereally above task accomplishment. If the division of labor were truly examined, Gronn (2000, 2002) reasons, leadership would surface as a more distributed phenomenon and the hero-anointing tendencies of, for example, neo-charismatic leadership theories would be in check.

Can Hosking and Gronn start from the same literature body and arrive at two different senses of agency? Yes, and both have a point. Gronn (2000) is correct, as others have noted the strong individualism and overstatement associated with the heroic capabilities of charismatic and transformational leaders (Beyer, 1999; Yukl, 1999). Yet Hosking (1988) is also correct because, across this genre of leadership theories and most others, agency is never explicitly theorized, the organization ontological status is assumed, and the disconnect between leader and organization perpetuates itself with inattention to the processes of organizing (Fairhurst & Putnam, 2004). Leadership is still seen as a phenomenon embodied in persons, not as an organizing process grounded in task accomplishment (Fairhurst, 2006).

Yet the move to study leadership as an organizing process cannot be done in the absence of discourse/Discourse and communication, a fact to which Gronn (2000, 2002) and Hosking (1988) only indirectly allude. As Bateson (1972) observes, what else do people have between them but the exchange of messages? Bateson argues that communication *is* the relationship because, following Schegloff (2001), it is the cellular biology or granularity from which perceptions are formed. As later discussion in this book makes clear, this is not to bias the study of leadership in the direction of social process over cognitive operations. It is to suggest alternating the lenses so that one does not mistake the individual for the social in leadership study, as when survey or interview data substitute for a codefined leadership process.

Importantly, the study of *leadership* discourse, not solely *leader* discourse, creates the kind of window in which to study the reflexive agency of its actors.[22] Such a view is based on the more general ethnomethodological argument of Garfinkel (1967) that action is organized from within—meaning that leadership actors are knowledgeable agents, who reflexively monitor the ongoing character of social life as they continuously orient to and position themselves vis-à-vis specific norms, rules, procedures, and values in interaction with others. What often seems paradoxical from the outside view of the researcher is logical and reasonable from the inside view of the actor, leading Garfinkel (1967), Giddens (1984), and others to object to the widespread derogation of the lay actor throughout much of the social sciences. With actors' language use, in particular, most discursive approaches view it as a window on human agency because "actions and the interpretations of their meanings are inseparable and occur simultaneously in the course of their production" (Boden, 1994, p. 47). Although discursive approaches certainly vary in how much knowledgeability they attribute to actors, most acknowledge that actors can be viewed as responsible agents who still do not fully comprehend or intend the nature of unfolding events (Giddens, 1979, 1984; Ranson, Hinnings, & Greenwood, 1980).

Second, to attribute knowledgeability and reflexivity to actors is to put them in charge of their own affairs in a way that is marked by constraint as much as by freedom. As such, leadership actors must continuously manage the tensions between agency and constraint or structure (Giddens, 1984). As with actor knowledgeability, the issue of constraint is the subject of considerable debate. Charges of relativism have been ascribed to constructionist approaches generally and poststructuralist approaches specifically (Reed, 2000, 2001). Relativism suggests an exaggerated form of agency, an "anything goes" ability to construct reality despite the constraints of a material world (Gergen, 1991). By contrast, more realist constructionist approaches conceive of agency as constrained by material forces such as the brute facts of a physical world (for example, buildings, mountains, hurricanes, and so forth) or macro social contexts of institutions and power relations (Edwards, 1997; Hacking, 1999; Searle, 1995). Just how the material intervenes to constrain action continues to be the subject of considerable debate in constructionist thought in and around organizations.[23]

TEXTUAL, CON-TEXTUAL VERSUS THE VARIABLE ANALYTIC

As discussed above, leadership psychologists focus on the individual and a search for essences. A search for essences coalesces nicely with the variable analytic tradition, which holds that complex phenomena like leadership are best understood in terms of a fine-grained analysis of parts. As part of this research tradition, analysts value generalizable over local knowledge and are far more interested in answering cause-and-effect 'why' questions than the more descriptively oriented 'how' questions (as in, how is leadership brought off?). Consequently, leadership researchers in the variable analytic tradition try to capture the experience of leadership by forming and statistically analyzing a host of cognitive, affective, and conative variables and their causal connections. Context is not unimportant, but too much attention to its contingencies produces more local than generalizable knowledge. As a result, there is often less attention to leadership's historical and cultural/political conditions, while a heavy reliance on cross-sectional designs and quantitative methods further enable analysts to aggregate across contexts in the search for the generalizable (Bryman, Bresnen, Beardsworth, & Keil, 1988; Conger, 1998; Parry, 1998).

It should surprise no one that survey researchers (many of whom are leadership psychologists) often view discourse analyses as fuzzy, unwieldy, and without a tangible payoff (Oswick, Keenoy, & Grant, 1997). Unconcerned with the search for essences or causal connections among variables, discourse analysts want to know *how* a text functions pragmatically, *how* leadership is brought off in some here-and-now moment of localized interaction. In complementary fashion, Discourse analysts ask, *what* kind of leadership are we talking about and how have the forces of history and culture shaped it? Both types of analysts reject prediction and control as key functions of theory, while never viewing description as *mere* description or prelude to the real work of theory building. Without the immediate concern of building generalizable theory, discourse scholars feel freer to embrace the context and its historical and cultural/political aspects. As Biggart and Hamilton (1987) write, "Leadership is a relationship among persons *in a social setting at a given historic moment*" (p. 438, emphasis added). Thus, local knowledge is key as text and context inevitably merge. Most discourse analysts take their cues from Bateson (1972) on this point, who argues that each action (which, once materialized, becomes text) is "*part* of the ecological subsystem called context and not . . . the product or effect of what remains of the context after the piece which we want to explain has been cut from it" (p. 338, emphasis original). Thus, what is text one moment for the discourse analyst is con-text the very next.[24]

What may also be particularly disturbing to the survey researcher is the protean nature of 'text' versus that of the 'variable.' A variable usually refers to a well-defined class of behaviors that can take on different values. The concept of 'text' has great currency in the organizational discourse literature precisely because it assumes myriad forms such as written records, memory traces, materialized spoken discourse, verbal routines, and so on where size or amount of text matters little. Texts also possess qualities like inscription and *restance*, which defines a text's "staying quality" (Derrida, 1988). Texts may even become a metaphor for the organization itself with their capacity to layer and interweave (Cooren, 2001; J. R. Taylor & Van Every, 2000). Unlike variables, texts may or may not have a unitary property whose order and coherence is the subject of analysis.

Does a textual analysis preclude or supercede the need for variable analysis or vice versa? No, they often address different kinds of questions even with the same subject matter. For example, Schegloff (2001) suggests that in variable analytic studies connecting status/power and interruption behavior (Kollock, Blumstein, & Schwartz, 1985; Smith-Lovin & Brody, 1989), "what is lacking is the 'cellular biology' that 'closes the connection,' which explicates the mechanism linking the outcomes being studied, initiating interruptions and 'succeeding' with them, and the variables which assertedly engender these outcomes" (p. 315). Thus, Schegloff is not discounting the variable analytic work in this area. Rather, he is suggesting that it is *how* parties achieve the relevance of their status and power vis-à-vis linguistic forms like turn taking and category memberships (for example, based on gender) in a series of interactional moments that usefully provide this 'cellular biology' or granularity that he finds so missing in variable analytic studies. Thus, the variable analytic connection between power/status and interruption behavior serves as a useful starting point for a more fine-grained textual analysis, such as conversation analysis.

One of the desired goals of this book is that discursive scholars and leadership psychologists will find more complementary connections. Some of these connections will be made explicit in the chapters on sequence and temporal form (Chapter 2), membership categorization (Chapter 3), and narrative logics (Chapter 6), all chapters focusing on little 'd' discourse. Chapters focusing on big 'D' Discourse appear less amenable to variable analytic tie-ins. However, they certainly contribute to the discussions of leadership psychologists regarding how best to conceptualize leadership and explicate its practices. As outside the mainstream, their role is an important one in challenging taken-for-granted assumptions and suggesting alternative ways in which leadership may be usefully conceived.

COMMUNICATION AS PRIMARY VERSUS SUBSIDIARY

More than the variable analytic tradition, it is the psychological orientation of mainstream leadership researchers that predisposes them to view the social and the communicative as subsidiary to individual (and broadly) cognitive operations. Communication merely plays out the cognitive and only partially, at best. This is part of the "received view" of communication, which Cronen (1995a) suggests "cannot be the site of the most important avenues of social inquiry because psychological, sociological, and cultural variables determine it . . . we [referring to psychologists primarily] only care about communication because it can have consequences for other matters that are our real concerns" (p. 310). Stated otherwise, communication is of interest only to the extent that actors can impact each other's *cognitive* operations.

Communication is of primary interest to discursive leadership scholars, although interest in human interaction varies as the distinction between 'discourse' and 'Discourse' makes clear. Interestingly, there is also substantial disagreement over the terms 'communication' and 'discourse' among discourse scholars. For example, in writing about the emphasis of conversation analysis on talk-as-action, Edwards (1997) views it as antithetical to what he called a "communication model," in which communication is strictly a means of expressing speaker intentions and an act of transmission. For conversation analysis and discursive psychology, speaker intentions are at issue in the talk-in-interaction of participants: "intentions, goals, mental contents, and their inter-subjective 'sharing' are analyzed as kinds of business that talk attends to, rather than being the analyst's stock assumption concerning what is actually going on" (Edwards, 1997, p. 107). As such, Edwards's "minds-in-communication" view is quite consistent with the received view of communication as depicted by Cronen (1995a). Yet most theorists in the discipline of communication neither *endorse* a strict transmission model of communication, nor *equate* the study of communication with speaker intentionality and its transmission aspects.[25]

In contrast to Edwards (1997), some organizational communication theorists like J. R. Taylor (personal communication, May 2002) actually prefer the term 'communication' over 'discourse' because the latter term obscures the relationship between interactive speech and text, a relationship that he believes explains the way the organization emerges in communication (J. R. Taylor & Van Every, 2000). Preferences for 'communication' or 'discourse' aside, most discursive approaches eschew a strict emphasis on speaker intentionality and communication as a simple act of transmission, while embracing more meaning-centered models of communication. However, one can hardly resist essentializing leadership and then turn right around and claim that a meaning-centered model is the 'true' model of communication—even if 'meaning' itself has been a contested term when it comes to the interpretations, understandings, and readings of texts within different genres of discourse analysis (Putnam & Fairhurst, 2001). Like Grint (2000), Craig (1999) denies "that any concept has a true essence except as constituted within the communication process" (p. 127). He suggests that, in the case of 'communication,' warrant can be found for both transmission and meaning-centered definitions of communication, depending upon the causes they serve.[26]

The Path Forward

Now that I have sketched a broad outline of the differences between discursive leadership and leadership psychology, each of the chapters that follow will address a key concept from the discourse/Discourse literature and apply it to leadership. The concept may or may not be tied to one specific discursive theory or approach; in fact, it could be several. As mentioned, Appendixes A1–A7 offer summaries for the uninitiated to discourse analyses and are designed for quick and easy reference.

Echoing Edwards (1997), those who are new to this literature may find that some of the discourse concepts I have selected to build chapters around may appear a bit mundane at first. For example, when effective leadership can impact life-and-death struggles in high-reliability organizations like police units, conversational turn taking or category use may seem rather unremarkable in the grand scheme of things. But to borrow a distinction made by Staw (1985), it is when these concepts become *problem driven* through case analysis that they develop import and relevance for leadership. In that sense, they will seem far less *literature driven* than concepts from leadership psychology, whose debates are about gaps in the literature, inconsistencies, challenges to conventional wisdom, fresh perspectives, and so on. For this reason, my treatment of the discourse concepts is more heavily weighted toward enlightening examples and the use of theory not specifically designed to study leadership per se.[27] However, where relevant in the chapters, one or more theories or approaches from leadership psychology will enter the discussion of the concept; thus its literature base will be important to consider. My stance toward leadership psychology in the ensuing chapters is both appreciative and critical in this regard.

With these caveats in mind, Chapter 2's discursive concept is *sequence and temporal form* in social interaction (little 'd' discourse). In leadership psychology, there is a tendency to study leadership apart from the tasks being performed, and in this chapter we will examine how a sequential orientation to leadership interaction can address this problem. There are a number of discourse approaches that focus on sequencing, but with different kinds of temporal units. Those units include (a) the act-interact-double interact, (b) turn taking and adjacency pairs, (c) narrative schemas and episodes, (d) scripts, and (e) script formulations. These units form the foundation of this chapter and collectively suggest that studying leaders' actions alone yields incomplete and ultimately distorting views of leadership interaction. This chapter also makes the case for distributed leadership and the sequential foundation of leadership command presence. From leadership psychology, Judi Komaki's work on performance monitoring also makes an interesting contribution to this chapter.

Chapter 3's discursive concept is *membership categorization* (also little 'd' discourse). In contrast to leadership psychology theories that focus on the cognitive processes underlying categorization and its consequences for leadership, a discursive approach like conversation analysis examines the performative nature of categories. In other words, how are categories invoked, created, modified, or rejected in everyday leadership discourse and for what purpose? This chapter considers the consequences of category use, especially for organizational role and identity management in the leadership relationship, and how category work as a discursive activity can add some much-needed specificity to leadership as the management of meaning.

While Chapters 2 and 3 focus on language in use and interaction process (little 'd' discourse), Chapters 4 and 5 explore those powerful historical and cultural forces that lie beyond language and interaction, yet serve as important resources for actors as they communicate (big 'D' Discourse). Chapter 4 addresses the role of history in the organizational sciences, including the study of leadership, and contrasts it with the work of Foucault, which is featured in this chapter. Through his conception of Discourse and disciplinary power, leadership actors are shown as subjects and objects of their relationships, organizations, and societies. It makes for quite an interesting contrast with leadership psychology's view of leaders as crucial agents. The resonances of Foucault's examination and confessional technologies are argued to operate in modern day performance management approaches such as 360-degree feedback and executive coaching. Moreover, the emerging executive coaching literature demonstrates how even the alpha males among leaders may be tamed and disciplined through the power of Discourse.

Chapter 5's focus is on the self and identity. The conception of the self in many leadership psychology theories is very different from the self in discursive leadership. In a discussion of these differences, we will continue to draw from the work of Foucault and his view of Discourse. However, the focus is also on the role played by multiple Discourses, including authentic leadership and gendered management Discourses, in the self-identity work of leadership actors. To carry out this task, we will adopt the translation of 'Discourse' into 'interpretative repertoire' by discursive psychology in order to understand the linguistic resources made available to leadership actors.

Chapter 6's study of narrative explores the intersection of both discourse and Discourse. The chapter title, "Narrative Logics," addresses itself to narrative as found in leadership interaction as well as the narrative resources afforded by various Discourses. Leader–member exchange (LMX) theory from leadership psychology is an ideal candidate in which to explore these narrative ties. Chapter 6 demonstrates that a narrative approach adds nuance and detailed meaning to the character and quality of LMX, particularly for the less well-understood, medium quality LMXs. It also reveals coconstructed, terse storytelling in LMX dialogue, and cultural contributions to LMX via the uniqueness paradox wherein culturally scripted narratives feel idiosyncratic.

Chapter 7 addresses material mediations in leadership discourse. This chapter begins by examining the elusiveness of charismatic leadership and proposes that a discursive approach rooted in actor-network theory, known as the Montreal school, be used to study charisma. This approach recasts charismatic leadership in textual, scenic, technological, cultural, and embodied terms. Rudy Giuliani's leadership during 9/11 will be used to demonstrate that charisma is perhaps best seen not as residing in a single person, but as an attributed product or outcome of a continuous networking strategy of human and nonhuman entities. Along the way, this chapter explores the criticism of discourse analyses vis-à-vis materialist concerns.

Finally, Chapter 8 has two goals. First, the implications of discursive leadership research for leadership practice must be articulated, which suggests more conversation between discursive leadership scholars and practitioners. Second, I am looking to keep the conversation going between discursive leadership scholars and leadership psychologists. It seemed fitting to ask scholars from both groups to offer their take on the possible interplay between discursive leadership and leadership psychology. I am grateful to Boas Shamir, Stephen Green, Robert Liden, James (Jerry) Hunt, Donna Chrobot-Mason, François Cooren, Kevin Barge, and Linda Putnam for their agreement to participate in this dialogue. As the ensuing chapters will make clear, and I hope readers will agree, discursive leadership is an interesting and powerful lens in which to view leadership and, speaking for myself and other discursive leadership scholars, our conversation with leadership psychologists has only just begun.

NOTES

1. For example, see work by Carlson (1951), Sayles (1964), and Stewart (1967).

2. Mintzberg's (1973) observations of managers produced a taxonomy in which there were three roles that dealt with managers' interpersonal behavior (leader, liaison, figurehead), three roles that dealt with information processing (monitor, disseminator, spokesman), and four roles dealing with decision making (entrepreneur, disturbance handler, resource allocator, negotiator).

3. Mintzberg's research was incomplete and is now outdated in many respects. For example, see Gronn (2000), Hales (1986), Reed (1984), Stewart (1983), and Willmott (1984).

4. For especially good introductions to the linguistic turn in the communication sciences, see Bochner (1985) and Deetz (1992), and in the organizational sciences, see Alvesson and Kärreman (2000a).

5. This point echoes the debate over paradigm incommensurability in the organizational sciences (Burrell & Morgan, 1979; Conrad & Haynes, 2001; Corman & Poole, 2000; Deetz, 1996; Gioia & Pitre, 1990; Hassard, 1988, 1991; N. Jackson & Carter, 1991; Parker & McHugh, 1991; Scherer, 1998; Weaver & Gioia, 1994).

6. This would also include ignoring other spheres of joint influence such as the economic, biological, or physical aspects of leadership.

7. Albert et al.'s (1986) principle of 'complementary holism' derives from the work of physicist David Bohm and modern quantum physics. Among other things, it emphasizes "that reality is not a collection of separate entities but a vast and intricate 'unbroken whole'" (p. 12).

8. At least one writer has suggested that discursive approaches such as conversation analysis and discursive psychology be seen as methodologies (Hammersley, 2003a, 2003b), which is counter to the view expressed here.

9. See *Leadership Quarterly*'s 2005 (16:3) special issue on authentic leadership.

10. In Meindl's (1993) 'radical' social psychological approach to leadership, he concludes, "A key to understanding and conceptualizing leadership must be built on the foundation of a naïve psychological perspective. How leadership is constructed by both naïve organizational actors and by sophisticated researchers should constitute the study of leadership. For it is these very constructions on which the effects of leadership, defined in conventional terms, are like to depend"(p. 97).

11. Analysts often falsely assume a consensus instead of a range of positions regarding the meaning of 'discourse/Discourses.' See Alvesson and Kärreman (2000b) for further discussion.

12. Texts have the capacity to layer and interweave processes of organizing, thus creating the notion of organizations writ large as texts layered within macro texts (Putnam & Fairhurst, 2001).

13. For a review of the organizational literature on these discourse approaches, see Putnam and Fairhurst (2001).

14. Thus, this excludes leadership theory and research where cognition and perceptual processing are the primary focus, such as implicit leadership theories (Lord & Emrich, 2001).

15. An example of focusing on the play of mental operations can be found in the practice of modeling psychological variables and behavioral outcomes. For examples, see the June 2005 issue of *Leadership Quarterly* devoted to authentic leadership (Gardner et al., 2005; Ilies, Morgeson, & Nahrgang, 2005).

16. One currently prominent example of this is leader–member exchange theory, which often focuses solely on the member's perspective in assessing the quality of the exchange (Graen & Scandura, 1987; Graen & Uhl-Bien, 1995). However, a discursive approach may fall prey to this same criticism if it focuses exclusively on one-sided interview data, which may report more interactional detail, yet show only one person's definition of the situation or the relationship.

17. Yammarino et al. (2005) reviewed 348 journal articles and book chapters on leadership from the last 10 years in 17 areas of leadership study. They coded them for the degree of appropriate inclusion and use of levels of analysis in theory, measurement, data analysis, and inference drawing. They concluded that 91% of the publications reviewed failed to adequately address levels of analysis issues. They characterized these findings as "troubling," given that the 'levels' issue has been around for some 20 years (Dansereau, Alutto, & Yammarino, 1984).

18. Cronen (1995a) provides a particularly good example of essentialist thinking with factor analysis: "Some researchers argue that the factors—mathematically derived vectors through n-dimensional space—stand for the common essence shared by variables loading on the factor. When this interpretation is carried to the extent of treating the mathematically created factors as the most important reality, we have Platonism masquerading as empiricism" (p. 43). For Cronen, the factor or essence is not the reality, although it is frequently treated as such by empiricists.

19. Although not specifically addressed by Grint (2000), neo-charismatic models of leadership appear to essentialize leaders and leader-context combinations.

20. To what extent is essentializing as activity or thinking exercise just a natural part of attributional processes or the assignment of meaning in sensemaking processes? For example, Meindl, Ehrlich, and Dukerich (1985) observed that in causally indeterminate and ambiguous organizational conditions, leadership assumes a romanticized, exaggerated role in accounting for successful or failed outcomes. The attribution made

here is essentializing in that the people in this study drew 'hero-making' themes from the flow of experience in their sensemaking. However, here I would draw a distinction between essentializing as a sensemaking activity and essentialism, which is a philosophical position dating back to Aristotle and the phenomenology of Husserl (1962). Modern day versions of essentialism view social objects, in this case leadership, as given objects in the world—innately possessing a true nature or 'essence' whose meanings must be grasped/discovered rather than viewed as constructed. While any assignment of meaning by the actor or observer asked to reflect upon leadership essentializes it, it is one meaning assignment in a milieu of many others that may coincide, contradict, or lack any relation whatsoever. Essentialism in leadership study is thus counterbalanced by recognizing that which is contested about leadership, questioning the solidity or facticity of the social world, and viewing leadership as a situated, ongoing practical accomplishment (Garfinkel, 1967).

21. Rorty (1979) argued that conversation between alternative standards of justification can ultimately affect changes in those standards. Further, by abandoning the notion of knowledge as representation, our task as scientists is not the endless search for essences, but vocabularies and languages suitable for particular aims and goals (Rorty, 1982).

22. However, more empiricist discourse approaches like interaction analysis, if they theorize agency at all, embrace an externalized conception of agency, one that depends on a connection or relation in a network/system of relations thus ascribing constrained choice to actors but deemphasizing their active interpretive role in making those choices (Fairhurst, 2004).

23. There are several sources on this point (Astley, 1985; Chia, 2000; Conrad, 2004; Conrad & Haynes, 2001; Deetz, 1992; Foucault, 1972, 1980, 1995; Gergen, 2001; Gioia, 2003; Hacking, 1999; Parker, 1998; Potter, 1996; Reed, 2000, 2001, 2004; Shotter, 1993; Tsoukas, 2000).

24. Discourse analyses vary greatly in how much of the immediate context is incorporated into their analyses; interaction analysis and conversation analysis are particularly adept at accounting for the immediate communicative context (Fairhurst, 2004).

25. A number of communication scholars make this clear (Ashcraft & Mumby, 2004; Cooren, 2001; Craig, 1999; Cronen, 1995a; Deetz, 1992; Fairhurst, 2001; Pearce, 1995; Putnam, 1983; Putnam & Boys, 2006; Stohl & Cheney, 2001; Taylor & Van Every, 2000).

26. According to Craig (1999), transmissional views of communication possess great cultural currency and may bolster the authority of technical experts, while meaning-centered views promote the cause of freedom, tolerance, and democracy. From this vantage point, Craig does not view these definitions as mutually exclusive.

27. It is quite common in the little 'd' discourse literature for argument to proceed from example (S. Jackson, 1986; Jacobs, 1986, 1988, 1990; Pomerantz, 1990). Those adopting this practice are chiefly conversation analysts, speech act theorists, and discursive psychologists who, it must be remembered, are not making claims about behavioral regularities in the way that the more quantitative interaction analysts are—or leadership psychologists for that matter. Instead, the emphasis is on claims about structural possibilities and coherent configurations generated by the particular system of discourse in question (Jacobs, 1986).

2

Sequence and Temporal Form

Within the organizational sciences, the study of leadership is sometimes depicted as a discipline unto itself. For example, in his review of the literature, Bryman (1996) asserts that, "Leadership theory and research have been remarkably and surprisingly uncoupled from the more general field in which they are located" (p. 289). Both Gronn (2000) and Robinson (2001) concur and attribute it to an undertheorized view of task performance. However, Hosking (1988) argues that leadership researchers also err by conceptualizing the organization as an already formed entity, instead of one that is in a state of becoming.[1] As such, they fail to conceptualize leaders as agents whose actions, as Giddens (1984) would say, "make a difference" in the ongoing course of events. By contrast, when researchers embrace the processes of organizing, leadership becomes intrinsic to it because the skills of leadership are the skills of organizing (Hosking & Morley, 1988). As Hosking (1988) explains

> it is not enough to understand what leaders do. Rather it is essential to focus on leadership processes: processes in which influential 'acts of organizing' contribute to the structuring of interactions and relationships, activities and sentiments; processes in which definitions of social order are negotiated, found acceptable, implemented and renegotiated; processes in which interdependencies are organized in ways which, to a greater or lesser degree, promote the values and interests of the social order. In sum, leadership can be seen as a certain kind of organizing activity. (p. 147)

Hosking's view restores agency to leadership theorizing because the organization is in a constant state of becoming only through the actions of its agents, thus making it difficult to cast leadership study in isolationist or epiphenomenal terms.[2]

Although Hosking was not particularly oriented to organizational discourse, her arguments take on new meaning with the study of sequence and temporal form in social interaction. To study sequence and temporal form is to study *interaction process,* the dance between leader and led and its language of connectedness, temporalness, patternedness, and embeddedness (L. E. Rogers & Escudero, 2004b). Hinde (1979) offers a deceptively simple example of this orientation by observing that it makes a relational difference whether a husband and wife consistently kiss after they quarrel or quarrel after they kiss, even though the total amount of quarreling and kissing may be the same.

Too often, survey or interview data are used as a proxy for interaction process as if there is a single relational reality that can be presumed.[3] According to L. E. Rogers, Millar, and Bavelas (1985), this equates a description from the part (one member) with the description of the whole (the relationship itself), a slip that is especially seductive in dyad study where there are only two people in the relationship. From an interactional perspective, relational patterns are always codefined. This is because individuals in a leadership relationship do not relate and then communicate, they relate *in* communication (McDermott & Roth, 1978). A leader or a member's action is thus of little consequence unless it is a reaction or antecedent to the other's action.[4]

Interaction analysis is the study of interaction process. McDermott and Roth (1978) define interaction analysis as when *"a person's behavior is best described in terms of the behavior of those immediately about that person, those with whom the person is doing interactional work in the construction of recognizable social scenes or events"* (p. 321; emphasis original). McDermott and Roth were actually describing a number of approaches in the 1970s, with an emerging emphasis on sequence and temporal form, including ethnomethodology, conversation analysis, sociolinguistics, exchange theory, and network analysis.

While the definition of interaction analysis has been narrowed significantly over the years (Fairhurst, 2004), the more general point remains. There is a loose confederation of discursive approaches, with seemingly few ties to any one theoretical tradition, that focus on the sequence and temporal form of behavior. These approaches currently include interaction analysis (in the form of coded interaction), conversation analysis, speech act schematics, and discursive psychology (for brief overviews, see Appendixes A1–4). Their emphases on sequence and temporal form include acts, interacts, and double interacts; turn taking and adjacency pairs; narrative schemas and episodes; scripts; and script formulations. These temporal forms serve as the basis for this chapter's organization.

Collectively, they will demonstrate why the individual leader or follower is no longer the unit of analysis. Individually, they will have much to say that goes to the heart of Hosking's (1988) enjoinder to study the organizing potential of leader–follower actions.[5] For example, the study of acts, interacts, and double interacts in interaction analysis can inform the study of collective mind in high-reliability organizations as a global structure emerges from local interactions (Weick & Roberts, 1993). The study of turn taking and adjacency pairs in conversation analysis creates a stage for distributed leadership to emerge.

Because turn taking reveals the articulation points of action, it is leadership-as-it-happens, however distributed or asymmetric the influence patterns (Boden, 1994). The study of narrative schemas and episodes in speech act schematics argues strongly for the sequential foundation of leadership command presence and treatment of it as a strategic response, not a trait-like characterization such as we find in neo-charisma theories. Finally, the study of script and script formulations tells us about the organizational scripts of leadership actors, improvisation around their timing and pacing, and actors' reflexivity surrounding them. While topics such as collective mind, distributed leadership, command presence, scripts, and script formulations are present in varying degrees in the mainstream leadership literature, this chapter's emphasis on sequence and temporal form makes the case for a relational view of leadership, quite different from the individualism of leadership psychology. Consider first Weick's (1979) now familiar *double interact.*

Act, Interact, Double Interact

While a number of social scientists lay claim to the above title's terminology, Weick (1979) is perhaps best known for popularizing it within the organizational sciences. An 'act' is the behavior of one person, an 'interact' is the response of another to that behavior, and a 'double interact' is the response to the response. Consider one of his early examples:

> [S]uppose that a supervisor wants to get a worker to stop doing task A and start doing task B. The worker's action is the doing of task A; the supervisor tries to influence the worker to do task B. Obviously, we must know how the worker responds to this directive before we can make any statement about the complete influence attempt. But to determine the worker's response, we need a specific description of the original activity as a basis for comparison. The worker's typical response pattern will probably be altered in some way by the supervisor's directive, and before we can understand the meaning of this alteration, we need to know the action that was already under way. (p. 89)

Weick's (1979) model of organizing is built upon contingent response patterns like the double interact (in this case, how the worker responds to the directive), which he views as the building block of organizational growth and decline. For Weick, sets of double interacts aimed at reducing equivocality assemble into processes that become stable collective structures the more they are repeated (a point to which we shall return).

Although Weick (1979) does not concern himself with organizational discourse very much,[6] there are discourse analysts who hold Weick's appreciation for the value of interacts and double interacts. Interaction analysts form one such group (for a brief overview, see Appendix A2). To study acts, interacts, and double interacts, they first code verbal behavior according to a predefined set of codes in order to analyze the patterns that form over the course of several minutes and multiple conversations.[7] More specifically, coding enables interaction analysts to quantitatively analyze the sequences (interact, double interact, and beyond) and stages of interaction, their redundancy and predictability, and the link between interactional structures and aspects of the organizational context (Fairhurst, 2004; Putnam & Fairhurst, 2001).

For example, one type of interaction analysis utilizes a system known as relational control coding (L. E. Rogers & Escudero, 2004a; L. E. Rogers & Farace, 1975). This coding system codes each turn at talk as to whether it asserts control (designated 'one-up'), acquiesces or requests control ('one-down'), or neutralizes the control move of the previous utterance ('one-across'). In this scheme, the form of the utterance counts, not the content. To understand this, think of how the exact same words from a manager, "Gee, you're looking good today," can be given as a compliment or, with a little voiced sarcasm, an insult. The way in which words are delivered defines self in relation to other and simultaneously (re)produces the ongoing relationship. Although content is expected to vary widely across conversations, the form of a person's utterance, that is, *how* a message is delivered, is thought to produce relatively fixed and reproducible patterns. Thus, the tone of the "you're looking good" comment, whether it is compliment or sarcasm, is expected to reproduce itself time and again within the leader–member relationship.

Using L. E. Rogers and Farace's (1975) relational control coding system, an act is a single one-up ($\uparrow$), one-down ($\downarrow$), or one-across code ($\rightarrow$). For example, a police supervisor's order to a junior officer to "Check on the victim's condition," is coded a one-up move because it asserts control ($\uparrow$). However, this lone control move really tells us little because we do not know how the act was received.[8]

In relational control analyses, the interact (that is, two contiguous control moves) serves as the most basic unit of analysis, and it is easy to see why. It makes a huge difference whether the one-up orders by the police supervisor are responded to with compliance by the junior officer ($\uparrow\downarrow$) or if they are met with resistance ($\uparrow\uparrow$).[9] In the first instance, the evolving relationship is one of junior officer subordination to the supervisor, while the second relationship is marked by competition or resistance. Relational control analyses also have the capability of examining more extended interactional sequences (that is, double interacts and beyond such as a conflict sequence, $\uparrow\uparrow\uparrow\uparrow\uparrow$) through Markov chain or lag sequential analyses.

What are the implications of relational control and other types of interaction analyses for leadership study? In interaction analysis, organizational constructs like leadership evolve from message patterns and evolving communication systems. Theoretically, what constitutes a 'system' could be a leadership relationship, a work unit (such as a team, department, or plant), or a whole organization. All are predicated on the view that systems emerge over repeated interactions that evolve into multileveled orders of pattern (Bateson, 1972). Interaction analysts assess the actual *redundancy* of message patterns that most other discourse analysts (and Weick) just assume and that leadership psychologists capture through self-reports.

By way of example, consider a conversation that Cooren and I analyzed (Fairhurst & Cooren, 2004). The data involve a police rescue of a Cincinnati, Ohio, female police officer named Officer Conway.[10] Conway was shot four times by an assailant who then took control of her cruiser. In the midst of a violent struggle in which she eventually killed her assailant, she radioed for help. That call and the ensuing search and rescue form the transcript that can be found in Appendix B.

What would an interactional orientation mean for our police rescue? For starters, interaction analysts would want to study longer interactions (for example, 20 minutes or more) and several of them in order to establish pattern repetition. Thus, the analysis of this police radio transcript is only suggestive of the type of analysis to be undertaken with more data. My colleague and I (Fairhurst & Cooren, 2004) began by focusing on the role of the dispatcher. She is not a police officer, and with the exception of Conway, she interacts only with police supervisors. Thus, we might expect that she would defer to police authorities, which she appears to do (Police $\uparrow$ Dispatcher $\downarrow$, .44), much more so than collectively they defer to her (D $\uparrow$ P $\downarrow$, .11).[11] She never challenges any of the police supervisors (P $\uparrow$ D $\uparrow$ or D $\uparrow$ P $\uparrow$, .00), and she engages in little discussion (D $\rightarrow$ P $\rightarrow$.00, P $\rightarrow$ D $\rightarrow$, .12). Clearly there is an authority relationship here that plays itself out.

However, the dispatcher (Dis) also plays a key role in eliciting information and confirming its receipt. When these moves are sequenced with the questions and acknowledgments of the police supervisors (1215, 1230), a submissive symmetry pattern of successive one-down moves ($\downarrow\downarrow\downarrow$ or more) emerges. The need to acknowledge ("Copy 1627 Central"), assist ("Car 15 responding"), question ("Is homicide responding?"), and confirm ("I'm notifying now") occurs in this unfolding submissive pattern as Excerpts 2.1a and 2.1b reveal:

2.1a Submissive Symmetry

			Act	Sequence
85	Dis:	Copy 1627 Central		$\downarrow$
86		(1.0)		
87	1215:	Car 15 responding	$\downarrow$	$\downarrow\downarrow$
88		(1.0)		
89	Dis:	Car 15 copy.	$\downarrow$	$\downarrow\downarrow\downarrow$

2.1b Submissive Symmetry After an Order

			Act	Sequence
95	1230:	Get the aircare to standby. And we have the night chief responding	↑	
96		(0.5)		
97	**Dis:**	The night chief is responding	↓	↑↓
98	1230:	Is homicide responding?	↓	↑↓↓
99		(2.5)		
100	**Dis:**	I'm notifying now.	↓	↑↓↓↓
101	( ):	Ok, so do you know who might have done this?	↓	↑↓↓↓↓

Submissive symmetry appears to play an instrumental role in eliciting information and building sufficient redundancy to avoid error in the coordination of messages from multiple officers. This makes sense because these actors are not copresent communicators; they are communicating via police radio. Moreover, high-reliability organizations (HROs) like police and firefighting organizations need communication redundancy to guard against simplification, complacency, and missed information (Weick, Sutcliffe, & Obstfeld, 1999). Unlike the concern for profit and efficiency in high-efficiency organizations, it is the safety of human lives at stake that requires reliable performances in HROs.

Certainly, patterns other than submissive symmetry, dispatcher deference to authority, and the absence of discussion may be detectable from larger samples of dialogue.[12] However, taken together they demonstrate the ways in which a global structure emerges from local interactions.[13] To the extent that coding schemes sensitively reflect interactional dynamics, the redundancies found through interaction analysis can be strong indicators of habitual performance. Such patterns can then be assessed against the expectations for reliability. According to Weick and Roberts (1993), "patterns of interrelating are as close to a physical substrate for collective mind as we are likely to find" (p. 365). This is because reliable performances signal a group of interrelating actors who are constantly inferring a changing self-interrelation, which they project back into the system.

Finally, while relational control analyses focus on *how* messages are delivered, other coding schemes tap into more content-related message features. Indeed, most coding schemes do not restrict themselves to the control function of messages, nor is this true of discourse analyses in general (Fairhurst, 2004). Nevertheless, in different ways interaction analyses make the point that the actions of the actors only make sense *from the perspective of the overall pattern*. Thus, the individual leader's or follower's acts are considered partial, incomplete, and ultimately distorted views of the leadership process because leadership patterns must always be codefined.

Turn Taking, Adjacency Pairs

Conversation analysts also key in on the unfolding scene of action, but they eschew coding schemes to focus instead on the social organization of talk-in-interaction[14] and how it enables actors to make sense of their worlds (for a brief overview, see Appendix A1). Staying with the police rescue example, conversation analysts would have no a priori interest in control (as in relational control coding) or any other topic unless the actors themselves make it an issue. Instead, these analysts would notice immediately how the business of a police rescue is 'brought off' through a series of quick, orderly turns at talk. For example, consider Excerpt 2.2 below from the very start of the radio call by Conway (Cy, car 1212) to the dispatcher (Dis) and police supervisors (1030, 1080, 12400). (See Appendix A1 for details of the transcription notation system for conversation analysis.)

2.2 Searching for Conway

1	Cy:	Help! I need assistance! I'm shot in the (car)!
2		(2.0)
3	Dis:	*Where* do you need it?
4	Cy:	Help! I need help!
5		(1.5)
6	1030:	1238 Elm. I believe, 1030, I believe I heard shots fired there.
7	Cy:	[((Unintelligible screaming)) please!
8	Dis:	[-Location?
9		(1.0)
10	Dis:	1212, what's your location?
11		(6.5)
12	1080:	1080, we got a location?
13		(1.0)
14	Dis:	Negative
15		((line sounds))

16	**Dis:**	Officer needs assistance, District One, unknown location. 12 12th and Elm.
17		Officer needs assistance, 12th and Elm. Possibly shots fired.
18		(3.0)
19	**1080:**	1080 35, 12th and Elm, do not *see* them
20		(2.5)
21	**1240:**	1240. Play the tape back

In these first minutes of dialogue, the injured Conway, the dispatcher, and police supervisors 1030, 1080, and 1240 occupy the radio traffic. The assailant and Conway are engaged in a struggle, while her supervisors search for her frantically. The above sequence of talk raises a lot of questions for the conversation analyst. For example, if the radio is their only means of communication at this point, what prevents them from all talking at once? Every on-duty officer in Cincinnati's District 1 (where Conway resided) heard Conway's cry for help. Moreover, the other four districts have heard the line sounds that are the prelude to countywide emergency announcements (line 15). What prevents them from joining in the radio traffic, especially the many other beat officers in District 1? How is it decided which speaker gets to talk at all? Further, exactly how does Conway's location come to be jointly formulated by the dispatcher and the participating officers?

These are important questions, the answers to which are suggested by Boden (1994) in *The Business of Talk*. Drawing from ethnomethodology and conversation analysis, she calls our attention to the sequential pacing that talk gives to tasks and how it signals the organization's presence: "The ways in which verbal rhythms anchor the unseen organization makes that abstract entity available and directly observable" (p. 206). How so? There are two prominent ways in which we can observe the 'organization' in the above sequence. First, there is an unspoken orientation to hierarchy by all police officers within earshot of District 1's radio traffic. For example, no beat officers (other than Conway) join the radio traffic because protocol dictates that proximate police supervisors take over the rescue. Clearly, the other beat officers are observing what Sacks (1992) would call the 'category-bound' activities of the hierarchy, a subject taken up more directly in Chapter 3.

Second, these actors not only orient to the organization's categories, but also to its rules and procedures. Given the coordination demands of a rescue, the dispatcher and police supervisors' training in emergency response prioritizes location formulation over other relevant tasks for good reason: a rescue is impossible without a location. The actors formulate a location through turn taking in an interrogative series composed of short questions and answers. In this series we see what Sacks, Schegloff, and Jefferson (1974) call *context-free* and *context-sensitive* action. Sacks et al. noted that the general organization of turn taking in everyday language is guided by a number of context-free rules; for example, there is a bias toward short economical turns, variability in the number and order of speakers, variability in turn sizes, and few gaps and over-laps in turn transition. Moreover, certain kinds of utterances in everyday talk are part of *adjacency pairs* where the first pair part (for example, a question) builds in a preference for a second pair part (an answer).[15] Culturally, we are taught these rules, and they help us to understand the sequential pacing of this interrogative series.

However, the general organization of turn taking in everyday speech is also quite context-sensitive. For example, the parties to this radio traffic are all trained to routinize emergencies, but in this particular case it means that the dispatcher must ignore Conway's intense emotions (lines 1, 4, and 7) and initi-ate short, pointed location questions to facilitate a speedy rescue (lines 3, 8, 10, and 12). Routinization could mean something quite different in less emotion-ridden scenarios or where location was already known. Importantly, initial speaker order is dictated by the participant with the most pertinent informa-tion at that moment. For example, after Conway's initial cry for help (line 1), the dispatcher is the only one with the technology to readily identify Conway without an announced car number.[16] Because of this informational capability, the dispatcher's general role is to facilitate the radio traffic of participating offi-cers until they arrive on scene. Until such a time, three participating police supervisors search and relay information (lines 6, 19) or clarify/direct the dis-patcher accordingly (lines 12, 21, 27), but thereafter form a speaking order based upon who is first on the scene to comment on the precise circumstances (1080 followed by 1240, lines 41–62, see Appendix B). Clearly, initial speaking order and location formulation are two context-sensitive actions that dictate the taking of turns—and signal the organization's presence.

Boden (1994) observed that "action *coheres* as sequence . . . turn taking mechanisms . . . reveal the *articulation points* of action and thus its structuring properties" (p. 206, emphasis original). We see in this brief example just *how* action coheres as a sequence of turns-at-talk. The task, which is to address Conway's pleas for help, triggers a multi-party turn-taking sequence to formu-late her location that, in turn, leads ultimately to the rescue, which entails the subtasks of securing the crime scene and requesting medical assistance. Inter-estingly, in the sequencing of the task, the complete transcript (see Appendix B) reveals that no one supervisor takes charge; rather, they appear in successive waves of command and control action (1030, 1080, 1240, and then the night chief in Car 15). This is by design because an emergency response team is desig-nated to be first on scene followed by other shift supervisors who may or may not be in their cars when emergency calls come in.[17] The lesson of this and other police rescues is that studying turn taking reveals the sequential pacing of the task that, in turn, allows leadership to emerge in its more distributed forms as specific police supervisors advance the task in various ways. Should asymmetric influence by one or more of the supervisors manifest itself, the mechanics of turn taking, including interruption behavior, requests/demands to speak, and floor dominance (time speaking), would reveal this as well.[18]

Too often in survey research, leadership comes off as a social or relational phenomenon quite divorced from task accomplishment. Yet, as we see in conversation analysis, task-related actions are always also task interactions (Engestrom, 1999). Even the most solitary of task performances requires instruction, coordination, integration, and/or delivery vis-à-vis other performances. Importantly, when the study of interaction process is embraced, the focus on language in use means that the study of *constraint* emphasizes those forces that operate on 'next action.' For example, when Officer Conway was asked by her dispatcher, "1212, what's your location?", that question and the force with which it was delivered (normatively) constrained Conway to answer the question, assuming she was capable of answering, in order to further the rescue. In the study of interaction process then, the scope of task activity under scrutiny is specifically dictated by the unfolding sequence of next actions.

By contrast, the operation of 'constraint' for much mainstream leadership research focuses on the creation of variables from aspects of the context—environmental, organizational, or relational—as they impact various relational states or outcomes. The scope of task activity is quite broad and glossed by the retrospective summarizing of behavior required for an overall rating's judgment. Arguable benefits notwithstanding, the operation of 'constraint' has none of the specificity directed toward *next action* and all of the generality of an overarching influence. For Robinson (2001), this is a prime example of how the leadership literature overemphasizes decontextualized processes of interpersonal influence and downplays actors' situated task skills and expertise.[19] Grounding the study of leadership in the task at hand is much more likely to reveal what Hosking (1988) terms "influential acts of organizing" because of the level of detail that a conversation analysis makes available. A similar conclusion may be drawn from the episodic analysis below.

Narrative Schemas, Episodes

Conversation analysts have a long tradition of studying 911 calls to emergency services in which they configure the beginning, middle, and closing organization of entire calls (Whalen & Zimmerman, 1998; Zimmerman, 1992). We could perform just such an analysis of Conway's search and rescue. However, 'search and rescue' is suggestive of a larger temporal unit than a turn-at-talk or even a double interact. The most commonly used unit is that of an *episode*. As Harré and Secord (1972) note, episodes appear as natural divisions of social life because certain sequences of events are perceived as distinct wholes. They also possess their own logics, often with recognizable openings and closings (Gumperz, 1972). The study of episodes has been particularly important to cognitive researchers because memory is narratively organized (Bruner, 1986, 1990), and a major issue for cognitive script or schema theories is how one moves from single episodes to more general patterns of schema formulations (Schank & Abelson, 1977).

However, the study of episodic structure is also important to discourse analyses, one of which is Speech Act Schematics (SAS) (Cooren, 2001) (for a brief overview, see Appendix A3). SAS is a relatively new form of discourse analysis that merges the speech act tradition (Austin, 1962, 1975; Searle, 1969, 1979) with Greimas's (1987) structural narratology. It does so by analyzing the larger episodic or schematic forms that arise from stringing speech acts together. Simply stated, *speech acts* focus on the actions performed through our language. Following Cooren (2001),[20] there are six types of speech acts as 2.3 reveals.

2.3 Types of Speech Acts

Assertives   Represent as actual a state of affairs ("It is raining.")

Commissives   Commit to a future course of action ("I'll be right there.")

Directives   Attempt to get the hearer to do something ("Check on her safety.")

Declaratives   Bring a state of affairs into existence by representing oneself as performing that action ("I baptize you.")

Expressives   Express the attitudes of the speaker about a state of affairs ("Thank you.")

Accreditives   Transfer permission or authorization from one agent to a recipient ("You have my permission to leave.")

The modus operandi for combining speech acts draws from Greimas's (1987, 1988; Greimas & Courtes, 1982) generalized schema for narratives. Greimas's narratology is not a property of a particular kind of storytelling, but delineates instead a set of generalizable structural relationships between actors and objects involved in goal-directed action. Because the schema specifically helps us to understand the sequencing of goal-directed action, it also becomes the means by which we make sense of any given text involving goal-directed actors. As 2.4 demonstrates, Greimas's narrative schema has five phases:

2.4 Greimas's Narrative Schema

Manipulation phase:	X has to or is requested/invited by Y to perform an action A (having to do)
Commitment phase:	X decides or agrees to perform A (wanting to do)
Competence phase:	X needs to know how to perform A (knowing how to do), and X needs to be able to perform A (being able to do)
Performance phase:	X performs A (to do)
Sanction phase:	X is assessed by Y regarding her performing of A

Greimas (1987) also articulates a set of roles or *actants* in these phases, a subject that will be taken up more directly in Chapter 7. Presently, what is interesting about Greimas's narrative schema is the way in which it highlights the conditions of action (known as 'modalities') in sequential form; that is, to coordinate action there must be necessity (manipulation), willingness (commitment), knowhow (competence), and means (competence).

SAS utilizes Greimas's narrative schema as a generalizable template for all organizing.[21] To achieve this, Cooren (2001) asserts that different categories of speech acts correspond with the phases identified in the narrative schema. Example 2.5 extends Weick's (1979) earlier Task A/Task B example in this regard. According to SAS, directives and assertives often open schemas by establishing the necessity of some action. Note the supervisor's directive that marks the manipulation phase in the dialogue below ("Please stop Task A and start Task B"). Commissives, accreditives, and assertives all contribute to schema enactment. Note the worker's commissive that marks the commitment phase in the example below ("I can do that for you, but . . . "), while the competence phase contains two assertives ("I'm newly trained on B, and I may need a little extra time to get up to speed"), all establishing willingness, know-how, and (possibly delayed) means for this worker. Declaratives also contribute to schema enactment with the performance ("Task B is complete!"). Finally, expressives contribute to the sanction phase and closure of schema through an evaluation of acknowledgment of the action performed, as demonstrated in the supervisor's expressive ("Thank you.").

2.5 SAS Example with Tasks A and B

Phase	Dialogue		Speech Act
Manipulation	*Supervisor:*	Please stop Task A and start Task B.	Directive
Commitment	*Worker:*	I can do that for you, but . . .	Commissive
Competence	*Worker:*	. . . I'm newly trained on B, and I may need extra time to get up to speed.	Assertive Assertive
Performance	*Worker:*	(Performing Task B) Task B is complete!	Declarative
Sanction	*Supervisor:*	Thank you.	Expressive

Clearly, not all schemas are as simple as the above example. Complexity in schematic analyses derives from the way in which schemas embed themselves in one another. Embedding is possible precisely because there might be some secondary tasks to complete before the requested action can be performed. For example, the worker in our example could (1) delay fulfilling the supervisor's request until she finishes Task A, (2) modify/amend the request if time is of the essence, or (3) ignore the request if Task B was already done. At any phase of the schema, a specific interruption can take place if the actors fail to understand the request (manipulation), be willing to cooperate (commitment), be capable of cooperating (competence), perform the action correctly (performance), or be acknowledged appropriately (sanction). These different phases do not determine behavior, but they reliably indicate potential sources of trouble in the completion of a sequence (Cooren & Fairhurst, 2004). Because each initiation of a schema opens a specific time and space whose closure can be anticipated and forecasted (although never predetermined), the anticipated closure of a schema makes it possible to embed it in larger schematic forms (Cooren, 2001). Cooren and Fairhurst (2004) use the term 'spatio-temporal closures' to signify both the spatial and temporal elements of episodic closure. For leadership, this raises questions concerning the ways in which actors open, close, and embed episodes within one another. Consider once again the initial phases of the search and rescue involving Officer Conway (Cy, car 1212), the police dispatcher (Dis), and police supervisors (1030, 1080, 1240).

2.6 Schema Development in Conway's Rescue

1	Cy:	Help! I need assistance! I'm shot in the (car)!	**CY OPENS SCHEMA 'A'**
2		(2.0)	
3	Dis:	*Where* do you need it?	**DIS OPENS SCHEMA 'B'**
4	Cy:	Help! I need help!	
5		(1.5)	
6	1030:	1238 Elm. I believe, 1030, I believe I heard shots fired there.	
7	Cy:	[((Unintelligible screaming)) please!	
8	Dis:	[-Location?	
9		(1.0)	
10	Dis:	1212, what's your location?	
11		(6.5)	
12	1080:	1080, we got a location?	
13		(1.0)	

14	Dis:	Negative
15		((line sounds))
16	Dis:	Officer needs assistance, District One, unknown location. 12 12th and Elm.
17		Officer needs assistance, 12th and Elm. Possibly shots fired.
18		(3.0)
19	1080:	1080 35, 12th and Elm, do not *see* them
20		(2.5)
21	1240:	1240. Play the tape back
22		(2.5)
23	Dis:	1212, what's your location?
24	Cy:	Distress. I've been involved in a shooting (0.3) on Central
25		Parkway (0.5) north (.) of Liberty. I need some help hhh

CY CLOSES 'B'

26		(0.5)
27	1080:	1080, I [copy that. Check on her safety. **1080 OPENS SCHEMA 'C'**
28	Dis:	[are you hurt?
29		(0.5)
30	Dis:	1212, are you hurt?
31		(0.3)
32	Cy:	That's affirmative.
33		(0.5)
34	1080:	1080, I'll be there in five seconds. Blockin' it off with four cars.

1080 CLOSES 'A' AND 'C'

Fairhurst and Cooren (2004) argue that Conway's assertives at line 1 ("Help! I need assistance! I'm shot in the (car)!") open a schema (Schema 'A' opens) by creating a tension to be resolved only at the moment she receives help. However, Conway cannot receive that help until her location is determined, thus the dispatcher issues a directive to Conway at line 3 ("*Where* do you need it?") that effectively opens a second schema, a 'sub-schema' that is now embedded in the first (Schema 'B' opens). Unfortunately, Conway cannot immediately respond to that question because she is struggling with her assailant. The dispatcher and police supervisors try many things to determine that location including repeating the question to Conway (lines 10, 23), speculating as to the location of shots fired (line 6), and issuing a request to play the tape back of Conway's plea (21). All of this is for naught until Conway shoots and kills her attacker (not recorded), at which point she is able to answer the dispatcher (lines 24–25), providing her location and closing the 'location' sub-schema (Schema 'B' closes).

From there, Officer 1080 initiates a second sub-schema with the directive to the dispatcher to "Check on her safety" (line 27) (Schema 'C' opens), which the dispatcher promptly asks and Conway answers (lines 28–32). Officer 1080 then responds with "1080, I'll be there in five seconds. Blockin' it off with four cars" (line 34). This commissive, or commitment to immediately respond, deftly closes two schemas—the schema he initiated, but also the schema Conway initiated at the start of the radio call seeking help (Schemas 'A' and 'C' closes).[22]

This kind of spatio-temporal closure of an episode by 1080 proved significant in police supervisors' accounts of this search and rescue.[23] Police supervisors noted that 1080's "I'll be there in 5 seconds" statement (line 34) reflected *command presence* at that moment because he simultaneously communicated to the dispatcher, other supervisors, and most importantly to Conway that help was moments away. This statement reflects the multifunctionality of message behavior at its best when a timely, efficient message can satisfy multiple parties and the attendant coordination demands. Moreover, for these supervisors, command presence was seen in the context of the unfolding scene of action; an exigency for leadership that emerged was met with an authoritative response signaling that the chaos of the preceding moments was under control. Presence was felt as *episodic closure* because a leader's response relieved an earlier tension created by a previously set goal, thus enabling forward progress.

But what is command presence as a leadership construct? Police textbooks are scarce on the subject, but Dunn's (1999) firefighting textbook describes it as not "achieved by behaving or speaking a certain way during fires," but by "commanding and controlling a firefighting operation" (p. 6).[24] Yet, this definition of command presence seems vague and ambiguous as does the frequent use of 'presence' to describe the magically gifted qualities of charismatic leaders (Conger, 1989; Conger & Kanungo, 1987).

However, the SAS analysis suggests an interpretation more in line with *rhetorical presence,* a term denoting the joining of several rhetorical strategies that coalesce to respond to some situational exigency (Karon, 1976; Murphy, 1994; Perelman & Olbrechts-Tyteca, 1969). These strategies include *stylistic choices* (in the police case, multifunctional messages, parsimony in word choice), *structural concerns* (episodic closure), *substantive issues* (locating an injured Conway and attending to her medical status), and *delivery skills* (even, authoritative tone and lack of nonfluencies), all of which come together to heighten others' consciousness of another's 'performance.' If one's bias is strictly psychological, that is, if we are looking at command presence only through a lens focused on individual qualities or predictors, the more nuanced insight that presence is as much about sequential timing and a confluence of rhetorical strategies may regrettably be overlooked. Such a view limits our ability to discern the undeniably efficient organizing potential of command presence.

Scripts

Cooren and Fairhurst (2004) observe some interesting parallels between Greimas's (1987, 1988) conception of a schema and North American conceptualizations of same, beginning with the work of Schank and Abelson (1977). Although they come from radically different traditions (Greimas's structural analysis of folk tales versus Schank and Abelson's research on artificial intelligence), both focus on schemas as knowledge structures used in human understanding and behavior. Greimas's concept of narrative schema may seem akin to Schank and Abelson's (1977) concept of event schemata or *script* because both deal with ordered sequences of events. However, Greimas's concern is with the presentation of narrativity as a basic mechanism of sensemaking, which SAS appropriates as a generalized sequential template for all organizing. By contrast, scripts are knowledge structures that are more concretely tied to specific contexts, content, and sequenced actions (Abelson, 1981; Schank & Abelson, 1977). Restaurant behavior forms the prototypical example,[25] but in the organizational context, scripted behavior is associated with performance appraisals, selection interviews, upward communication, formal meetings, and decision-making processes (Gioia & Poole, 1984).

Gioia and Poole (1984) suggest that operationally, a *cognitive script* is a "mental representation of behaviors and behavior sequences appropriate for given contexts and retained in memory," while a *behavioral script* is the "performance of the observable stream of behaviors retained in an activated cognitive script" (p. 456). Further, behavioral scripts are *performative* if based in actor perceptions, and *inferred* if derived from observers of patterned, sequential behavior. Language analysis has been used to study behavioral scripts in performance appraisals, task coordination, and negotiations (Putnam & Fairhurst, 2001). However, Komaki's performance-monitoring studies are instructive for inferred leader behavioral script analysis because she uses interaction analysis to study effectiveness in patterned sequential behavior (Komaki, 1986, 1998; Komaki & Citera, 1990; Komaki, Zlotnick, & Jensen, 1986).[26]

Komaki is basically interested in one critical question: How can leaders most effectively improve the performance of their employees? Trained as a psychologist, Komaki draws from the principles of operant conditioning, the theory of which directly links consequences to behavior (Skinner, 1957, 1974). However, one of the unique contributions of her work is performance monitoring (for example, through work sampling, questioning the employee, and so on), which reportedly gives leaders more accurate information about specific performances, thus enhancing their ability to provide *contingent* consequences to employees. Because feedback from leaders to employees is often only tenuously linked to their performances, her research breaks new ground in linking effectiveness to the combined use of performance monitors and consequences *in the midst of employee task performance* (Komaki, 1986). The task performances that she and her colleagues studied ranged from sailboat races to theater productions to more standard manufacturing operations (Komaki, 1998).

The temporality of Komaki's work is captured in her use of musical scales to capture an AMC sequence where 'A' stands for an antecedent (a leader's order or instruction), 'M' stands for monitor (usually through work sampling), and 'C' stands for consequence (leaders' positive, negative, or neutral judgments of the performance). According to Komaki (1998), the most effective leaders deliver their AMC sequence quickly and in close succession as in the following:

2.7a Effective AMC Sequence

A | ● - - |

M| - ● - |

C | - - ● |

Like a musical score, movement from left to right denotes time. The vertical lines denote the beginning and ending of the score, while 'A,' 'M,' and 'C' are 'notes' (●) delivered in close succession. According to Komaki (1998), effective leaders initiate rapid sequences in which they "deliver an antecedent, follow quickly with a monitor, and then, after more discussion about performance, deliver a consequence" (p. 193). Monitoring has been shown to stimulate employees to talk about their own performances, which encourages further monitoring (Komaki & Citera, 1990). By contrast, ineffective leaders reportedly take much more time to deliver this same sequence:

2.7b Ineffective AMC Sequence

A | ● - o - o - - - - - - - - o - - |

M| - - - - - - - - - - - - - - ● - |

C | - - - - - - - - - - - - - - ● |

Komaki's (1998) description of the above 'sluggish' and 'lackluster' leader shows three antecedents delivered in a row before a monitor and consequence are delivered, taking five times as long to deliver the AMC sequence (p. 27). Similar to the point made about sequentiality in command presence, Komaki demonstrates the utility of sequential pacing in the distribution of effective and ineffective performance monitors and consequences over time.

Why is Komaki's work relevant for inferred behavioral script analysis, especially given its basis in operant conditioning theory? Two reasons stand out. First, while several of her studies highlight the sequential aspects of leader and follower behavior, Komaki's (1998) explanatory focus appears to be solely on the sequenced behavior of effective and lackluster leaders. It is reasonable to infer from her scaled graphs and Komaki's (1998) narrative that effective leaders (should) follow a behavioral script with a strict monitoring and reinforcement schedule.[27] Her profile of *effective* leaders suggests that they hold expectations regarding both the need for monitoring and reinforcement to achieve maximum performance, and a progressive sequencing of events tightly scripted in terms of AMC pacing and placement. By contrast, her profile of *lackluster* leaders reflects sluggish AMC sequences, loosely scripted at best because they are either isolated, laconic, under-communicating performance expectations (antecedents), or stressing the details of the work over the performance before commencing monitoring. They show little sensitivity to the sequencing of performance monitoring and reinforcement as concerns.

Second, she chooses interaction analysis to study the redundancies in sequential pacing, but with a twist. Too often discourse analysts generally view language and nonlinguistic action as disjoint activities and underrepresent them in their analyses (Putnam & Fairhurst, 2001). However, Komaki codes time-sampled (at 15-second intervals), observed linguistic and nonlinguistic behavior because not all performance monitoring is verbalized (for example, work sampling), and manager self-reports have proven unreliable (Komaki, 1998).[28] Through her Operant Supervisory Taxonomy and Index, Komaki codes the language and action of leaders in the midst of employee task performance, assesses baseline frequencies, and forms script-like sequences that yield her AMC model. She helps refine notions of leader effectiveness by explicating its sequential properties when trying to improve employee performance. Indeed, using interaction analysis for inferred behavioral script analysis can offer a lens on effectiveness in terms of sequential pacing and placement that is too rarely observed.

However, Komaki's time sampling techniques restrict one key insight about leaders' antecedent activities. Unlike other forms of discourse analysis, we do not have transcripts of what leaders and followers actually said to one another. Such a transcription could reveal what Sanders (2006) calls "a certain artfulness in the way speakers sequentially place and phrase what they say for the sake of being responsive to what has gone before, and at the same time anticipatory of fostering desired consequences for the ensuing interaction and for their presentation of self" (p. 169). What Sanders is calling attention to here is the notion of *interactional consequences*, which may or may not be the same as the *performance consequences* that Komaki is coding. Komaki's coding of antecedents, monitors, and consequences gives us the bold strokes, or raw outline of the interaction between leader and led; it gives us none of the details regarding what future course the interaction can relevantly and coherently take when antecedents are first communicated and/or performance monitoring conversations occur. Ineffective leaders are considered sluggish and lackluster for the extra time they take to deliver them without considering the kinds of constraints that members may be introducing into the interaction, thus potentially explaining the leaders' additional time spent in the antecedent phase— or perhaps better explaining the 'artfulness' with which certain leaders can overcome them.

The organizing potential of the leaders' actions are explicit in Komaki's work, but a full discussion of this issue requires that we also address the related notion of 'script formulations.'

Script Formulations

In the previous section, I used script theory as it relates to behavior observation to explicate Komaki's (1998) AMC sequences for shaping employee performance. As generalized event schemata, scripts are knowledge structures that are abstracted from experience when action becomes recognizable, expected, and routinely ordered (Nelson, 1986). This is because living in an ordered world requires actors to generalize from experience to form schematic understandings that allow them to move into new situations with reasonable expectations for what may unfold. While scripts are considered perception-and-action schemas, the emphasis in script theory is often on the cognitive representation of cultural or organizational scripts (Edwards, 1994; Gioia & Poole, 1984).

However, Edwards (1994) challenges the primacy of perception over language, arguing instead that, "Although events that conform to script expectations start to pass largely unnoticed, the things we notice, remark on, and remember are the exceptions or anomalies, and these in turn can become, with sufficient regularity, the basis of new schematic scripts or subscripts" (p. 212). Hence, *script formulations* surface in ordinary conversation when event sequences are depicted as more or less routine, and *breach formulations* appear when these sequences are contrasted with some norm or routine. Both are pragmatically formulated constructions; that is, script talk and breach talk are rhetorical moves designed to achieve some interactional goal when specifically introduced into the conversation. Both also recount the experience of sequence and temporal form through some kind of sequential mapping or perspective framing as that of a routine or anomaly (Hoskin, 2004). For Edwards (1994), the challenge is to discover how scripts and breaches function less as mental representations and more as *linguistic resources* for communicating actors.

Edwards's (1994, 1997) approach is that of discursive psychology, first popularized by Potter and Wetherell (1987) (see Appendix A4 for a brief overview). Discursive psychology builds on ethnomethodology-informed conversation analysis, yet also includes a more Foucauldian emphasis on Discourse to source the origins of the particular linguistic resources deployed (Potter & Wetherell, 1987; Wetherell, 1998). With this approach, narratives from recorded oral histories and talk-in-interaction may be analyzed for script or breach talk where such formulations can serve a key role in the very construction of events. Edwards (1994) explains, "It is not only that script theorists deal mostly with invented or idealized texts, or ones reconstructed anecdotally, but that script theory pays scant attention to the nature of descriptions as potentially arbitrary and variable, rhetorically designed, or interactionally occasioned *constructions* of events" (p. 214, emphasis original).

For example, consider the following conversational excerpt from Fairhurst (1993a) on the introduction of Total Quality (TQ) into a U.S. manufacturing plant.[29] The leader, Pete, and his direct report, Ken, are discussing the introduction of statistical quality control. Previous to this excerpt, they discussed the use of audits, graphs, and data recording to assist Ken's team in monitoring the quality of their work.

2.8 Pete and Ken on TQM

1	Pete:	We gotta do a lotta managin' around it though, Ken (.6)
2		I mean
3	Ken:	Yeah
4	Pete:	just manage the *hell* out of it. (.7) You know in
5		a lot of case- If they had their way they would just be out
6		there and uh (.) you know eight hours (.) exchange (.1)
7		whatever information they need to and then leave. And
8		and there's no- there's no kind of consolidating information
9	Ken:	[Yeah
10	Pete:	[and reviewing it and helpin' 'em look at it and (1.7) we just gotta
11		reinforce it and oh *kill* it (.4) with 'em
12	Ken:	[Oh yeah

13   **Pete:**   [every time we talk to 'em

14   **Ken:**   *Sure* (1.3) like we gotta make sure they they *know* it's there and

15   they're gonna use it right. And if they don't wanna use it you

16   know at least come and *ask* (.4) 'Hey, (.2) I got a problem here,'

17   (.6) you know, 'What can I do about it?' (.7) 'Have you checked

18   the book? (.4) You know, 'Have you checked your uh- your audit

19   book your (.4) process audit, your glue audit book?' And if they hadn't,

20   'Well let's go *look* at it . . . If we can get 'em to use the uh things

21   that are in place (.9) I think they can help themselves a lot

22   more than they do now

Pete scripts the team's standard operating practices, which lacks the consolidation that TQ affords through statistical monitoring, as a breach of TQ (lines 4–8: "If they had their way they would just be out there . . . eight hours (.) exchange . . . whatever information they need to and then leave. . . . And there's no . . . kind of consolidating information"). With this remark, Pete claims a consensus that serves to normalize past practices as a pathology (Edwards, 1994). The breach formulation also supplies the warrant for his enjoinder to Ken that they must "manage the *hell* out of it" (line 4) and "*kill* it with 'em" (line 11) "every time we talk to 'em" (line 13) to force change. Ken follows by formulating a TQ script as a sequence of steps that takes into account the team's recalcitrance (lines 15–20: "And if they don't want to use it . . . at least come and ask, 'Hey . . . I got a problem here. . . . What can I do about it?' . . . [I will ask] 'Have you checked . . . your audit book?'"), thus responding to the breach formulation as a previously introduced interactional contingency. Based on previous conversation, the script that Ken formulates also presumes a prior scripted sequence of data collection, analysis, and recording in order for the 'audit book' to serve as a resource when a problem arises. Thus, technically lines 14–20 constitute a subscript of a larger TQ script for statistical quality control.

Nevertheless, Pete's breach talk and Ken's TQ script talk reveal a new script in the making for Ken's team, which is vital to organizational change in two ways. First, Pete's metaphorically strong language (line 4: "manage the *hell* out of it" and line 11: "*kill* it with 'em") is an unmistakable sign for Ken about his manager's commitments to Total Quality. Pete's words possess none of the ambivalence that may provide Ken with an excuse for a halfhearted TQ change effort.

Second, the more these managers discuss TQ solutions to the team's problems vis-à-vis new scripted event sequences, the more they expand their ideas about what might be possible. In turn, envisioning possible futures should have a priming effect on future team conversations with Ken (Fairhurst & Sarr, 1996). Team members will introduce their own contingencies, which they and Ken will negotiate, the outcome of which will likely be more major or minor adjustments that establish the conditions of TQ's relevance. However, Ken's ability to negotiate is a function of how much he develops his mental models for the use of TQ, draws from its linguistic repertoire, and recognizes large and small opportunities for adoption, some or all of which may be instigated by these very conversations with his manager. As Barrett, Thomas, and Hocevar's (1995) argue

> An interpretive community is, by definition, always transforming the horizon into ingredients for its own practices, but the practices themselves are being transformed by the very work they do. When members reach out to absorb ideas for their own projects, they are simultaneously extending those projects and altering them. (p. 367)

Organizational change here is more evolutionary than revolutionary because it is grounded in ways of talking and constituting reality. As such, Tsoukas and Chia (2002) have argued strongly for a view of change that gives theoretical priority to the microscopic and has analysts looking for "creep," "slippage," "drift," and natural "spread" (p. 580), or what Orlikowski (1996) and Weick (1998) label ongoing improvisation.[30] Script and breach formulations are instrumental indicators in this regard.

A Backward Glance—Final Thoughts

In one way or another, all of the discursive approaches reviewed in this chapter suggest that the organizing potential of leadership discourse is based on sequence and temporal form in leadership interaction. For example

- Interaction analyses suggest that relational patterns are always codefined from an interactional view, and the actions of leaders only make sense from the perspective of the overall pattern.
  - Interaction analyses can be used to study collective mind in high-reliability organizations because these analyses produce a global structure that emerges from local interactions. Such a structure can be assessed against the expectations for reliable performances.
- In conversation analysis, we can observe the sequential pacing given to tasks through turn taking. By allowing the task back into the study of leadership, leadership is also free to emerge in more distributed forms if more than one leadership actor advances the task.
  - The mechanics of turn taking, including interruptions, requests/demands for the floor, and floor dominance, reveal leadership-as-it-happens however distributed or asymmetric the influence patterns.

- From speech act schematics, we can observe the episodic ordering of interaction as episodes nest within one another.
  - Studying episodic closure can demonstrate command presence when an actor steps into the unfolding scene of action at those precise moments that can best alter its trajectory toward goal resolution.
  - Like rhetorical presence, command presence is sequentially grounded and represents an interaction of rhetorical strategies including stylistic choices, structural concerns, substantive issues, and delivery skills.
- When interaction analysis is used for an inferred script analysis, effectiveness can be defined in terms of the sequential pacing and placement of key behaviors
  - Komaki's performance-monitoring research lends itself to an inferred script analysis by specifying supervisory effectiveness in terms of performance antecedent, monitoring, and consequence sequences.
- *Script formulations* surface in ordinary conversations when event sequences are depicted as more or less routine, or as *breach formulations* when contrasted with some norm or routine. Both are pragmatically formulated constructions; that is, script talk and breach talk are rhetorical moves designed to carry out some kind of interactional business (for example, organizational change) when specifically introduced into the conversation.
  - Script and breach formulations reveal actors' reflexivity around these acts of organizing.

To suggest that order matters in leadership study is not to assert the primacy of the interactional tradition (broadly defined) over leadership psychology. It is to suggest that there are certain kinds of questions for which each is ideally suited. Recall from the introduction that Hosking (1988) argued that the skills of leadership are the skills of organizing. Such a view emphasizes the agency in theorizing leadership because the organization is in a constant state of becoming, and leadership is about making that happen in varying degrees. Whether one studies the iterability of interact/double interact sequences, turn taking/adjacency pairs, spatio-temporal closures, scripts and script formulations, we are studying what is organizing about leadership discourse and formative of organizations. Chapter 3, on membership categorization, continues with the organizing potential of discourse.

NOTES

1. For further discussion of organizations as entities versus a becoming view, see Fairhurst and Putnam (2004) and Tsoukas and Chia (2002).

2. The phrase "leadership theorizing" is important here because Gronn (1995), Yukl (1999), and others have certainly made the case for exaggerated agency in neo-charisma theories. However, as Chapter 1 suggests, agency is rarely explicitly theorized (Hosking, 1988).

3. However, it should be noted that some discourse analysts rely heavily on interview data that, unless positioned appropriately, may be susceptible to the same criticism.

4. This is much as we see in Mead's (1934) concept of the social act, Bateson's (1972) ecology of form, and Weick's (1979) model of organizing.

5. Because Hosking (1988) focused heavily on leadership process, one can extrapolate that the organizing potential of both leader and follower actions require study.

6. However, see Weick (2004) on this point.

7. By this is meant that a typical sample includes conversations from multiple dyads with some 20 to 30 minutes of conversation per dyad.

8. Even if we knew that this supervisor ordered this officer around a lot, it still tells us little other than that this supervisor generally seeks control of his junior officer. We can only guess at the outcomes.

9. However, the designation of any specific act, interact, or double interact always depends on where the analyst punctuates the interaction sequence.

10. The 4-minute and 15-second transcript depicts the 1998 shooting of a 23-year-old Cincinnati, Ohio, police officer, Katie Conway, by a 41-year-old male assailant who hijacked her cruiser. The officer was shot four times with a .357 magnum handgun after which she returned fire, killing the suspect with her gun. The transcript in Appendix B describes the officer's initial panicked call for help when the assailant was still in control of her cruiser, the police dispatcher's efforts to identify her location, and conversations with police supervisors who sought to assist her. This conversation is a matter of public record and was obtained from the Cincinnati Police Department.

11. The dispatcher was compared to the police supervisors as a group, given so little data on individual police supervisors.

12. Such analyses could examine how specific police officers respond and are responded to when they communicate. This would make a particularly interesting analysis of the distributed and/or asymmetric nature of the influence exerted given that police supervisors of different rank gather together to coordinate rescues. Should leadership emerge from unexpected quarters (for example, a beat officer), this would be easily discerned. One could also assess relationships between specific distributed or asymmetric interactional patterns and a host of perceptual variables, including relationship judgments like leader–member exchange, job performance, communication satisfaction, perceived decision-making control, and so on (Fairhurst, Rogers, & Sarr, 1987). Such analyses could supply many of the specifics around judgments of effective or ineffective leader–member relationships.

13. Again, this is assuming multiple interactions. For examples of relational control research in which global structures emerge from local interactions, see the work of Fairhurst and colleagues (Courtright, Fairhurst & Rogers, 1989; Fairhurst, Green, & Courtright, 1995).

14. Despite their label, conversation analysts prefer the term 'talk-in-interaction' to 'conversation.'

15. Other types of adjacency pairs include request-grant/rejection, invitation-acceptance/refusal, and greetings (Woodilla, 1998).

16. Conway's car number appears automatically on the dispatcher's computerized caller identification system.

17. However, the protocol of this roll-out may be superseded at any time by the evolving nature of the crisis.

18. These indicators are not necessarily the only ones. For an interesting example of a request/demand to speak, see line 48 in Appendix B.

19. For an in-depth treatment of this issue, see Robinson (2001).

20. Cooren (2001) derives his list from Vanderveken (1990–1991), but adds a sixth in the form of accreditives.

21. See also Robichaud (2003), Soderberg (2003), and J. R. Taylor and Van Every (2000).

22. The use of commissives to close a schema seems specific to emergency situations where communication is by necessity efficient and absent the social conventions of everyday speech.

23. According to Harré and Secord (1972), accounts are simply actor or observer statements of why certain actions get performed and the social meanings attached to them.

24. Since both police and firefighting units are examples of high-reliability organizations, parallels in command presence are argued to exist.

25. The restaurant behavior to which I refer includes the individual scripts associated with seating, ordering food, bill paying, and so forth.

26. To be perfectly clear, Komaki (1998) does not associate her work with script analysis.

27. For example, see Komaki's (1998) first chapter.

28. Managers typically overestimate the amount of time they spend monitoring and providing consequences, but underestimate the amount of time they spend alone (Komaki, 1998).

29. Total Quality is an approach to management that seeks to improve product quality and increase customer satisfaction largely through strong quality-oriented leadership, a more efficient use of resources, participation in team-based structures, and statistical monitoring of work processes (Deming, 1982; Juran, 1964, 1988). Note that organizational participants can refer to Total Quality as "TQ" or "TQM," which stands for "Total Quality Management."

30. A number of writers argue for reconceptualizing organizational change by moving away from the presumption of stability before and after an intervention and toward continuous change and ongoing improvisation (Feldman, 2000; Orlikowski, 1996; Tsoukas & Chia, 2002; Weick, 1998). Tsoukas and Chia (2002) depict traditional change models as synoptic, in which change is a fait accompli and triggered externally as it progresses through distinct stages at different points in time. They argue that a synoptic view, "does not do justice to the open-ended micro-processes that underlay the trajectories described; it does not quite capture the distinguishing features of change—its fluidity, pervasiveness, open-endedness, and indivisibility" (p. 570).

3

Membership Categorization

Categorization theories are nothing new to the study of leadership. They explain how our implicit theories of leadership, or presuppositions about leadership effectiveness, function in judging others' abilities. For example, *leader categorization theory* (LCT) suggests that the decision to label someone a leader involves matching another's observed behavior to the prototypes that define our 'leader' category, such as 'influential,' 'visionary,' 'change agent,' and so on (Lord, Foti, & Phillips, 1982; Lord & Maher, 1991). Drawing from Rosch (1978), Lord and colleagues suggest that leadership knowledge structures are not just a single category, but a hierarchical cluster of three levels: perceivers' most broad categorization of leaders is at a superordinate level (such as 'leader' versus 'non-leader'); at a basic level, perceivers distinguish leaders between context (for example, 'military,' 'political,' 'business,' and so on); and at a subordinate level, they distinguish leaders within context (for example, 'senior manager,' 'middle manager,' 'supervisor,' 'team leader,' and so on) (Lord, Foti, & De Vader, 1984). As actors come to understand the world through abstracted categories of information organized around prototypes, category assignments in LCT are less algorithmic and more like a fuzzy set in which category members may be both similar to and different from the prototype (Cantor & Mischel, 1977, 1979).[1]

Social identity theory (SIT) examines the means by which individuals transform (self and other) social identities by adopting the categories of the group as membership becomes more salient (Hogg, 2001; Hogg & Terry, 2000). Leaders, in effect, emerge as the quintessential group members. For example, Platow, Haslam, Foddy, and Grace (2003) report on a set of idealized behaviors such as greater influence, trust, fairness, and charisma that appear typical of all in-group members to whom leadership may be attributed. Perceptions and judgments about leadership depend upon how closely an actor's behavior matches the behaviors of the in-group, a prototype matching process for all intents and purposes. SIT and LCT are not necessarily incompatible, although the latter views group identity as only one of many factors that may contribute to the construction of a leadership prototype (Lord & Hall, 2003).

As described by Edwards (1997), the basic model in cognitive categorization theories (like LCT and SIT) is a "lone, sensemaking perceiver" who extracts sensory information, recognizes patterns, stores mental representations of phenomena in the world, compares new sensory input to those stored representations, and then talks about them (p. 230–231).[2] Rooted in individual psychological functioning and pre-linguistic perceptual processing, *categorical expression* in discourse appears secondary and epiphenomenal. This is because communication is viewed as a simple transmission of a mental representation, thus ignoring its potential role in meaning creation (Billig, 1985; Potter & Wetherell, 1987). As such, cognitive categorization approaches appear blind with respect to the role of language in perceptual processing. Edwards (1997) suggests that this becomes obvious as soon as one asks

> a prototype of? A typical what? An exemplar of what? . . . The perceptual processes that supposedly produce and define verbal categories are themselves dependent on those categories, in order to identify what should count as an instance or exemplar. (pp. 233–234)[3]

If Edwards is correct and we are trading in language and word meaning right from the start in category conception, then perhaps there is a far greater role for the linguistic performance of categories than has been acknowledged by leadership psychology to date.

Although LCT and SIT treat categories as decontextualized and idealized, the fact that both research programs concern themselves with the actual content of leadership categories strongly suggests that they might be treated as *flexible linguistic resources,* not just cognitive ones by leadership actors. By doing so, categorization is not only an automatic thought process for simplifying a complex world (Potter & Wetherell, 1987). There is also interactional work involved when categories get performed, and it involves the management of meaning at a most fundamental level. As this chapter will make clear, categorization work in social interaction is one way to operationalize leadership as the management of meaning in rather concrete terms because leadership actors are incessant category users. The topics in this chapter on role and identity management, organizational coordination, sensemaking, and relationship and task structuring ably demonstrate this. However, in order to understand how categories get performed, we must turn from categorization in leadership psychology toward its role in more discursive approaches such as ethnomethodology, conversation analysis, and discursive psychology.

Membership Categorization Defined

It was Sacks's (1972, 1992) work on membership categorization that first spurred interest in this topic, although a number of conversation analysts (and a few discursive psychologists; see Appendixes A1 and A4) have further developed his ideas (Hester & Eglin, 1997; Jayyusi, 1984; Schegloff, 2001). A *category* or *membership category* (the terms will be used interchangeably) is simply a class or type of persons, such as 'leaders' or 'females.' However, collectivities, objects, and activities also fall into membership categories, such as 'middle management,' 'quarterly reports,' or 'gate-keeping.'

Categories are often linked to form classes or *membership categorization devices* (MCDs), which are collections of categories together with members' rules for application (Sacks, 1992).[4] For example, MCDs can be found in standardized relational pairs like 'manager–employee,' which employs an organizational hierarchy device; 'husband–wife,' which employs a marriage device; or 'teacher–student,' which employs a pedagogy device. All of these paired categories are frequently heard and used as "going together" (Sacks, 1972). However, there are also MCDs for multiple categories such as those involving employee grades: 'salaried,' 'part-time,' 'temporary,' 'intern,' 'retired,' and so on. MCDs can even unite categories as seemingly disparate as 'leadership books' 'music,' and 'ice-skating,' if the device is 'my favorite things.'

Membership categorization refers to the interactional work of actors who use categories to make claims and/or their actions accountable. Often they will move beyond the simple use of categories to characterize or reconstitute categories as the occasion warrants (Jayyusi, 1984). Thus, membership categorization is a socially situated accomplishment. Categories serve more than just a referential function here because they are methods for organizing and communicating knowledge about the world. This categorical knowledge comes in the form of *predicates* or category features involving attributes, motives, competencies, obligations, rights, entitlements, and so forth, but also actions or activities that are *category-bound* or *category-generated* through particular obligations and rights tied to a category (Hester & Eglin, 1997; Jayyusi, 1984; Sacks, 1972). For example, certain safety and rescue activities in and around water are routinely associated with the category 'life guard,' and thus are bound to that category. However, the category 'safety manager' generates more local meanings from specific site-based actions in equipment or material operations when protecting people, natural resources, and so on. In either case, category predicates thus reveal the stock of culturally based, commonsense knowledge that accompanies category membership (Sacks, 1992). As Schegloff (2001) argues, it is not just that categories can be used to name, describe, or refer to actors, but that categories "are one major repository, perhaps the major repository, for commonsense knowledge of the society by members of the society *as* members of the society" (p. 308, emphasis in original).

In organizational interactions especially, formulating or invoking a category is data because it is infrequently capricious or impulsive.[5] Categories thus tend to be finely ordered and consequential because *how leadership actors categorize their world is how they orient to it* (Boden, 1994), as the next section describes.

Categories and Organizational Coordination

Coordination demands in the leadership relationship require that leaders and followers categorize their work tasks in similar ways. Note that this does not necessarily presume shared category meaning, simply enough overlap to give participants the sense of shared meaning (Ellis, 1995). Shared category meaning is a presupposition, but a powerful one because it allows members of a discourse community (broadly or narrowly defined) to coordinate their behavior without specifying every warranting assumption or feature of a category.

Consider once again the case of Officer Conway who was shot repeatedly by an assailant as she struggled to regain control of her police cruiser (Appendix B). Chapter 2's discussion of this example mentioned an unspoken orientation to hierarchy by beat officers because protocol required proximate police supervisors to take over the rescue. Indeed, Appendix B shows that the only speakers besides the injured Conway (Cy, car 1212) and the dispatcher (Dis) were supervisors, all of whom had call signs with a '0' as their last digit (1030, 1080).[6] The silence of the beat officers speaks volumes here as they orient to supervisor call signs and observe their category-bound activities. Ironically, remaining silent and standing by can be a form of orienting to a role category for an organization in crisis mode.

While sharing a category system was clearly necessary for effective coordination between supervisors and beat officers, category use was also critical for Conway herself. Her use of a membership category was a turning point in her life-and-death rescue as the following excerpts demonstrate. (Transcription details are provided in Appendix A1.)

3.1a Conway's First Request for Help

1   Cy: Help! I need assistance! I'm shot in the (car)!

2   (2.0)

3   Dis: *Where* do you need it?

4   Cy: Help! I need help!

5   (1.5)

6   1030:   1238 Elm. I believe, 1030, I believe I heard shots fired there.

7   Cy: [(((Unintelligible screaming)) please!

3.1b Conway's Second Request for Help

23	**Dis:**	1212, what's your location?
24	**Cy:**	Distress. I've been involved in a shooting (0.3) on Central
25		Parkway (0.5) north (.) of Liberty. I need some help hhh
26		(0.5)
27	**1080:**	1080, I [copy that. Check on her safety.
28	**Dis:**	[are you hurt?
29		(0.5)
30	**Dis:**	1212, are you hurt?
31		(0.3)
32	**Cy:**	That's affirmative.

Cooren and I have written about Conway's use of the membership category 'distress' (line 24).[7] Prior to this utterance, Conway's only contact with the dispatcher was a hysterical plea for help (lines 1, 4, and 7).[8] In those early moments of the crisis, her assailant took control of her cruiser, and a struggle ensued until she shot and killed him (not recorded). Understandably, police protocol for radio communication was not a priority. However, that changed quickly when, after repeated attempts to reach Conway, her first word to the dispatcher (in response to the latter's query at line 23, "1212, what's your location?") was "Distress" as in the category 'distress call.' This terminology was routinely used by police to designate emergencies requiring immediate assistance (line 24). In much calmer tones and slower speech rate, Conway only then answers the dispatcher's question about her location and continues the use of police jargon when queried again (line 32).

The use of the 'distress' category was an attempt by Conway to routinize her own emergency. As mentioned in Chapter 2, police organizations are high-reliability organizations (HROs) whose effectiveness requires a commitment to resilience, including the ability to cope with surprises and bounce back from errors (Weick, Sutcliffe, & Obstfeld, 1999). One mark of the success of Conway's training by her supervisors was when she shifted from victim to police officer with this category use, despite the four bullets lodged within her. By invoking the 'distress' category, she effectively joined the search for her own bullet-ridden body and further instantiates the reliability that is *sine qua non* for effective HROs. It also demonstrates how categories serve as repositories of both common sense and role-based knowledge (Schegloff, 2001), in this case involving emergency responses by police supervisors and officers. But what is the difference between a membership category and an organizational role? That question is addressed below.

Categories and Organizational Role/Identity

Leadership psychologists might question the differences between a membership category and more familiar concepts like 'role' or 'identity.' *Role* usually refers to a recurring set of behaviors prescribed for a particular position or office (Katz & Kahn, 1978). *Identity* is often cast as the part of the self-concept that derives from membership in one or more social groups, along with the value and emotional weight attached to that membership (Tajfel, 1978).

The answer to the question over differences lies first in distinguishing 'role' (and related terms like 'role set,' 'role conflict,' 'role strain') and 'identity' as *analytic concepts* used by social scientists from their *everyday use* by members of society in social interaction (Edwards, 1997; Halkowski, 1990; Sacks, 1992). Regarding the latter for the concept of role, Hilbert (1981) sees its utility in terms of what actors can do with it in social interaction, such as "clear up confusion, sanction troublemakers, instruct others in the ways of the world, and so forth" (p. 565). Similarly, for the concept of identity, Antaki, Condor, and Levine (1996) suggest that cognitivists will see it as a mental state for how people *think* of themselves, while ethnomethodologists take it to be how people *describe* themselves, "a description available for people to invoke and deploy in mundane interactions" (p. 474). However, recall that membership categorization refers to how actors use categories interactionally to make claims or actions accountable. Membership categorization is the social process in which actors constantly position themselves with respect to membership (or lack thereof) in one kind, group, or class where quite often they define the very terms of membership by specifying the boundaries, predicates, or prototypes of that kind, group, or class. Categories are thus the malleable and putty-like structural forms, while 'role' and 'identity' speak more to their content or the type of category they reflect.[9] For example, a business leader who says, "I am a Republican, not a Democrat, because I am anti-tax and oppose big government," is making a statement about his identification with a U.S. political party. Yet he deploys two categories ('Republican' and 'Democrat') and two distinguishing predicates (anti-tax and big government) to achieve this, thus delineating the interactional work that categories perform for a concept like identity.

Halkowski (1990) found that actors engage in category shifting from an initial role-defining reference term to a new one when there is a question over the motives to be attributed to an actor. Antaki et al. (1996) speak of the plasticity of identity categories, finding that the enactments of actors' identities are far more subtle than analyst-assigned category labels suggested and that "they change rapidly as a function of the ephemeral (but socially consequential) demands of the situation" (p. 473). Actors even avowed contradictory identities and invoked both group distinctiveness and similarity as they tactically positioned themselves within the ebb and flow of interaction. Because the force of any role or identity description is *indexical,* or dependent upon local reference points, only the actors themselves can define the latitude associated with any role or identity category label. Antaki et al. (1996) explain further for the concept of identity:

> Ephemeral as they [identity categories] might be . . . speakers are doing three things at once: invoking social identities, negotiating what the features or boundaries of those identities are and accumulating a record of having those identities. They will be able, in the next round of their interactional history, to draw on having all been exposed to this conversational display of identities. (p. 488)

Identity or role categories can thus be flexibly defined in situ, yet seen to be stable to the degree actors consistently orient to particular features or boundaries across interactions. Moreover, conceptions of organizational roles and identities are usually a part of larger Discourses serving as linguistic resources for communicating actors. The interactive accomplishment of roles and identities through categorization work will thus function to sustain these larger Discourses in one form or another. Membership categorization is a common process to both role and identity management in these various ways.

Importantly, certain role and identity categories can be oriented to, although not specifically mentioned by, leadership actors. For example, consider hierarchical role. Throughout this book, there are excerpts from long, recorded work conversations in which the categories of 'manager,' 'direct report' (the actual terms used by one of the organizations to denote a reporting relationship), or their equivalents are never mentioned. Yet the sequences enacted were quite typical of paired relational role categories like 'manager' and 'one who reports to the manager.' These examples demonstrate how the role categories of 'manager' and 'direct report' get enacted *en passant,* a term employed by Schegloff (1979) to suggest 'in the doing.' Psathas (1999) translates:

> That is, there is no explicit naming of who I am need be done by either party. Rather, the who I am is accomplished in the doing of the action. What one person does, provides for the other person an answer to who I am for present purposes. (p. 148)

From this perspective, membership categorization is an ongoing, interactive accomplishment between leaders and their direct reports who, by their actions, signal to one another a role or identity that is subsequently affirmed. Most of the examples in this chapter will reflect en passant enactments; however, the attendant problem of establishing the relevance of a category amidst many possible others presents itself and will be discussed later in the chapter. There is still much to say about the interactional work involved in membership categorization, starting with sensemaking and meaning management.

Categories, Sensemaking, and Meaning Management

Several leadership scholars have described leadership as the *management of meaning*. Fundamentally, it is a sensemaking, reality-defining activity in which leaders identify what is important (for example, vision, mission, and values), communicate about the meaning of events, and seek consensus (Pondy, 1978; Smircich & Morgan, 1982; Weick, 1979). Shotter (1993) has perhaps the most elegant formulation of this approach. In his views of *practical authorship*, leaders who are faced with "unchosen" conditions create a landscape of enabling constraints and a network of moral positions, and are able to argue persuasively with those for whom it applies.[10] However, in his review of qualitative leadership research, Bryman (2004) characterizes leadership as the management of meaning as a "lofty and slightly nebulous" notion, quite divorced from mundane, immediate, instrumental, and material concerns, and perhaps the sole province of senior leaders charged with organizational change (p. 754).

It is unfortunate that within this literature, leaders are often depicted as the only symbolizing agents (Fairhurst, 2001). However, membership categorization as a discursive activity not only corrects this problem, but also adds much-needed specificity to leadership as the management of meaning because of its link to sensemaking. Importantly, sensemaking is not just a psychological process; it is also social and systemic (Weick, Sutcliffe, & Obstfeld, 2005). It is social because meanings are managed in interaction through the contested interpretation of events vis-à-vis the categories deployed and the resulting distinctions that emerge. It is systemic because categories often derive from stocks of knowledge commonly held by organizational members. According to Weick et al. (2005), "Sensemaking is about labeling and categorizing to stabilize the streaming of experience" in communication with others (p. 411). Like Antaki et al. (1996), they argue for the plasticity of categories because they are socially defined and must be flexibly adapted to local circumstances and changing conditions.

To take a simple example, categories are particularly useful in *social theorizing*, a communicative activity that organizational members engage in to explain others' behavior. As Jayyusi (1984) suggests, we engage in social theorizing by producing and providing for collectivities in talk "as morally organized groups and the characterization and description of individuals and their actions as relative to, and accountable in terms of, their membership in such groups" (p. 52). In other words, the work of invoking the character of collectivities or turning collections of individuals into collectivities produces sense as the meanings of group membership become clear.

Consider one such example from Fairhurst and Sarr (1996) in which this author led a group of Kroger managers in a Prisoner's Dilemma game. As is well-known, in this game four groups must choose to compete or cooperate with one another. Cooperation has its rewards, but the choice to compete could result in even greater rewards should one group play the game strictly on these terms. That is exactly what happened with one group of managers who scored the most points, claimed victory, and then returned for an afternoon session with the other three groups only to find their diplomas, chairs, and table missing from the seminar room. A spokesperson for the three groups announced that they had named the winning group the 'Judas' group, after the disciple who betrayed Jesus Christ. He said such a designation was fitting because they had betrayed the other groups, which warranted a dismissal from the class.

Through casting a collection of fellow managers as a morally bankrupt lot organized by a philosophy of unbridled competitiveness and winning at all costs, the category 'Judas group' was social theorizing and clearly explanatory of the other groups' felt betrayal. Note the emergence of leadership vis-à-vis the management of meaning here. All three remaining groups passed judgment on the fourth, collectively embraced this morally bound interpretation (despite their formerly competitive posture), and united behind the spokesperson cum leader, who perfectly captured 'the situation here and now' with the creation of the Judas category. According to Shotter (1993), leadership emerges exactly in these moments of providing an "intelligible formulation" of what for others may be "a chaotic welter of impressions" (p. 157). This notion strikes at the very heart of leadership as the management of meaning.

Key to managing meaning is Weick's (1979) view that actors must understand that the context is not something one responds to as an immutable given, but becomes an enactment of the possible and envisioned. Regarding membership categorization, this suggests a need to understand the occasioned, constitutive features of categories (Jayyusi, 1984), often in the midst of what Weick et al. (2005) suggest is evolving disorder. What they mean by this is that knowledge and technique are repeatedly fitted and retrofitted to circumstances and changing conditions where, through category work, actors "interpret their knowledge with trusted frameworks, yet mistrust those very same frameworks by testing new frameworks and new interpretations. The underlying assumption . . . is that ignorance and knowledge coexist" (p. 412).

One cannot hope to capture this evolving disorder with faulty assumptions about the leader's role as the sole symbolizing agent. To be clear, leadership actors may display an asymmetric use of linguistic resources to achieve disproportionate influence in any given encounter, but sensemaking as a social activity requires a communicative environment of at least two symbolizing agents. Consequently, membership categorization is never unilateral; it is always a product of social interaction.

For example, consider a conversation from Fairhurst (1993) in which a leader (L) listens to a team member's (TM) concerns about the applicability of Total Quality Assessment (TQA)[11] to his job in an internal support function (supplying plant energy) to the plant's manufacturing operation.

3.2 The 'Customers' in Total Quality[12]

1	TM:	If this- if we're getting the savings *now* with the system we *got*,
2		why even look at the damn (TQA) thing? (.9) I'm- I'm struggling
3		with that
4	L:	We::ll (1.0) maybe [(Indistinguishable)
5	TM:	[(Indistinguishable) in the quality method. In
6		TQA, lookin' at it though in TQA. I'm struggling with that=
7	L:	= Okay
8	TM:	for- for *savings*, pure out and outright savings. *Yes.* We may be
9		able to get something out of there, but is it- (.6) is it- is it contributing
10		to the quality of (.6) product, whatever product we're puttin'
11		out here (1.0) [okay
12	L:	[Well (.8) think about (.8) think about(hhh) though, what
13		is the product we're providing? *We're not making soap.* You're
14		not. I'm not, okay?
15		(1.1)
16	TM:	The plant is.
17		(.9)
18	L:	*Yeah* the plant is and- but- but you and I:: indirectly are. (2.2) You
19		know, one of the things is this- this thing and I- I believe you
20		have- have a copy of that=
21	TM:	= I have a copy
22	L:	the seven fundamental questions, you know. (1.0) Who are my
23		customers? What do they need? What's my- *my* product or
24		service, not the *plant's?*(.6) *Your* product or service. (1.6) What are
25		our expectations? (1.7) What's the process for providing my product
26		or service? What action is required to improve? So it deals with
27		*your* specific- don't worry if I turn it around, *my* (1.1)
28		specific product. (1.6) And right now that's a *service*, and the

29		service is project engineering, project management, project
30		development. (1.8) So in this specific piece okay, (3.5) what do
31		your customers need? If you think about it, *who* are your customers
32		if you think about it that way.
33	( ):	((sigh)) (3.0)
34	L:	Would it be like- people like ICD, liquid ((product name)),
35		accounting, everybody (3.0) that will utilize energy in the future.
36		(3.0) And their needs- I- you know, this is ((full name)) kinda
37		off the top of his *head* making this up, but it would seem to
38		me *their* needs (1.4) are to have a cheap source of *energy,* (2.2) okay?
39		(1.6) To be able to *make* their products. (1.8) But what they *need* is
40		they need a way get to a cheaper source of energy than right
41		now.

In this excerpt, the member is experiencing concern over the relevance of Total Quality (TQ) and its assessment methods to his project on downsizing, which is to provide cheaper steam, water, and utilities to the manufacturing lines and support functions of the plant. The leader then begins a tutorial with an initial series of questions that reframes the utilities function from one of not making product (because the plant does) to indirectly making product (lines 12–18). He then invokes the seven fundamental questions surrounding TQ from which he reconstitutes the category 'customer,' shifting from the plant's former definition as 'consumers of our product' to a more general view of any 'consumer of our services' (lines 22–32). By creating a new class of 'customers' consistent with Total Quality principles, sensemaking becomes possible.

Is the leader the only symbolizing agent here? No, even though the leader may be a momentary sensegiver as a category provider for this change effort (Gioia & Chittipeddi, 1991), and thus display an asymmetric use of TQ linguistic resources to achieve influence. However, the opportunity was created by the member's communicated predicament over the relevance of TQ, and meaning is negotiated in light of it (Fairhurst, 1993). The sensemaking process here is social and systemic, an organizationally informed coconstruction despite asymmetric influence. It is also worth noting that, especially if asked, the leader must reinforce the criticality of this TQ change effort vis-à-vis an ongoing series of job relevancies if it is to survive, but it is just as easy to envision a role reversal between the leader and an informed member.

This Total Quality example also shows how certain categories like 'customers' remain open-ended so that with different tasks or circumstances, a category may be reconstituted (Tsoukas & Chia, 2002). Thus, the distinction between membership categories and membership categorization outlined earlier is useful here (Jayyusi, 1984; Sacks, 1992). While the former are culturally available category concepts like 'customers,' the latter refers to the interactional work of categorizing. Thus, in a TQ context the category 'customers' was broadened to include any consumer of one's services.

Oftentimes categorization work depicts a *characterization* of a category in explicitly evaluative terms. It is what Jayyusi (1984) calls "the unrelievedly judgmental character of descriptions and of categorization work" (p. 40). As she suggests, characterized categories play a critical role in actors' sensemaking accounts (to justify or explain their thoughts and actions to others) because they simultaneously function as inferences, descriptions, and judgments. Such category use enables actors to complain and set problems (to be discussed later).

The example below displays a generated category whose features function as a complaint. It is the same organization in the midst of implementing Total Quality implementation as in the previous example. The following excerpt is taken from a conflict between two female leaders (in a reporting relationship) over whether to confront a male higher-up with the 'old style' management philosophy (Fairhurst, 1993; Wilhelm & Fairhurst, 1997). The women heard through a confidential source that the male higher-up was displeased because their plant was not sending a team to attend a TQ training session that he was promoting. In the excerpt, the leader, Pat, wants to send a team to the session or confront the higher-up directly, thereby breaking the confidence of their source. The more junior manager (Jane) is against both courses of action. Observe how Pat constructs the 'old style' management category through attributes and projected next actions for this male higher-up:

3.3 'Old Style' Management

1	Pat:	I guess I know ((higher up's name)), (1.3) and I know a little how he
2		he operates (2.2) and=
3	Jane:	=okay tell me about that.
4	Pat:	I just think [he's
5	Jane:	[How does he operate? What do you know?
6		(1.5)
7	Pat:	He is just uhm to me a good ol' boyish (1.8) kind of. Uhm (.8)
8		you know, he sat behind me at June meetings and was

9		very much in the old style of the division manager.
10		And (1.8) not like Skip at all ((Indistinguishable)) participative
11	**Jane:**	((Indistinguishable))
12	**Pat:**	No
13	**Jane:**	((Heh-huh-huh))
14	**Pat:**	Uhm (1.6) not like- he's not like Skip where he can work
15		through, I mean, he's very much in the old style of
16		it. (1.2) traditional.(1.0) So (2.0) you know he'll play the-
17		he'll play the game. He'll play the politics. He'll put the
18		pressure on. He'll put the fear in. He'll- he'll make
19		the comments and he's very much with the *comments*
20		and the jabs and things, and that will forever
21		be out in the system. And *we don't need that.* So
22		we have to either (1.2) have to go and solve it, or we need to
23		send someone to UT (for the training session).

Recall Weick et al.'s (2005) earlier words related to sensemaking as "labeling and categorizing to stabilize the streaming of experience" (p. 411). Pat is attempting just that by unequivocally positioning the higher-up through the category constitutive features of 'old style': three negative attributes ("traditional," line 16; but also earlier with "good ol' boyish," and not "participative" like Skip, lines 7, 10) and five projected next actions of which to be wary: "He'll play the game. He'll play the politics. He'll put the pressure on. He'll plug the fear in. He'll make the comments . . ." (lines 16–20). These attributes and projected actions—at once inferences, descriptions, and judgments—forcefully register the complaint against this higher-up that, in turn, effectively supplies the warrant for Pat's proposed dichotomized response (lines 21–23). Although Pat and Jane continued this conflict without resolution, this excerpt displays exactly the kind of specificity and detail that membership categorization as a discursive activity can add to the management of meaning.

Finally, Pat's reference to "very much the old style of it" (lines 15–16) and projection of the traditional higher-up's next actions also suggests she is constructing what Jayyusi (1984) would call a *type categorization.* In other words, Pat's description of the traditional male leader is really an ascription to a type (or prototype), in this case 'old style,' because in this excerpt and the remaining transcript, little of the higher-up's actual interactional history emerges.

Jayyusi's (1984) point that categorization work is not just descriptive but "through and through an *ascriptive* matter" raises an interesting observation about the situated use of prototypes (p. 27). The cognitive categorization theories discussed in the introduction to this chapter suggest that leadership actors carry implicit theories of leadership (Lord et al., 1984), but this example demonstrates why they matter so much: they are inevitably deployed for some kind of interactional purpose. Just like the Judas example, the 'old style' categorization in Excerpt 3.3 is social theorizing—simultaneously an inference, description, and judgment—used for a persuasive end and the vested interests of the speaker. One could well imagine other contexts such as performance appraisals, organizational succession, recruitment and retention of talented female leaders, and so on in which social theorizing of this kind would matter a great deal in terms of the outcomes.

Finally, invoking such a prototype also raises questions about how and why such categories come into play when they do in the interaction as in, why this category here? Chapter 5 addresses this matter more directly. However, first we must return to the potential problem that leadership actors face when multiple roles or identities apply to those with whom they communicate.

Categories and Social Structuring

Because actors are always subject to multiple categorizations, the task of referring to and categorizing them becomes profoundly equivocal (Sacks, 1992; Schegloff, 1991, 2001). For example, in an organizational setting, is it only one's work role that is relevant in social interaction? If not, then how do other categories involving gender, ethnicity, or education level, to name just a few, factor in? Schegloff (1991) defines the problem of *relevance* as how to show "from the details of the talk . . . that we are analyzing that those aspects of the scene are what the *parties* are oriented to . . . to show how the parties are embodying for one another the relevancies of the interaction and are thereby producing social structure" (p. 51, emphasis original). For conversation analysts then, a crucially important way to understand social structure is through the categories actors invoke and make relevant in social interaction. Such category use thus defines social structure as an ongoing, emergent accomplishment.

In most contexts, decision rules about which categories to invoke hinge on rather predictable factors like speaker goals, recipient design, task activities, and the like (Jayyusi, 1984; Sacks, 1992; Schegloff, 2001). However, in organizations there will also be relevance rules accorded to setting, in particular, role and identity categorizations that are omni-relevant. As mentioned at the start of the chapter, role categories associated with the organizational hierarchy are likely oriented to, although not specifically mentioned, as task activities are performed. Thus, standardized relational pairs such as 'leader' and 'direct report' get enacted *en passant*, recalling Schegloff's (1979) term for 'in the doing.' From this perspective, membership categorization is an ongoing, inter-active accomplishment between a leader and her or his direct report who, by their actions, signal to one another their respective roles that are subsequently affirmed. It is here that the sequencing of interaction and category construc-tion are almost inseparable except through analysis (Hester & Eglin, 1997; Schegloff, 2001; R. Watson, 1997). However, two interesting implications surface from this observation.

First, if hierarchical membership categories are affirmed en passant, so too should qualifications that further categorize the relationship. This is the foundation of leader–member exchange (LMX) theory, in which high- or low-quality relationships purportedly form based on an ongoing exchange of resources between a leader and a member (Graen & Scandura, 1987; Graen & Uhl-Bien, 1995). That LMX relationships are enacted en passant is hardly news within this genre of research (as the specter of role theory can also attest), but the documented variety in the enactments is another matter, given so few discursive LMX studies. By and large, researchers are more concerned with LMX predictors and outcomes than in exploring what LMX relationships actually look like 'in the doing' as they go about their work. Two earlier studies suggest quite a lot of variety exists in individual enactments (Fairhurst, 1993b; Fairhurst & Chandler, 1989), a subject discussed further in Chapter 6.

Second, given that hierarchy categorizations are often unspoken, it is inter-esting to observe the circumstances in which they are overtly made relevant. J. R. Taylor and Robichaud (2006) supply just such a scenario as they analyze a senior executive conversation between Sam Steinberg, Canada's one-time answer to Wal-Mart, and his vice presidents over the issue of his successor. Throughout the 77-minute videotape that chronicles the discussion of succes-sion, everyone is on a first-name basis in this family-owned and operated firm except Sam Steinberg, whom everyone refers to as "Mr. Sam."[13] Usually, English speakers pair the courtesy title "Mr." with a surname, full name, or title; how-ever, in this case everyone pairs it with his first name, thus minimizing the dis-tance that a courtesy title introduces. However, in the excerpt below, Mr. Sam complains about an anonymous "they" who are increasing prices in one of his regions, thus violating his lowest-cost pricing philosophy. The "they" is actually Jack Levine, a vice president and non-family member who abruptly switches categories by referring to Mr. Sam as "Mr. President" as he charges back. Here is the segment of dialogue in which "Mr. President" is used:

3.4 Mr. Sam and Jack Levine

1   **Sam S:**   This is exactly how I feel (0.5). Now listen to what I'm telling,

2   each and every one of you. (0.5) Evidently over the past four o' five

3   weeks, (0.5) a hundred or two hundred items (0.5) have to be increased in

4		price
5	Jack L:	\<Seventy-two items\> =
6	Sam S:	= Alright, well, I'm telling you what I heard. [so- .
7	Jack L:	[(accumulated) on four
8		weeks, seventy-two items =
9	Sam S:	= Okay. Let's (0.2) let's say it's seventy-two items. (1.0) So here's what
10		happens. I meet one of our managers having lunch upstairs who's the
11		manager of St-Lawrence and Cremazie. I walked over an' say "Hello, how
12		are you?" and everything else, "How is it going?" He says "Very fine,
13		sales are up thirteen or (0.2) fourteen percent" but he says "He's terribly
14		dis*turbed.*" (0.5) They got in a wh:ole list of items that they have to
15		increase the prices on (0.5) and he's disturbed because now they'll be
16		going back to what they did in the past, erasing prices an' (.) putting on
17		higher prices an 'everything else.
18	Jack L:	Mr. President =
19	( ):	=[hhuhh
20	( ):	[Could I..Could I=
21	Jack L:	=No, [just a minute =
22	( ):	[Could I..could I..could I get
23	Jack L:	=Will you wait a minute? Mr. President look, this is what- this's *why*
24		I want to talk about structure first. (1.0) It happens that I and you
25		communicate. (0.5) > Twice a day three time a day four times a day- no
26		matter what time of day it is eh? <
27	Sam S:	Ri[ght.
28	Jack L:	[We communicate, I communicate to you, you com'nicate to me. And I
29		brought up to you (1.0) this perplex thing. 'Cause I have to have somebody
30		to speak to too (.) outside of my peers who we speak to, eh? So I
31		communicate with this. ((*Spoken with intensity and pointing finger*)) Have
32		you got the same problem in Toronto?
33		(1.0)
34	Jack L:	Do you know what's happening at Toron[to?
35	Sam S:	[No, (I don't).

36	Jack L:	((*Spoken with intensity and pointing finger.*)) Are you running one
37		company or two companies? Is the *struc*ture that's wrong? Is it
38		professional management's wrong? Is it a (box) wrong? *How* do you
39		communicate? *They* communicate an' listen to this an' an' I this is why I
40		say structure (.) is so important an' how we're gonna do it an' feedback an'
41		control. .hh *Th:ey* been raising prices from the first week. We kept prices
42		back four weeks, we did- though we got a co-co*st* increases, four (0.2)
43		three four weeks 'go three weeks 'go, so forth, we kept back four weeks.
44		They've been e- every week, putting in the price changes though they
45		come in- the same problem with- They discuss it with you?
46		(.)
47	Sam S:	No =
48	Jack L:	= Have they communicated with you? =
49	Sam S:	= No.
50	Jack L:	((*Spoken with intensity and pointing finger.*)) = Have they communicated
51		with anybody here? (0.5) How many companies are you running? (0.5)
52		*What* philosophy do you want? That's why my *first* thing on page *six* (0.2)
53		page *six* and I want you to go back and read it. This is exactly- I I am *very*
54		glad you brought it up. Because page six I say, for God sake, "the
55		*objec*tives and goals and corporate philosophy, the objectives and goals
56		must be spelled out. "↑*What* is your goals for Tor- ? Are you running one
57		business? Are you still running an- an Ontario business? You wanna be
58		the general manager here? Or do you want to act as the President? Do you
59		wanna act as a corporate- as a corporate President for everybody or for
60		one?

J. R. Taylor and Robichaud's (2006) analysis is incisive on this point. Jack Levine does not refute the pricing accusation, but he turns it into an indictment of Mr. Sam for failing to act presidential. Levine apparently believes that Mr. Sam neither treats his vice presidents equally nor fully understands what it means to run a corporation. Although Taylor and Robichaud perform a narrative analysis, we can be even more specific here because Levine formulates the problem vis-à-vis the simultaneous, practical relevance of two contextually opposing role categories: 'general manager' and 'president' (lines 57–60). The former is restrictive to Ontario and thus suffers by comparison to the latter corporate community of the whole. Jayyusi (1984) suggested that such contrasts and attending arguments may be describable as conflict, the resolution of which occurs through the assignment of categorical precedence. Levine does just that by faulting Mr. Sam for acting too much like a lower-level general manager (whose job duties include pricing policy) and not enough like a corporate leader (who would not micromanage such duties). Hence, Levine's earlier use of the role category "Mr. President" (lines 18, 23) appears to serve more as a reminder of the expectable duties and obligations of categorical incumbency than a polite, deferential form of address.[14]

Thus, as we see in the case of Mr. Sam, conversation analysis tackles the relevance problem in defining social structure through the sensemaking and coordination of the actors themselves. Such a focus puts the onus squarely on the categories they explicitly or implicitly invoke vis-à-vis their relationship to one another within the temporal flow of interaction. Ethnomethodology frequently informs the explanations of conversation analysts in this regard by recognizing categories as a means of organizing locally and temporally contingent knowledge about the world (Hester & Eglin, 1997; R. Watson, 1997). However, there is more to say about this example because of the task structuring that also takes place.

Categories in Task Structuring

In discussing how categories are made relevant by actors in a leadership relationship in the previous section, much attention was focused on social structure through an orientation to status differences in category use. However, actors also use category concepts in task structuring, the most important of which involves *problem setting*. This term was coined by Schön (1983) to describe the process by which we define decisions:

> When we set the problem, we select what we will treat as the "things" of the situation, we set the boundaries of our attention to it, and we impose upon it a coherence which allows us to say what is wrong and in what directions the situation needs to be changed. Problem setting is a process in which, interactively we name the things to which we will attend and frame the context in which we will attend to them. (p. 40)

Based on the arguments made in this chapter, naming and framing problems are inherently categorizing and characterizing activities due to the features tied to category use. Here it is useful to recall Jayyusi's (1984) observations about the morally organized character of categorization work such that, "some categorizations are usable in explicitly moral ways, so that the fulfillment of moral duties and commitments is basic for the assessment of the performance of category tasks" (p. 44). Of course, the failure to uphold certain moral obligations can also define category membership such as the category 'murder,' whose moral entailments usually demand a legal and judicial remedy.

However, problems can also be set through *categorical contrasts* much as we saw with the Mr. Sam example and Jack Levine's pairing of two contextually opposing role categories, 'general manager' and 'president,' and their expectable duties (lines 57–60). Levine deftly set the problem as a choice between two unequal categorical alternatives that gave Mr. Sam little maneuverability. Mr. Sam *was* the president and to even suggest that he was not acting presidential rendered a moral judgment of his performance that Levine effectively linked to the debate on lowest-cost pricing philosophy. Levine's argument was simple: "Disagree with me, and you're acting like a general manager would (in managing pricing policies), which is morally wrong. Agree with me, and you're acting like a president should (who refrains from such micromanagement), which is morally right." Levine contrasted both role categories and marked his preference as the only obvious choice.

Problem setting in this example is also interesting because Jack Levine's contrast of opposing role categories was the denouement to a series of questions interspersed with argument and the finger-pointing "you" (for example, "How many companies are you running? (0.5) *What* philosophy do you want?" lines 51–52). Robinson (2001) notes that in the process of problem setting, ill-structured problems gain structure the more constraints are introduced because, "Constraints narrow the solution alternatives by specifying the conditions that are to be satisfied" (p. 94). *Constraint sets* may vary widely (involving, for example, value systems, regulatory requirements, resource availability, organizational structure, and cultural practices, to name a few) and assume a categorical form. This is exactly what occurs in the dialogue preliminary to Levine's role category contrast. When Levine announces to Mr. Sam and his senior staff, "I want to talk about structure first" (line 24), he introduces a constraint vis-à-vis the membership category 'structure' that his proposed solution—acting presidential—must satisfy.

Levine generates the 'structure' category with a number of items, including queries about pricing policy communication among units (lines 24–34, 38–51); how many companies Mr. Sam is running (36–37, 51, 56–57); professional management (line 38); the organizational chart (the box pointed to, line 38); and corporate philosophy, goals, and objectives (lines 52–56). Levine generates neither a simple nor a straightforward category list because he elaborates in places, especially on the communication issues (lines 24–34, 38–51), and contradicts himself by using the word "structure" as both category and member (lines 24, 37). Perhaps because Levine's emotions are running high, it is also not crystal clear whether the foregoing items are members of, or related to, the category 'structure,' a distinction that may be of little practical utility here. However, his rapid-fire delivery of some 21 questions and his three interspersed queries about the number of companies Mr. Sam is running (lines 36–37, 51,

56–57), a structural concern fundamentally, gives the listed items a sense of category coherence. The interrogative series delivers the membership category 'structure' that, in turn, functions as a constraint on the preferred solution to the problem set between 'general manager' and 'president,' such that the latter takes precedence. A president (in this case) is the leader of only one company whose management philosophy, organizational chart, communication flow, pricing policies, and corporate philosophy and goals are aligned accordingly.

In the same way that listing can deliver a constraint set, so too can problems be set from the *listing* activities of actors as they generate and characterize categories. Earlier in the chapter, we noted that the judgmental character of categorization work often sets up complainability by virtue of the proposed actions that are judged negatively. Frequently, this is done through the composition of a list whose items are selected to provide the grounds for and features of a complaint (Jayyusi, 1984). Listing can involve a set of *sequential* steps, but in Excerpt 3.3, it was the *cumulative* listing of the male higher-up's projected next actions, each one a complainable, that delivered the category 'old style' management in gestalt fashion. Each listed item appeared to have been selected so as to reinforce the others: "He'll play the game. He'll play the politics. He'll put the pressure on. He'll plug the fear in. He'll make the comments. I mean, he's very much with the comments and the jabs and things." From these examples, we see that a complaint *sets* a specific kind of problem because it expresses actors' grievances, pain, dissatisfaction, or resentment associated with the task at hand. Listing is a way to modulate the intensity of the complaint, either through itemization or cumulativity of the features of the membership category in use (Jayyusi, 1984). It is also the means by which actors display their knowledge of the context and task at hand.

Regarding one final issue, Jayyusi (1984) argues that listing concerns also deal with the translation of a set of particulars into a categorization. In order to achieve the preferred response from hearers, speakers routinely orient themselves to the *practical translation problem* "so as to provide in the selection of descriptive items both the solution and the puzzle for which that is a proper solution" (p. 92). However, the solutions that speakers or hearers proffer are always defeasible or capable of being annulled. Consider a discussion between a warehouse manager (WM) and one of his reporting supervisors (Tom) concerning the category 'lay-ons,' a term used by their manufacturing organization to denote an order or command.

3.5 'Lay-ons' in the Warehouse

1	Tom:	There was a STACK OF ((PRODUCT NAME)) that had ta
2		be moved, and that was it. And then say, 'Folks, (.6) this is it.
3		(1.0) It's a lay-on (.6) to a large extent. (.6) We won't allow
4		tractors ta be left (.4) sitting idle in the warehouse.' And people

5		hafta do certain clean-up functions at certain times, and
6		certain inspection functions at certain times. Uh, but
7		the implementation of it would be relatively *simple*
8		I believe.
9		(1.2)
10	**WM:**	I gotta feeling we could implement that in a manner
11		other than a *lay-on* . . . There've just been so darn many lay-ons
12		around here lately that I'd like ta
13		(1.0)
14	**Tom:**	back away from some of [the lay-ons?
15	**WM:**	[Yeah do some of these things uh in
16		a- in a different way if we could
17		(3.8)
18	**Tom:**	Yeah I- I think you're a little bit- (.8) I don't have any problem
19		with lay-ons, and I honestly don't think my men have much of a
20		problem with certain lay-ons. (1.0) If they're *absurd,* they- it's
21		a *very* tough pill to swallow. But by and large they ah
22		(1.4)
23	**WM:**	Ya know, they become a way of life after awhile.
24	**Tom:**	Yes they can be.
25		(2.0)
26	**WM:**	And that's not the direction we wanna go. We're wanting to go
27		in a different direction (1.5) to get our employees to *own the business*
28		and ah assume more responsibility for making decisions an- and
29		their own actions. And that just directionally doesn't *happen* when
30		you're giving more and more and more orders (.7) about what you
31		want done and how you want it done.
32		(1.7)
33	**Tom:**	I don't know I just uh- (1.4) That's uh- We could have a *long*
34		conversation on this,
35	**WM:**	Yep we could=

36	Tom:	=ya know. I think once we reach minimum *standards*
37		there need not be any lay-ons. (4.0) But if we assume that we're
38		gonna achieve minimum standards on a voluntary basis (1.0) I think
39		we're really *mistaken*, and I think that's part of our problem right
40		*now*. Our standards *are* are *well* below what we would call minimally
41		acceptable. And in order to *get* to that acceptable *point*, I think
42		it's gonna take some *lay-ons*. (1.8) It's gonna take some
43		*practice* (.8) It's gonna take *breaking* old habits, and those
44		are *done* in a lay-on=
45	WM:	=Yeah you're *right*. We can spend an
46		awful lot of [time
47	Tom:	[Sure
48	WM:	talking that I don't think we have [time today
49	Tom:	[Right.

In Excerpt 3.5, Tom introduces the category 'lay-on' by listing such particulars as "not allowing tractors to be left sitting idle in the warehouse," and people having "to do certain clean-up functions . . . and certain inspection functions at certain times" (lines 1–6). The warehouse manager then sets the problem of "so darn many lay-ons around here lately" (lines 10–11). This prompts Tom to draw a subcategory contrast between "certain" versus "absurd" lay-ons (lines 20–22), which the manager rejects through a nonspecific but opposing membership category, "a different direction," whose constraint set on a solution appears to be getting "employees to own the business" and "assume more responsibility for making decisions and their own actions" (lines 27–33).

In a fascinating turnabout, Tom resets the problem as one of not yet achieving minimum daily standards (lines 38–44), the solution to which is more lay-ons. However, he does this by noting, "it's gonna take some *practice*. It's gonna take *breaking* old habits, and those are *done* in a lay-on" (lines 42–44). Note here the different, more general set of items listed for the lay-on category as compared with the set of particulars he initially offered (lines 1–8). In effect, Tom treats his manager's problem with lay-ons as a *translation problem* that when seen in the context of reaching minimum standards, is really about "practice" and "breaking old habits." Meeting minimum standards trumps change initiatives most any day in this organization as both actors are aware.

However, the warehouse manager shuts the conversation down on the subject perhaps because of the tape recorder present, too little time as he suggests (line 48), or, ironically, the authority he has to do so. Nevertheless, treating contested problem formulations as a matter of translation remains a potentially viable route to issue resolution. Finding ways to enhance clarity, reduce equivocality, or secure agreement are reasons why speakers continue to orient to the translation of a set of particulars into another categorization after one has failed.

Echoing the arguments of Chapter 2, we see influential acts of organizing by leadership actors through category use in task-based problem setting, constraint setting, and resolution of contested problem formulations. Analyzing categories created in discourse reveals how problems are set through categorical incumbency, contrast, or listing activities. Through the discourse, we see how in the process of problem setting, category-generated constraint sets suggest preferred solutions. We observe how contested problem formulations may potentially be resolved when they are treated as category translation problems. Finally, in the category-listing activities of actors, we see the ways in which the depth of organizational knowledge may be displayed. We also see *who* displays it. In ways that perhaps Robinson (2001) did not fully comprehend, through the discourse we discover leadership "wherever it lies" in the task-related expertise asymmetrically displayed by one or more leadership actors (p. 100).

A Backward Glance—Final Thoughts

The key aspects of membership categorization in leadership interaction include the following:

- A membership category (or simply, category) is a classification of persons, objects, or activities.
- Categories can form classes or membership categorization devices, which are collections of categories together with members' rules for application.
- Membership categorization refers to the interactional work of actors who use categories to make claims and/or their actions accountable. Often leadership actors will move beyond the simple use of category concepts to characterize or reconstitute categories as the occasion warrants.
- Category characterizations depict a category in explicitly evaluative terms. They are, at once, inferences, descriptions, and judgments.
- Categorical knowledge forms classes of predicates involving attributes, motives, competencies, obligations, rights, entitlements, and so forth, but also actions or activities that are category-bound or category-generated through particular obligations and rights tied to a category.
- At the level of social interaction, both 'role' and 'identity' assume a categorical form open to construction through membership categorization. Categories are thus malleable interactional structures, while roles and identities speak more to their content or the type of category they reflect.
- Some role and identity categories are enacted en passant or 'in the doing' (for example, those involving hierarchical relationships) versus an explicit mention of a category.

- Membership categorization as a discursive activity adds much-needed specificity to leadership as the management of meaning because much sensemaking is acted out conversationally through category work.
- The problem of categorical relevance in defining social structure is addressed in the categories that leadership actors explicitly or implicitly invoke vis-à-vis their relationship to one another.
- Leadership actors use categories in task structuring in the way they problem-set through categorical incumbency, contrast, or listing activities.
- In the process of problem setting, category-generated constraint sets often point toward preferred solutions. Contested problem formulations are often resolved when treated as category translation problems.

This chapter concentrated on the fundamentals regarding membership categorization and leadership, carefully avoiding the inevitable overlap among identification processes, role management, meaning management, organizational coordination, social structuring, and task structuring. However, organizational problems are not always so neat, and discourse analyses cannot always be so discretely partitioned. For example, Sheep's (2006) research on the leadership of the Episcopal Church in the United States, following the consent of its General Convention to the election of its first openly gay bishop in August of 2003, demonstrated the complexity of multifunctional category use during times of intense organizational conflict.[15] Through in-depth interviews with key leaders and group representatives, Sheep used discursive psychology to focus on church leaders' use of categories and broader Discourses as they attempted to position themselves and justify their views. He specifically demonstrated how the elasticity of membership categories may be used to accommodate complex positioning and multiple identification processes. As a result, meanings were managed with categories that stretch and accommodate a diverse leadership for some, but stretch to their breaking point for others. In the politicizing of "the event" by the leadership, roles and relationships changed as factions formed—as did the identity work of leaders as they confronted the issues surrounding Discourses of difference (Ashcraft & Mumby, 2004). These Discourses, in this case involving gay/straight and masculine/feminine, also triggered broader societal Discourses associated with Western family values. Sheep's research clearly demonstrates the powerful discursive lens afforded by membership categorization, especially during times of organizational conflict and change. Yet, despite increased attention to talk-in-interaction in institutional settings, especially by conversation analysts (Boden, 1994; Drew & Heritage, 1992; Heritage, 1997), there remains a paucity of this type of research to date. The subject of membership categorization will be taken up again in Chapter 5 as we examine how categories can become products

of various management Discourses. However, Chapter 4 must first introduce us to a Foucauldian view of Discourse.

NOTES

1. Eschewing early work that assumed rather rigid categorical structures,
current LCT theorizing utilizes neural network or connectionist representations of
leadership prototypes to demonstrate the ready application of categories as tasks or
situations shift in the flow of interaction. In contrast to memory retrieval views of
leadership categorization, connectionist models are better at capturing the situational
nature of prototype construction (Lord & Hall, 2003).

2. Edwards (1997) draws heavily from Roth (1995) in this area.

3. See Edwards (1997) for an extensive critique of cognitive categorization
theories.

4. For example, Sacks (1992) wrote about the *economy rule*, which holds that
even a single category will suffice in describing a person, although multiple categories
will always apply. Thus, team members may orient to the category 'team leader' in work
interaction even though 'married,' 'Duke graduate,' and 'marathoner' also apply. The
consistency rule holds that a first member's category use usually remains consistent
across further members' category uses. Thus, if rank is used to describe one military
officer, it is usually held across all officers' descriptions.

5. However, I do not wish to suggest that all category use is necessarily conscious.
For example, category use can sometimes reflect an unconscious gender bias as when
the expression 'girls in the office' is repeatedly used, or a bias toward organizational
hierarchy when terms such as 'superiors and subordinates' are consistently invoked.

6. However, this is with the exception of 'Car 15,' a designator for another police
supervisor.

7. See Cooren and Fairhurst (2004) and Fairhurst and Cooren (2004) for more
details.

8. In the context of 911 calls, Whalen and Zimmerman (1998) define hysteria as
sobbing, screaming, using profanity and 'shock tokens' such as "Oh God!", or pleading
for immediate assistance.

9. I am not suggesting that membership category replace concepts like role or
identity as analytic concepts. Certainly, there are capital and material benefits that social
role explains better than membership category. The value added of membership category surfaces primarily in the interactional work surrounding roles and identities in
social interaction.

10. For an extensive discussion of the work of Shotter on practical authoring, see
Holman and Thorpe (2003).

11. Total Quality is an approach to management that seeks to improve product
quality and increase customer satisfaction largely through strong quality-oriented leadership, a more efficient use of resources, participation in team-based structures, and
statistical monitoring of work processes (Deming, 1982; Juran, 1964, 1988). The term
'Total Quality Assessment' in the dialogue appears to refer to the statistical monitoring
aspects of Total Quality.

12. From "Social structure in leader-member interaction" by T. Gail, et al., *Communication Monographs, 56,* 1989. Reprinted with permission of Taylor and Francis, www.tandf.co.uk.

13. The author would like to thank François Cooren and the National Film Board of Canada for making this transcription available. From *Interacting and Organizing: Analyses of a Board Meeting,* edited by Cooren, F., copyright © 2006, Lawrence Erlbaum. Reprinted with permission. Videotape used with permission of the National Film Board of Canada.

14. A person's title also introduces more social distance between communicators, which some find useful in a conflict.

15. Sheep's dissertation is part of a larger project with Elaine Hollensbe and Glen Kreiner. Their research was funded as part of the Episcopal Identity Project by The CREDO Institute, Inc., and the College for Bishops.

4

Disciplinary Power

In previous chapters, we focused on sequentiality and membership categorization in leader–member language use and interaction. In this chapter, we explore those powerful cultural forces that lie beyond interaction, yet serve as important resources for leadership actors as they communicate. The writings of Michel Foucault are the touchstone here, and in this chapter we explore his conception of Discourse and through it how leadership actors may become objects and subjects of their relationships, organizations, and societies. In this context, the forces of history and culture produce disciplinary power.

Ironically, the organizational sciences and history could be considered strange bedfellows (F. N. Brady, 1997). As Goldman (1994) observes, organizational researchers and practitioners are "quintessential creatures of the present" (p. 621). Theirs is a utilitarian science whose relevance is based on solving problems and "where old problems are no longer problems" (F. N. Brady, 1997, p. 160). To understand this rejection of the past, Kieser (1994) recalls early tensions between sociology and history. The former favored the kind of grand theorizing that could tie organizations to society, much as we saw in Mills's (1951) *White Collar* and Whyte's (1956) *The Organization Man,* while the latter absorbed itself in historical details and organizational uniqueness. When the organizational sciences were formed, they migrated away from the disciplines and into applied fields (such as management science) largely bereft of history concerns and theories tying organizations to society (Goldman, 1994).[1] While one might argue that leadership researchers and practitioners have always had an affinity for history and its leaders, the strong influence of psychology in the management sciences made this interest primarily individualist ('great man' theories) and psychological (Bass, Avolio, & Goodheim, 1987; Gronn, 1993; Kets de Vries, 1990a).[2]

A turn to Foucault to study leadership revives Mills's (1951) and Whyte's (1956) early interest in disciplined behavior,[3] but goes much further in turning leadership actors into 'quintessential creatures of history and culture.' Such a move does not seem out of step with the early sociologists until we confront

Foucault's own brand of unique and powerful theorizing, which Shapiro (1992) aptly characterizes as "defamiliarizing." For example, in leadership psychology the terms 'leaders' and 'agents' are nearly synonymous; yet, Foucault's work suggests that we also treat leaders as subjects—managers of meaning *and* passive receptors. The mainstream leadership literature will ask, "Who is this leader?" (whom we seek to study), while Foucault's question is, "Which one?" because there is no essence of leadership to capture, only the multiple leader-manager selves who emerge in Discourse. Likewise, Foucault substitutes violent imagery for the rather benign representations of social learning processes accepted by many social scientists (Shapiro, 1992).[4] For Foucault (1995), the human body is docile, an object to be manipulated, and is where disciplinary technologies inscribe themselves. The history of the human body and the exercise of power parallel one another for Foucault.

In this chapter, there is much to learn from Foucault's defamiliarizing impact on subject matter such as leadership. The resonances of the violence in Foucault's (1995) *Discipline and Punish,* in which he traces the history of French penal systems and punishment of society's lawbreakers, will be shown to carry over to key performance management technologies within the leadership literature, including the performance appraisal, 360-degree feedback, and executive coaching. This new lens offers a fresh perspective on the power dynamics in these technologies with important insights into leadership development practices. However, a brief introduction to Foucault is first necessary.

A Primer on Foucault

If Foucault was writing about leadership today, he would advise us to look for relations of power and domination and insist that leadership is a kind of labor power produced by systems of subjection. As we will later see, leaders who are made into 'subjects' are an interesting counterweight to leaders as crucial 'agents'—transformational leaders, visionaries, change masters, and the like. To understand Foucault's (1983) central concern with subjectivity, we begin with his view of Discourse.[5]

Foucault's *Discourse,* signified by a capital 'D' (Alvesson & Kärreman, 2000b), is a set of statements surrounding the formation and articulation of ideas in a historically situated time. *Discursive formation* is the term Foucault (1972) uses to capture the relationships among the statements and how they combine to produce truth claims about some subject matter, generate claims of meaning between material and cultural conditions, and transform themselves over time. Less abstractly, Knights and Morgan (1991) characterize Foucault's Discourse as a "set of ideas and practices which condition our ways of relating to, and acting upon, particular phenomena" (p. 253).

In his early writings especially, Foucault (1972) advocated a type of historical analysis, termed *archeology*, in which we treat Discourses as relatively autonomous systems of thought apart from whatever uses individuals may have for them (for a brief overview, see Appendix A5). As Foucault (1972) wrote, "The analysis of statements, then, is a historical analysis . . . it questions them as to their mode of existence . . . what it means for them to have appeared when and where they did—they and no others" (p. 109).

Bennis and Thomas's (2002) *Geeks and Geezers: How Era, Values, and Defining Moments Shape Leaders,* mentioned in Chapter 1, is a business press example of an archeological analysis. Here the authors focus heavily on describing two eras that produced radical generational differences in today's crop of leaders. They argue that *geezers* are products of the Depression and World War II 'analogic' era, characterized by linear narrative and thinking, maps, system mechanics, controlling management styles, an emphasis on experience, conventional warfare techniques, and specialization. By contrast, *geeks* are products of the 'digital' era of the Internet and the end of the Cold War, characterized by nonlinear thinking, compasses that impart only a general sense of direction (unlike maps), living systems, empowerment (over control), a beginner's mind (over experience), terrorism and cyberwarfare, and deep generalization (over specialization). The conceptualization of this generational divide demonstrates the allure of an archeological analysis.

However, in a move that would characterize his later work in *genealogy* (for a brief overview, see Appendix A5), Foucault argued that Discourses tend to resist idealization because they are always embedded in the social practices that constitute the key experiences defining the context.[6] For Foucault, those key experiences are madness, illness, death, crime, and sexuality. Through examples from these topics areas, Foucault urges us to see how power and knowledge are intertwined because what is 'true' or 'right' about some phenomenon is not driven by its essence, but by how it is represented through the language and practices of a Discourse. Unlike the assumptions of modernism (upon which so much of the mainstream leadership literature is based), language does not reflect a material reality for Foucault; it is the means by which we construct it. For this reason, he (1980) argues, "Truth is not outside power . . . each society has its regime of truth, its 'general politics' of truth" (p. 13).

For example, du Gay and Salaman (1996) argue that management Discourses construct what management 'is' and how it is to be performed. We could go back a century or more to demonstrate this, beginning with the Discourses of the Industrial Revolution in the early twentieth century, the human relations Discourses of the 1940s and 1950s,[7] the human resources Discourses of the 1960s, Total Quality and organizational culture Discourses of the 1980s, and the neo-charisma Discourses[8] beginning in the 1980s and proceeding through the early twenty-first century.[9] Interestingly, organizational change has been an abiding concern for some time, yet only in the neo-charisma Discourses do we see that it is the *sine qua non* of 'leadership,' which is quite distinct from 'management.' True 'leaders' are now change masters,[10] who through their visions and ability to communicate are capable of sweeping organizational transformations, while 'managers' are the technicians with know-how and process skills. However, 'leader' and 'manager' are interchangeable in all other management Discourses (and in this book unless otherwise specified), thus demonstrating how the politics of truth varies by Discourse.

When considering the power effects of Discourses, Foucault (1983) also urges us to look for them where we find *resistance,* using it "as a chemical catalyst so as to bring to light power relations, locate their position, find out their point of application and the methods used" (p. 211). For Foucault, where we find resistance, so shall we find the effects of power. Significantly, he is not looking broadly at institutions here, but at their vehicles or *technologies* and the ways in which specific rituals of power weave knowledge, competence, and qualification together. Similarly, he is less concerned with overarching rationalities than with specific local rationalities around the technologies through which power is deployed and resisted—as we will soon see in performance management technologies like the performance appraisal, 360-degree feedback, and executive coaching.

A genealogical analysis aids us in understanding the constitution of leadership through its various technologies. History is put to a different use in genealogy as the focus turns toward the constitutive or productive role of cultural practices in defining social phenomena. From this vantage, cultural practices are more basic than discursive formations. As Dreyfus and Rabinow (1983) explain,

> We are trying to understand the practices of our culture, practices which are by definition interpretations. They quite literally and materially embody a historically constituted "form of life," to use Wittgenstein's phrase. This form of life has no essence, no fixity, no hidden underlying unity. But it nonetheless has its own specific coherence. (p. 125)

How does genealogy apply to leadership? Grint (1997, 2000) supplies one answer by focusing on the philosophical, fine, martial, and performing arts of those whose leadership performances were ultimately believed.[11] He argues that scientific approaches fail to grasp the complexity of the interpretive process where for both actors and analysts alike, leadership, like art, remains in the eye of the beholder. To paraphrase Wittgenstein, leadership as a "form of life" has no essence, no fixity, no hidden underlying unity, but it does indeed have its own specific coherence in the formulations of its many beholders.

SUBJECTS AND OBJECTS

One of Foucault's key points with respect to Discourse is that it produces the *objects* about which it speaks, giving it a "public reality" (Dreyfus &

Rabinow, 1983). At least for the social sciences, objects do not have an existence outside of Discourse.[12] For example, replace what Foucault (1972) says about mental illness with leadership:

> mental illness [leadership] was constituted by all that was said in all the statements that named it, divided it up, described it, explained it, traced its developments, indicated its various correlations, judged it, and possibly gave it speech by articulating, in its name, [D]iscourses that were to be taken as its own. (p. 32)

Have we who study and write about leadership not done the same? We have named the field in which a few influence the performance of the many as leadership, although please do not ask us to agree on a precise definition (Alvesson & Sveningsson, 2003b; Rost, 1991). Our dividing practices associated with its forms take on jigsaw puzzle proportions to which countless leadership style inventories can attest. There is a virtual industry of business press books devoted to describing and explaining it, and an army of organizational consultants who will offer this up as advice in person. Countless textbooks trace its developments, and a steady stream of publications in scholarly journals records its correlations with other weighty phenomena. Critics over the years have judged its utility, even for a time suggesting its usefulness had run its course (Kerr & Jermier, 1978). All along the way, they and others have given voice to leadership, as the language and practices of the Discourses of neo-charisma, TQM, human resources, human relations, and Taylorism bear testimony. These and other management discourses treat leadership or management as conceptual objects of study and targets of expertise (du Gay & Salaman, 1996). As historically situated bodies of knowledge, they produce the objects about which they speak and objectify those for whom they apply.

While it is through Discourse that human beings are treated as objects, they are also constituted as *subjects*. Importantly, for leadership study there is no subject, individual or collective, "moving history" in Foucault's genealogy (Dreyfus & Rabinow, 1983, p. 109). Such a statement is clearly at odds with the ascribed heroism bias in neo-charisma Discourses (Gronn, 2002; Yukl, 1999)[13] and more general attributional processes that may be at work (Meindl, Ehrlich, & Dukerich, 1985). But if the extant leadership literature reflects a pendulum that exaggerates agency (Gronn, 2002), Foucault's thoughts on the modern subject are an interesting and important counterweight to consider for leadership study.

Foucault's (1983) central aim was to "create a history of the different modes by which, in our culture, human beings are made subjects. . . . [specifically] three modes of objectification which transform human beings into subjects" (p. 208). Two ways should already be somewhat familiar. The first way is the objectification of the speaking subject in Discourses, much the way a visionary CEO gets captured in neo-charisma Discourses as a true 'leader.' For Foucault (1983), it is the specifics of knowledge found within these Discourses that represent a form of power that "categorizes the individual, marks him out by his own individuality, attaches him to his identity, imposes a law of truth on him which he must recognize and which others have to recognize in him" (p. 212).

The second way is through norm-producing, dividing practices that partition a subject either inside him- or herself or from others. Again, the CEO searches that divide worthy 'leader' candidates from unworthy 'managers' draw from the norm-producing, neo-charisma Discourses that supply distinct meanings for these categories. Finally, the third way involves how humans turn themselves into subjects, a topic that merits considerable attention from Foucault and requires further explanation.

In communication, speaking subjects skillfully position themselves within various Discourses as they coordinate their actions with others. Discourses thus serve as linguistic resources for speaking subjects, who are afforded a space for action generally within the scope defined by one or more Discourses (Daudi, 1986). Yet these resources are always shifting; Discourses inevitably change and evolve as subjects creatively adapt them to suit their changing circumstances. Despite the agency manifested here, the power effects of Discourses still reproduce themselves. Importantly, this is not done in an oppressive or omnipotent way, but in the way Discourses become the basis for the subject's own self-understandings (Knights & Morgan, 1991). Subjugation occurs when, through their language and behavior, individuals begin to understand themselves in relation to the produced objects of one or more Discourses. Thus, for the aspiring CEO who wants very much to be a 'leader' (not 'manager'),[14] she is likely to subjugate herself to the demands of acquiring both visioning and industry expertise in order to be seen as a force for change.

For Foucault (1983), subjects only emerge within these Discourses, forsaking any notion of a 'true' reality behind the scenes. Such a claim will seem odd to many leadership researchers who view 'leader' and 'agent' as nearly synonymous terms and where agency must therefore derive from a conception of the self that is unitary, coherent, and ultimately autonomous (a topic addressed in Chapter 5). However, Foucault's genealogy forsakes this kind of agency in favor of a decentered self and a central concern with social practices, as displayed in a play among conflicting or complementary Discourses, and the space or field that they clear in order for subjects to emerge.[15] As Dreyfus and Rabinow (1983) explain, "Subjects do not first preexist and later enter into combat or harmony . . . subjects emerge on a field of battle and play their roles, there and there alone" (p. 109). The implications of such a stance dictate that we look less at the leader as crucial agent and more at the structural field of Discourses and their power to discipline.

In order to understand this better, consider that Foucault's (1990) view of power is likely foreign to those who might view it in terms of authority or position,[16] a commodity that is a potential or what one possesses, or the ability to act strategically or instrumentally.[17] On the contrary, Foucault's power is *relational* because it reveals itself in its application with others vis-à-vis specific practices, techniques, or procedures. Power is thus diffuse and rarely formulated in a continuous systematic Discourse because it enlists disparate tools and methods (Foucault, 1995). Importantly, Foucault's concept of *power/knowledge* highlights the key role of knowledge in rendering aspects of our existence thinkable and thus governable through intervention (Miller & Rose, 1990).

There is little need to ontologically privilege leadership (broadly or narrowly defined) as a construct because its very construction is laid out before us in various governing practices that build one upon the other in ever more general mechanisms or technologies of power (a subject to which we shall return in later discussion of Foucault's governmentality). Townley (1993b) and Gordon (1980) thus attribute to Foucault an ascending view of power, in which power-laced minutiae aggregate and build. By articulating the many technologies of power in all of its rich detail, it is no longer a question of 'who has power' but 'how are power effects produced by these many technologies.' To address the latter, Foucault (1980) introduces us to *disciplinary power*, which turns on two meanings of the word 'discipline.' As both a branch of knowledge and a system of regulation, training, and control, disciplinary power is again testimony to the inextricability of power/knowledge relations. That is, the exercise of power creates knowledge, while the use of knowledge always engenders power.

In disciplinary technologies of power, the human body is docile and an object to be manipulated. Although not always visible, disciplinary power operates by means of the practices focused in the technologies and their innumerable instantiations. Disciplinary power is often aided by the *surveillance* capabilities of certain technologies, and nowhere is this more evident than in Bentham's Panopticon, which Foucault (1995) describes in *Discipline and Punish* as a model prison in which the prisoner can always be observed.[18] However, because the prisoner is never sure of precisely when observation occurs, he disciplines himself and becomes his own guard. Yet, because the guards who do the observing are themselves subject to administrative control, they too fall under the veil of disciplinary power.

The exercise of discipline requires mechanisms that coerce through some means of hierarchical observation. Once made visible, *normalizing judgment* can be applied to individuals as their behavior is compared to others' behavior, especially as averages or norms get established. Some form of examination "measures in quantitative terms and hierarchizes in terms of value the abilities, the level, the 'nature' of individuals," introducing through these measures "the constraint of a conformity that must be achieved" (Foucault, 1995,

p. 183). Foucault is quick to note that conformity can be achieved as much through meting out rewards as through punishment.

Foucault (1990, 1995) wrote extensively about rituals like the examination and the confession, which either separately or together combine the techniques of an observing hierarchy and normalizing judgment. The *examination* has a rich history in medical and school settings, the specific rituals of which make the individual visible in some way (such as knowledge of a topic, or heart rate, body temperature, weight, and so on). Once made visible, he or she can be qualified, classified, and sanctioned. Disciplinary power manifests itself in the hierarchy's power to gaze upon a subject who is treated as an object, primed and ready for classification through the means that the examination affords. The hierarchy's ability to maintain an unfettered gaze maintains the disciplined individual in his or her subjection (Foucault, 1995), much like the student who diligently studies for top grades or the patient who diets for fear of the doctor's rebuke and categorization as overweight.

Typically, the examination that subjects an individual to surveillance also situates him or her in a field of documentation. Individuals are constituted "as a describable, analyzable object, not in order to reduce him to 'specific' features . . . but in order to maintain him in his individual features . . . under the gaze of a permanent corpus of knowledge" (Foucault, 1995, p. 190). This body of knowledge includes ratings and measurement procedures, group category formations and descriptions, individuals' assessment vis-à-vis their distribution in a given population, and the understandings that accompany them. For Foucault, the examination is key among procedures that constitute the individual as an *effect* and *object* of power and knowledge.

By contrast, the *confession* has its roots in religion and the sacrament of penance, given the ritualized way in which the Catholic Church designed it to produce 'truth.' Yet, society still utilizes the confession for many forms of information that are difficult to disclose (such as crimes, secrets, and lies). Foucault (1990) himself was fascinated by the confession around sex that described its practices, classified and named them, rendered moral judgments, and traced its history and corollaries, in short, that transformed it into a Discourse. In confession, individuals are subjects in a double sense: They are the subjects of the confession, and they are subject to the gaze and judgment of an authority who requests or demands it, places a premium on it, and intercedes where necessary to reinforce, reward, punish, or empathize (Foucault, 1990).

For Foucault, the confession leads to self-understanding. As he describes it for sexuality, "It is no longer a question simply of saying what was done—the sexual act—and how it was done; but of reconstructing, in and around the act, the thoughts that recapitulated it, the obsessions that accompanied it, the images, desires, modulations, and quality of the pleasure that animated it" (Foucault, 1990, p. 63). Yet, in deriving this self-understanding, modern science's role as a powerful partner in formulating the truth must be acknowledged. For the truth is not solely what a confessor reveals; it is as much the person who, through the Discourse of science's canons, takes the testimony, assimilates it, labels it, and documents the 'findings.' That which emerges as the 'truth' is a coconstruction that always unfolds within a power relationship between confessor and his or her scientific interlocutor.

The resonances of Foucault's rituals of examination and confession can be found in three performance management technologies common within the field of leadership today: the performance appraisal, 360-degree feedback, and executive coaching. All three are *disciplinary technologies* that produce knowledge, develop and diversify Discourses, and generate the power to discipline (Foucault, 1990).

Discipline and Surveillance in Performance Management Technologies

Performance management generally includes both objective setting and formal appraisal, where the appraisal process is further subdivided into assessment and coaching (Bevan & Thompson, 1991). The centerpiece of performance management technologies, the *performance appraisal,* has been gaining in popularity since the 1970s. This is due to widespread organizational restructurings that increased job autonomy, discretion in decision making, and self-management, making managerial oversight more difficult (Bowles & Coates, 1993; Townley, 1989). As the ensuing discussion makes clear, 360-degree feedback and executive coaching enhance managerial oversight, especially when used in tandem with the appraisal.

PERFORMANCE APPRAISAL

In the performance appraisal, managers monitor work outputs, identify under-performers, and reward success (Barlow, 1989). Performance monitoring and work sampling enable the manager-appraiser to rate and categorize the appraisee in terms of a number of effectiveness measures that are critical to objective setting for future performance.

Research that has been critical of the appraisal process finds that management uses it not just to measure performance, but also to foster identification with corporate goals and objectives and inculcate organizational standards through the communication of expectations (Bowles & Coates, 1993; Offe, 1976; Townley, 1993b). Barlow (1989) asserts that the appraisal conveniently serves the organization's claims of a rational and efficient use of human resources, "albeit with varying and frequently criticized effectiveness" (p. 500). He observes that promotion decisions and performance appraisals often do not coincide, given the more narrow bounds of the appraisal relative to the political and personal criteria often used in promotion decisions. Finally, the form of the appraisal can either be quantitative or qualitative, as there are a large number of appraisal schemes from which to choose (Townley, 1993b). Despite their wide availability and numbers, under-skilled managers often resist rigorous appraisal of those who report to them (Barlow, 1989). Because appraisees are asked to join in the appraisal process (to enhance investment in their own development), the manager-appraiser is cast into the potentially conflicting roles of disciplinary judge and helpful counselor (McGregor, 1960; Newton & Findlay, 1996). These role enactments require a great deal of managerial skill as the appraisees' full participation may be inhibited if the information they disclose ends up being used against them.

Foucault's discussion of disciplinary power and the examination ritual lies at the heart of much of this critique. The appraisal process is often set within human resources Discourses from which the appraisal draws its emphasis on basic social values and the worth and dignity of the individual (Newton & Findlay, 1996),[19] and Discourses that apply psychological theory and techniques to personnel and human resource management (Barlow, 1989; Townley, 1993a, 1993b). The latter are designed to make the employee a "knowable, calculable and administrative object," a characterization of Miller and Rose (1990) that epitomizes management's desire for an employee who could be made visible through examination (assessment). Key also to the examination is a normalizing judgment, a function that the appraisal performs especially as under-performance is assessed and labeled. However, Newton and Findlay (1996) argue strongly for the panoptic power of the appraisal beyond assessment because manager-appraisers invite appraisees into the appraisal process so they can explore the 'why' behind substandard performance. As Newton and Findlay (1996) explain, "Answering this question requires an ability to gaze on the subjectivity of the worker, to know their feelings, anxieties, their identity and their consciousness" (p. 48). Appraisees have a lot to learn (read: discipline themselves) through the sharing of difficulties with the manager-appraiser, all the while this 'participative' appraisal "brings us closer to the celestial vision of a 'god' who 'knows' and 'sees' and 'guides'" (Newton & Findlay, 1996, p. 48).

360-DEGREE FEEDBACK

In 360-degree feedback, the goal is to distribute the hierarchic observation by the manager-appraiser among all members of a person's role set: direct reports, peers, team members, colleagues, supervisors, and customers/clients (Church & Bracken, 1997; Funderburg & Levy, 1997; London, Smither, & Adsit, 1997). It is a popular form of multi-rater assessment that may be used in the appraisal process or by itself. Not only is the very name '360-degree' emblematic of panoptic power, it also allows management and human resources specialists to accumulate a body of individualizing knowledge of increasingly finer distinctions vis-à-vis the observational method of multiple raters using 360-degree feedback instruments. With an unobstructed 360-degree view, the individual is permanently on show and open to examination—or at least he or she presumes as much as the individual ultimately disciplines him- or herself in response to the collective gaze of the role set. Yet, many who participate in extending the hierarchy's gaze to 360 degrees are their surrogates (such as coworkers, customers, and so on). Whether the role set defines the individual's job performance in their (360-degree) terms is always a potential point of resistance.

EXECUTIVE COACHING

The surrogate gaze takes on additional meaning with the advent of executive coaching, which has become enormously popular in new market economies and neo-charisma Discourses that associate 'leadership' with organizational change (Berglas, 2002; Cannon & Witherspoon, 2005; Kets de Vries, 2005).[20] In this era, organizations are downsizing their workforces and reengineering their work processes. The average blue- or white-collar worker is knowable, calculable, and expendable due to cost-saving labor practices like outsourcing and off-shoring. The workers' objectified status is that of 'waste' or 'fat' that needs to be cut so the now 'lean' organization can respond to change more quickly. By contrast, the senior executive who can pull off such sweeping changes is also objectified, but he or she becomes "a living vessel of 'intellectual capital'—a resource regarded as no less precious than money itself" (Sherman & Freas, 2004, p. 84). Thus, the average worker is surplus value while the right senior leader is a precious resource, ironically one who can convincingly invoke the human resources Discourses of employee worth for the downsizing survivors. More generally, it is a leader who can embrace relationship-oriented management practices as a way of building more commercially responsive organizational structures (for example, service quality, teams, and flattened hierarchies) (Kerfoot & Knights, 1996).

Executive coaching is yet another form of appraisal and development, but one that adds a confessional technology to the examination. The executive coach is brought in for the prospective leader (or work team) who is experiencing image or relational difficulties, but whom the organization wants to keep. Previous uses of the confessional technology in organizations found that, although voluntary, it encourages a narcissistic identification with the organization ideal (Casey, 1999). This would appear to be the case for executive coaching because leaders have their own individual coach who can drive that message home. The coach enters into a three-party contractual relationship (client, coach, coachee) with the organizational client who pays the costly fees, yet guarantees the confidentiality of the coach–leader relationship. Unless requested by the coachee, there is usually no further reporting to the client—a collection of interested parties (management, mentor, human resources, and so on) who should be able to witness firsthand the coachee's transformation over a several-month period (Sherman & Freas, 2004).

Although the coach is there at the behest of management, the hope is that a trusting relationship will develop with the leader, not unlike that of a psychotherapy relationship. The problems to be addressed are initially set by the client and leader, but are usually refined through examination techniques like 360-degree feedback. The many senior managers who cannot deliver quality feedback to coached leaders in the performance appraisal typically have little trouble delivering it through the 360-degree process or to executive coaches directly, who increasingly serve as "outsourced suppliers of candor, providing individual leaders with objective feedback needed to nourish their growth" (Sherman & Freas, 2004, p. 85). Similarly, the hope is that a coachee who holds back in the appraisal because of a perceived conflict between the potentially conflicting roles of 'helpful counselor' and 'disciplinary judge' of the manager-appraiser will be forthcoming to the executive coach, whose role is only cast as the former.

The confessional technology is instrumental to executive coaching because its very design is to get at the truth, as Foucault (1990) wrote, "corroborated by the obstacles and resistances it has had to surmount in order to be formulated" (p. 62). Just as for Foucault, the confessional technology turned sex into a Discourse and truth into a joint formulation between a confessor's avowal and its scientific uptake, so too executive coaching attempts to turn a person's leadership into a coaching Discourse whose 'truth' is a coconstructed product of the leader's disclosures and the coach's interpretations. Next we will consider the means by which this is done: the surrogate gaze of the executive coach, the regulation of coaching Discourses, and targeted objects of the Discourses like the 'alpha male.'

Surrogate Gaze of the Executive Coach

In charging executive coaches to 'grow' senior leaders, the coach is a surrogate or proxy for senior management who are either incapable or unwilling to expend the time and effort necessary to develop their people (Cannon & Witherspoon, 2005). Yet, the coach's stand-in role is a special one because the panoptic view into a coachee's job performance can surpass even management's view. The surrogate gaze of the executive coach derives from observing the coachee in action, his or her access to the knowledge generated from examination techniques like the 360-degree feedback and the performance appraisal, and the confessional technology endemic to the quasi-therapeutic coaching relationship. Similar to the participative appraisal, the latter affords the "ability to gaze on the subjectivity of the worker, to know their feelings, anxieties, their identity and their consciousness" (Newton & Findlay, 1996, p. 48). In many ways, this surrogate gaze is extraordinary for the unfettered view of the individual that executive coaching affords.

Regulating Executive Coaching 'Psychological' Discourses

It is perhaps because of this unfettered view that clinical psychologists have begun to patrol the boundaries of executive coaching Discourses— defining all problems as potentially psychological and reflective of unconscious conflict that only a psychological evaluation can detect and a coach trained in clinical psychology can safely address (Berglas, 2002; Kets de Vries, 2005; Ludeman & Erlandson, 2004). The very state of executive coaching today has been depicted by psychologist-coaches as a "wild West," a reference to the 'anything goes' nature of the early American West now applied to the diverse backgrounds and qualifications of executive coaches (Sherman & Freas, 2004). According to Kets de Vries (2005),

> A clinical orientation to leadership analysis and intervention . . . is therefore essential in the organizational context. The clinical orientation is solidly grounded in concepts of psychoanalytic psychology . . . short-term dynamic psychotherapy, cognitive theory, human development and family systems theory. (p. 72) . . . Self-styled leadership "coaches" may have good intentions, but real leadership coaching is built on a solid base of psychological under- standing and practice. Effective leadership coaches are attuned to the uncon- scious life of organizations. (p. 74, emphasis original)

Some admit that a psychiatrist is hardly necessary to develop an executive's strategic planning abilities or that a psychotherapist-coach without grounding in organizational management can be harmful (Berglas, 2002; Kets de Vries, 2005). However, these caveats do not outweigh the coaching narratives in this literature in which success is premised upon psychologists who immediately discern individual pathologies or dysfunctional group dynamics to safely guide the development effort, or psychologists to whom organizations turn to save the day when previous coaches with jock (as one writer described it), legal, aca- demic, or management backgrounds fail. As such, the confessional technology of executive coaching finds its absolution in psychology, the salvation science as it is sometimes known. The merits of this argument notwithstanding, Foucault's insight, that Discourse produces its own truth effects through artic- ulating a view of the world in which problems are defined that a Discourse can solve, is most relevant here. When psychologist-coach Steven Berglas chastised "unqualified" coaches for defining problems in (the nonpsychological) terms they understand best, clearly he was unaware that his adage, "If all you have is a hammer, everything looks like a nail," also applied to himself (p. 7).

Targeted Objects of Coaching Discourses: The 'Alpha Male'

Perhaps the most targeted object of executive coaching Discourses to date is the alpha male. The objectifying term *alpha male* is imported from the ani- mal kingdom as the male in charge of all others in his social group. While alpha females rival the power of alpha males in the animal world, Ludeman and Erlandson (2004) argue against the notion of alpha females in business (a point taken up more directly in Chapter 5). Writing in the *Harvard Business Review*, they suggest that alpha males represent some 70% of all senior executives. However, narrowly associating 'alpha' with 'male' is hardly surprising to students of the history of Western management practices. As Kerfoot and Knights (1996) argue, "masculinity and management are at once mutually embedded and reproductive of one another. Self-estrangement and emotional distance from others (features of a Masculinity Discourse) occurs not in some form of psychological vacuum: it is created, sustained and reproduced in social or managerial practices" (p. 92). Alpha males thus make prime targets for coaching because of their overriding need for control and reliance on masculinity Discourses, which maintain an instrumentalism and emotional distance in social relationships. As Kerfoot and Knights (1996) argue, these Discourses are clearly at odds with management practices that emphasize relationship skills and inclusiveness (suggestive of a more feminine Discourse) as the preferred means of control. The qualities that Ludeman and Erlandson (2004) ascribe to alpha males are exemplary of control and instrumentalism: alpha males are natural leaders, independent, action-oriented, poor listeners, opinionated, arrogant, unemotional, analytical, stubborn, resistant to feedback, prone to snap judgments, and oblivious to the effect that they have on others. While there are a number of variations on the enactment of masculinity Discourses (see Chapter 5 for more on this subject), the concern here is for the confessional technology deployed in coaching. The challenge for the executive coach in this regard is to not to undermine the alpha's drive for results, but to improve the means by which this is done.

For example, Ludeman and Erlandson (2004) posit that the right way to coach an alpha includes getting his attention, demanding commitment, speaking his language, hitting him hard enough to hurt, and engaging his curiosity and competitive instincts. Yet, these enjoinders are merely emblematic of the disciplinary techniques designed to subject an alpha to coaching Discourse. For instance, the coach should *get the alpha's attention* through 360-degree feedback gathering. Yet, based on earlier arguments, the 360's power to supply "undeniable proof that his behavior (to which he is much attached) doesn't work nearly as well as he thinks it does" is panoptic, resting in the collective gaze of the role set (p. 63).

Coaches must also calibrate the feedback from the 360 because alphas think in charts, graphs, and metrics. Yet, in order to *speak his language*, communicating in 'alpha speak' intensifies the impact of a normative judgment as coaches are urged to inundate alphas with quantitative data. Bar charts and plotted graphs are a favorite here not only because they visually display consensus around scaled categories, but also because the scales themselves are visually depicted to highlight deviation from the norm. For example, Ludeman and Erlandson's (2004) metric evaluates alphas on business leadership, vision, results-orientation, problem solving, empowerment, mentoring, motivation, peer collaboration, and integrity. They use a scale so that alphas can "see at a glance" *how much* an area is a 'strength,' 'improved,' 'neutral,' 'warning,' 'developmental area,' or 'serious risk' (p. 64). Note that at least four of the six scale categories are subpar.

Similarly, the ensuing delivery of the qualitative comments from the 360-degree feedback proceeds by using the full force of the verbatim, emotionally loaded language of the role set. Because alphas routinely use hard-hitting language with others, Ludeman and Erlandson (2004) argue that the coach must *hit him hard enough to hurt:* "We regulate the level of pain, keeping it high enough to get their full attention but also presenting the changes as attainable" (p. 63). One can't help but be reminded of Foucault's (1995) discussion of the art of torture, where a corpus of knowledge was developed to precisely measure and control the application of pain to the body so the person being tortured does not die too quickly. While pain is calibrated and applied to the body in the case of torture, it comes in calibrated emotional wallops to the psyche of the leader. Not unlike the forced confession at the end of a public torture, it is only after receiving these comments that the alpha is properly situated to realize or 'avow' the consequences of his behavior. The modus operandi of the torturer and the executive coach are clearly different, but the confessional technology is the same.

Finally, alpha males are a popular target of coaching Discourses because they are likely to be common, the most resistant to coaching, and arguably the most in need. Yet, in order to *engage his curiosity and competitive instincts,* the defensiveness that an alpha experiences as a result of blunt feedback must be confronted. Ludeman and Erlandson (2004) recommend a specialized alpha metric entitled, "How Defensive Are You?" that scales openness and defensiveness behaviors each on a 10-point scale. To take a few examples from the openness scale, a +1 is awarded if the alpha looks interested and demonstrates an open posture; a +4 if the alpha expresses genuine curiosity about the issue; a +7 if the alpha takes full responsibility for the problem; and a +10 if the alpha plans the change, engage with others, sets milestones, and implements. For the defensiveness scale, a −1 is awarded if the alpha shows polite, albeit superficial interest; a −2 if the alpha provides an overly detailed explanation; a −4 if the alpha interrupts to give his perspective; a −7 if the alpha reveals his irritation nonverbally; a −8 if he shifts the blame; and a −10 if he appears to comply with no intention of following through (p. 66). According to Ludeman and Erlandson (2004), "Asking the alpha to monitor his defensiveness motivates him to see how quickly he can catch himself and shift to a more open frame of mind (p. 63). . . . Alphas can use this tool to chart their progress" (p. 66).

Foucault's insights here are useful on several counts. First is that resistance is not just a source of "perpetual disorder," but it is also "through the articulation points of resistance that power spreads" (Dreyfus & Rabinow, 1983, p. 147).

Clearly, Ludeman and Erlandson (2004) have turned the alpha's defensiveness into a Discourse in which 'his' problems are defined in 'their' terms. The coach's use of this metric is shot through with power afforded by the opportunity that the alpha's resistance to coaching presents.

Second, the use of this metric is what Foucault (1995) would refer to as a disciplinary technology, the aim of which is to forge a "docile body that may be subjected, used, transformed, and improved" (p. 136). The alpha is not only the subject of this Discourse, but he is also being asked to subject himself to it by monitoring those feelings and behaviors that the Discourse defines as defensive in order to motivate him to "see how quickly he can catch himself and shift to a more open frame of mind" (Ludeman & Erlandson, 2004, p. 63). The embodied aspects of this exercise in self-discipline and self-regulation require the alpha to demonstrate genuine interest through even breathing, directed eye gaze, and an open posture. The alpha should also refrain from 'taking the floor' through interruptions, talk less, listen more, and restrain nonverbal signs of irritation or intimidation. As Foucault has suggested, disciplinary technology is inscribed on the human body and the spatio-temporal arrangement it occupies, whether it is eye gaze, body position, floor dominance, or more general scripts for interaction that regulate the content and procedural aspects of the spatio-temporal flow. In this way, the confessional technology of executive coaching combined with examination techniques like 360-degree feedback and performance appraisals unite knowledge, power, control of the body, and control of space into integrated disciplinary technologies. The coordinated use of performance management technologies like the appraisal, 360-degree feedback, and executive coaching call to mind Foucault's (1979) concept of governmentality, the subject of the next section.

Performance Management Governmentality

Foucault (1979) introduced the concept of *governmentality* to refer to the means by which economic, social, and individual conduct comes to align itself with socio-political concerns. His concern was population management and "the regulation of the processes proper to the population, the laws that modulate its wealth, health, longevity, its capacity to wage war and to engage in labour and so forth" (Miller & Rose, 1990, p. 2). However, governmentality can be widely applied because it is formed by a host of "institutions, procedures, analyses and reflections . . . calculations and tactics" (Foucault, 1979, p. 20). It sets problems in such a way that they carry a kind of 'political a priori,' in that authorities assume a political mandate that—through their Discourses—enables them to problematize the world in such a way that it becomes amenable to administration (Miller & Rose, 1990).

When applied to the government of the economic sphere, governmentality concerns itself as much with systems of economic production as with the cognitive calculations of economic actors (Miller & Rose, 1990). It is a *mentality* that relies upon knowledge based in Discourse and the inextricability of power/ knowledge relations that render aspects of the world visible, analyzable, and actionable. Within this frame, Miller and Rose heuristically exploit Foucault's governmentality in order to understand the changing techniques of organizational management, one of which is the performance appraisal. However, the arguments that Miller and Rose offer up extend well beyond the appraisal. This is because they pay particular attention to the ways in which governmentality achieves Latour's (1987) notion of 'action at a distance'—in this case, management at a distance vis-à-vis often indirect, mundane, and layered institutional technologies or mechanisms that make it possible for targeted objects of policy to be problematized and acted upon. To accomplish this, they explicate management's increasing reliance on *expertise*, not just to shape the technical features of production, but to shape the thinking and self-disciplining capacities of producing subjects.

Based on these ideas, governmentality usefully explains the ways in which the performance appraisal, 360-degree feedback, executive coaching, and countless other performance management technologies like assessment centers, incentive plans, bonus or merit pay, and even separation/termination policies, may work collectively through distinct or, more likely, overlapping languages and vocabularies to produce power/knowledge regimes. It is knowledge that translates to information—reports, charts, graphs, ratings, statistics, and so on that enable pertinent features of employee performances "to literally be re-presented in the place where decisions are to be made about them (the manager's office, the war room, the case conference and so forth)" (Miller & Rose, 1990, p. 7). All are part of the government of the business enterprise, interwoven further still with mechanisms of a more mundane nature: notation, computation, and calculation techniques; examination procedures and forms; presentational styles; standardized systems for training around work procedures and habits; professional vocabularies; and many more.

As we see in the case of surrogate-driven technologies like 360-degree feedback and executive coaching, many of today's performance management technologies are an indirect means of managerial action and intervention made possible by the presence of expertise. As an examination ritual, 360-degree feedback (like the appraisal) puts into play expert Discourses, while confession rituals like executive coaching send embodied experts into the field to coach. The function of expert Discourses and their emissaries are the same: apply a normalizing judgment to the behavior of individuals—specifically targeted through the individualizing knowledge that performance management technologies produce due to surrogate surveillance capability—in order to rein in substandard performances.

Importantly, the leader who is objectified and judged by these expert Discourses is also a subject who, in order to monitor and regulate him- or herself, requires a *translation* of authoritative norms and evaluative processes into his or her value base, assumptions, and decisional processes. But who does the translating? Although senior leaders are the obvious candidates, their translation skills may not match that of executive coaches whose gaze is more privileged. Although Miller and Rose (1990) did not write about executive coaching, their treatise on the role of the expert as 'translator' seems tailor-made:

> Experts . . . have elaborated the arguments that the personal capacities of individuals can be managed in order to achieve socially desirable goals. . . . They have latched on to existing political concerns, suggesting that they have the capacity to ameliorate problems, and achieve benefits. They have allied themselves with other powerful social authorities . . . translating their 'lay' problems into expert languages and suggesting that rational knowledges and planned techniques hold the key to success. They have problematized new aspects of existence, and in the very same moment, suggested that they can help overcome the problems that they have discovered. And they have acted as powerful translation devices between 'authorities' and 'individuals,' shaping conduct not through compulsion but through the power of truth, the potency of rationality and the alluring promises of effectivity. (p. 19)

Thus, senior management expects executive coaches to be powerful translators who can make authoritative, expert Discourses personally relevant to the work lives of coached leaders. However, by virtue of the indirect nature of this management at a distance, one also cannot minimize the opportunities that exist to resist the disciplinary techniques of executive coaching and other performance management technologies. As long as human beings are evaluating and coaching other human beings, planned outcomes may well diverge from that which is realized—a message that is true of any programmatic aspect of governmentality (Miller & Rose, 1990). The next chapter picks up on this theme more directly.

A Backward Glance—Final Thoughts

The key points of this chapter's Foucauldian look at leadership have been the following:

- *Discourse* is a historically and culturally situated way of thinking and talking about some subject matter.
- *Archeology* examines Discourses as relatively autonomous systems of thought, while g*enealogy* focuses upon the constitutive or productive role of cultural practices in defining social phenomena.
- *Power* and *knowledge* are intertwined in Discourse because once something is known in a particular way, it can be acted upon. Also, what is 'true' about a phenomenon is not driven by its essence, but by the way in which a Discourse represents it.

- The power effects of Discourse are revealed where there is *resistance*.
- Foucault's view of power is diffuse and relational. He recommends analyzing power relations via power *technologies* and the ways in which specific rituals of power weave knowledge, competence, and qualification together.
- Discourses produce the *objects* about which they speak. Discourses supply three modes of objectification by which human beings are transformed into *subjects*. These modes operate by (a) the objectification of the speaking subject, (b) norm-producing dividing practices, and (c) the ways in which humans turn themselves into subjects.
- In *disciplinary power*, the human body is docile and an object to be manipulated. Discourses are inscribed on the body.
- Disciplinary power is aided by the *surveillance* capabilities of certain technologies, much like Bentham's Panopticon. Once made visible, *normalizing judgments* compare and hierarchize an individual with respect to some norm or average.
- *Examination* rituals combine surveillance and normalizing judgment. They render an individual visible, primed and ready for classification in the way that the examination affords. They also situate him or her in a field of documentation.
  o The performance appraisal and 360-degree feedback are panoptic examination techniques designed to make an employee a knowable, calculable, and administrative object.
- The *confession* ritual also combines surveillance and normalizing judgment. It is a technology designed to produce 'truth' and self-understanding, but 'truth' is always a coconstruction of the confessor and an interlocutor.
  o Executive coaching utilizes examination techniques like the appraisal and 360-degree feedback, while also adopting a confessional technology based on the quasi-therapeutic relationship of the coach and leader.
  o This relationship is facilitated by (a) the surrogate gaze of the executive coach, which is extraordinary for its unfettered view of the leader, (b) psychologists who patrol the boundaries of executive coaching Discourses to define all important problems as psychological, and (c) targeted objects of executive coaching like the alpha male for whom interventions and metrics are designed.
- *Governmentality* refers to the means by which the economic, social, and individual conduct of a population becomes regulated and aligned with the sociopolitical concerns of authorities.
  o Governmentality can explicate the changing techniques of organizational performance management, which often take the form of *management at a distance*.

At this writing, executive coaching is exploding in popularity. Leaders proudly announce they have their own executive coach (D. Brady, 2006), and executive coaching spin-offs are taking root. For example, leaders are now hiring 'life coaches' to put their personal lives in order and even college admission coaches for their children, as early as the eighth grade, to assure their acceptance into the right colleges some five years down the line (Tergesen, 2006). Perhaps most remarkable of all is what *Business Week* is calling the "charm offensive" taking hold among America's CEOs who "are suddenly so eager to be loved" (D. Brady, 2006, p. 76). The lessons of executive coaching have taught them the 'likeability game,' recalling Wittgenstein (1953). According to *Business Week,* the rules require that CEOs "Take to calling [themselves] a 'servant leader'—never a 'philosopher king'—in interviews"; "Personally rush heavily branded equipment to a disaster site and talk about what a moving experience it was in your blog"; "Compliment every member of your team by name at the corporate picnic while handing out organic hot dogs"; "Make a personal and endearing confession at the townhall meeting, even if it's just about your teenager's tattoos"; "Bring your executive coach to the next board meeting to help you understand how to tap the hidden needs and desires of each member"; and "Focus on the next ad campaign on global warming, install solar panels at HQ, and rebrand your product line as 'green'" (D. Brady, 2006, p. 76).

When executive coaching can be parodied with organic foods, environmentalism, and Oprah-like moments of disaster relief and public confessions, there are some powerful discursive formations at hand. However, the real proof is in the rather creative ways in which 'free' individuals and 'private' spaces can be 'ruled' sans an apparent breach of their autonomy. Foucault's notion of disciplinary power thus has great relevance for the study of leadership, as hapless eighth graders with their own college coaches readily suggest.

NOTES

1. Labour process theory is the sole exception here (Kieser, 1994).

2. For example, see discussions of psychobiography (Gronn, 1993; Kets de Vries, 1990).

3. Sociologists William H. Whyte, Jr. (1956) in *The Organization Man* and C. Wright Mills (1951) in *White Collar* both predate Foucault on the subject of discipline. Whyte's (1956) call was for those who have "left home, spiritually as well as physically, to take the vows of organization life," to resist from within and fight the conformity, mediocrity, and neuroses that the disciplining system inevitably bestows (p. 3). Mills (1951) spoke less optimistically about the managerial demiurge, which symbolizes a subordinate deity and a subordinated deity in which managers carry an authority in which they are not its source (recalling the guards in the tower in Bentham's Panopticon).

4. To be clear, Shapiro (1992) wrote only about organizational sociologists; however, I am broadening this argument to other social scientists.

5. Because Foucault presupposed but was not interested in the communicative process per se, our previous conceptualization of discourse as language in use is too narrow.

6. Archeology was never abandoned by Foucault, but it came to be seen as secondary to genealogy (Dreyfus & Rabinow, 1983).

7. Human resources Discourses are sometimes referred to as 'neo-human relations' (Newton & Findlay, 1996)

8. 'Neo-charismatic' (House & Aditya, 1997) or 'new leadership' (Bryman, 1992) are the usual labels attached to this genre of theories that draw, in varying degrees, from Weber's original writings on charismatic authority.

9. For example, in early twentieth-century Discourses of the Industrial Revolution, including Weber's bureaucratic model, Fayol's (1949) classical management

functions, and F. Taylor's (1919) scientific management, work efficiency problems were thought to be solved by controlling employees' work output and treating them as rational economic beings. The manager's job was to plan, direct, and control others' work output (Fayol, 1949).

The human relations Discourses of the 1940s and 1950s, captured in Follett (as cited in Hurst, 1992), Barnard (1938), and Mayo (1945), celebrated democratic ideals and the importance of interpersonal relations. However, managers were ultimately focused on production needs; they were just asked to don velvet gloves to meet them (Miles, 1965).

The human resources Discourses of the 1960s were inspired by Maslow (1954) and included McGregor's (1960) Theory X and Theory Y, Likert's (1961, 1967) Systems 1-4, Blake and Mouton's (1964) managerial grid, and Herzberg's (1966, 1968) motivation-hygiene model. They cast workers as valuable human resources and urged managers to trust their employees to perform their jobs responsibly, participate in job design, and replace mechanistic structures with organic ones (Redding, 1973).

The Discourses of Total Quality Management (TQM) (Deming, 1982; Juran, 1964, 1988) in the 1970s and 1980s were inspired by the success of Japanese management techniques (Pascale & Athos, 1981). TQM emphasized a customer orientation, team structures like quality circles, and statistical monitoring of work output. Quality circles lasted only a short time in the United States, but in their place self-managing team Discourses based in socio-technical systems philosophy emerged (Trist, Higgin, Murray, & Pollock, 1963). When used in conjunction with TQM, teams were now charged with self-management, and the management function became everyone's responsibility.

Organizational culture Discourses also arrived on the scene in the early 1980s and centered on the role of corporate values in aligning the interests of employees with the organization (Deal & Kennedy, 1982; Peters & Waterman, 1982). Leaders were thought to be able to put their stamp on the culture by articulating a vision for the future, clear mission (or purpose), and core set of values (Schein, 1985).

Finally, neo-charisma Discourses emerged in the 1980s and continues on through the turn of the twenty-first century in new market economies (global outreach, technological advance, and cost-saving labor practices). Organizations sought senior executives who could effectively reshape their organizations to win market share in a globally competitive environment. 'Leaders' were cast as the change agents, capable of sweeping organizational transformation (Bennis & Nanus, 1985; Kotter, 1990; Kouzes & Posner, 1995). Theories of transformational leadership (Bass, 1985, 1988), charismatic leadership (Conger & Kanungo, 1987; House, 1977; Shamir, House, & Arthur, 1993), and visionary leadership (Bennis & Nanus, 1985; Westley & Mintzberg, 1989) explained the extraordinary capabilities of 'leaders' in terms of charisma, personal appeal, and a powerful vision to produce change. By contrast, 'managers' became the technicians with day-to-day know-how and skill, a particularly important function at middle and lower hierarchical levels.

10. See Kanter's (1983) book by the same name.

11. Grint (2000) points to the construction of a German identity by Adolph Hitler that "mobilized the fanatics and immobilized the skeptics" (p. 410); the catalyzing effect of Martin Luther King's "I Have a Dream Speech" on the Civil Rights Movement of the 1960s in the United States; the strategic inconsistencies of England's greatest military hero, Horatio Nelson; the organizational tactics of Florence Nightingale during the Crimean War that created a support network of public relations activism and compensated for her own weakness in this area; and the control of information that

reverberates around great leaders such as King, fueling their image long after they have departed the scene. Of course, Grint (2000) is not the first leadership scholar to arrive at the conclusion that leadership is a social construction (Calder, 1977; Meindl, 1993, 1995; Meindl et al., 1985). However, Foucault's (1980, 1983) influence on Grint is particularly apparent in the genealogical emphasis on cultural practices or leadership arts and in his view that the modern leader, as objectified, analyzed, and (re)constituted in various leadership Discourses, is a historical achievement.

12. When Foucault said that an object does not exist outside of Discourse, he nonetheless acknowledges the role played by nondiscursive practices and material conditions in forming some objects. However, at least for the social sciences, "discursive practices have a certain priority because they 'establish' relations between the other types of relations" (Dreyfus & Rabinow, 1983, p. 63).

13. Transformational and charismatic leaders are sometimes cast in heroic terms, exaggerating their impact (Gronn, 1995; Yukl, 1999).

14. Jack Welch was one such CEO who wanted to be called a leader rather than a manager (Hegele & Kieser, 2001).

15. See Holmer-Nadesan (1996) and Chapter 5 in this volume for further discussion of the space of action created by multiple Discourses.

16. As Foucault (1990) notes, "Power is not something that is acquired, seized, or shared, something one holds on to or allows to slip away" (p. 94).

17. Authoritative or positional power comes closest to Foucault's view of monarchic and juridical power wherein the exercise of power is seen in terms of law and the right to rule.

18. Bentham's concept of a Panopticon includes a central tower in an annular building that is subdivided into cells with inner and outer windows. The cells are backlit so that individuals are unable to tell when they are being observed from the tower.

19. Newton and Findlay (1996) specifically argue that human resources Discourses "can be seen as productively 'constituting' appraisers and appraisees in a discourse which emphasizes the 'learning' that can take place, through 'listening,' 'sharing' and through 'solving problems together'" (p. 48).

20. Estimates are that by 2004, annual spending for executive coaching was roughly at 1 billion (Sherman & Freas, 2004).

5

Self-Identities, Interpretative Repertoires

Having previously theorized about leadership traits, styles, situations, behaviors, and a host of contingencies, it was perhaps only a matter of time before leadership psychologists focused on the 'self' and 'identity' in their theorizing of leadership. Two emerging bodies of theory in leadership psychology exemplify this trend. They include follower self-identity theory (Lord & Brown, 2004; Lord, Brown, & Freiberg, 1999) and authentic leadership (Avolio & Gardner, 2005; Gardner et al., 2005; Ilies, Morgeson, & Nahrgang, 2005). As this chapter reveals, these theories reflect conceptions of the self that differ from those in discursive leadership. In a discussion of these differences, we continue to draw from the work of Foucault, but also the role played by multiple Discourses in self-identity work. As this chapter unfolds, authentic leadership, gendered Discourses, and interpretative repertoires take center stage.

The 'Self' in Leadership Psychology and Discursive Leadership

In *follower self-identity theory*, leadership becomes a process through which leaders change the way followers feel about themselves in order to elicit their best performances (Lord & Brown, 2004; Lord et al., 1999). Drawing from self-theorists in psychology, Lord and Brown (2004) define the self as an overarching knowledge structure that organizes memory and behavior, yielding an array of many compartmentalized selves (p. 14).[1] Because knowledge is inherently contextual and there are many possible situated selves, it is the *working self-concept* (WSC) that predominates at any specific point in time. The WSC is "a continually shifting combination of core self-schemas and peripheral aspects of the self made salient (i.e., activated) by context" (Lord et al., 1999, p. 176). Leaders are the primary context here. They are urged to address key components of a follower's WSC, including self-views as they measure against current goals or possible selves (both feared and ideal), to help the follower develop more integrated self-identities.

The emerging *authentic leadership* literature draws from the science of optimal human functioning, otherwise known as *positive psychology* (Seligman & Csikszentmihalyi, 2000). Because one of the keys to building life's positive qualities rests in authenticity, leaders are urged to get in tune with their 'basic nature' so they may see themselves clearly and act more consistently (Avolio et al., 2004; Gardner et al., 2005; Ilies et al., 2005). The authentic self is virtuous at its core, so genuine leaders must strive to 'know thyself (virtues)' in order to meet high personal standards of conduct and promote flow-like (working) capabilities in others.

Firmly rooted in humanistic psychology, authentic leadership's view of the self is centered in knowledge and experience, reflexive in its capacity to reflect upon itself, and more or less an integrated whole.[2] Writers in the humanist tradition, such as Carl Rogers (1961) and Abraham Maslow (1954, 1971), theorized the development of fully functioning or self-actualized individuals based on the unhindered operation of one's true or core self. Geertz (1984) captured this very Western conception of the self as a "bounded, unique, more or less integrated motivational and cognitive universe, a dynamic center of awareness, emotion, judgment, and action organized into a distinctive whole and set contrastively both against other such wholes and against its social and natural background" (p. 126).

In a marked contrast to these and other leadership psychology theories, Foucault and postmodern scholars like Holstein and Gubrium (2000) have called into question an integrated whole self in favor of the business of self-construction. Recall from the last chapter that Foucault's primary interest was the subject, its place in social life, its conceptual and agential status, and how it forms through the force of its bodily relations with others. In their theorizing, Holstein and Gubrium observed that Foucault was not particularly interested in the 'self' per se, but how it is that the body is seen as possessing a self with its own interests, one that rationally orients to itself and to the world (p. 76). In Foucault's (1995) *Discipline and Punish,* where he traces the history of French penal systems and punishment of lawbreakers, power/knowledge conceptions of a disciplined subject evolve from an appendage to the crown, controllable through bodily torture (so as to excise the diseased 'member'), to one colonized by contemporary institutions and its Discourses, controllable from a self within. For Foucault, the self cannot be the center of experience because the subject with a 'centered presence' is a historically based product of a humanist Discourse.[3]

Foucault's influence on Holstein and Gubrium (2000) is apparent as they cast the self as a form of *working subjectivity,* which "formulates a self that not only is a polysemic product of experience, but is also a byproduct of practices that diversely construct it in response to varied senses of what it could, or need, be" (p. 57).[4] Influenced by Wittgenstein (1953) as well, they see the self as a set of sited *language games* whose rules construct the semblance of a unified subjectivity centered in experience. To speak of a 'sited language game' in Wittgenstein's terms is to recognize the locally derived nature of meanings and word use and rules that give rise to forms of life—like selves or specific forms of leadership. Thus, the experientially-centered self of humanism, autonomous and enduring, gives way to an evanescent, communicated self located in Discourse in postmodernism. The latter is a self deployed, that is, put to work in context as it goes about the business of ordinary life. As such, ethnomethodology and Foucauldian theory are equal influences in Holstein and Gubrium's (2000) theorizing of the self. The former elucidates a self continuously under construction through language use and in social interaction (what we have earlier termed little 'd' discourse), while the latter articulates in Foucauldian terms the conditions of possibilities or linguistic resources that one or more Discourses make available to the communicating actor (termed big 'D' Discourse). More will be said about the interplay between the two as the chapter unfolds.

In turning toward the ordinary work of discursively constructing selves, many discourse analysts add to Foucault's work by adopting poststructuralist moorings, which cast Discourses of power as attempting to fix meanings in a struggle where several competing Discourses are always at play.[5] Taking their cues from structuralism, poststructuralists Laclau and Mouffe (1985) view the fixation of meaning as temporary because there are always other meaning potentials, hence the struggle against closure over which Discourses should prevail.[6] Because subjects attain their identities by being represented discursively, *identity* thus becomes a contingent identification with a subject position in a competitive discursive field. The term 'contingent' suggests that an identity could always be otherwise positioned.

The more competitive the discursive field, the greater the freedom to move or *space of action*, a term Daudi (1986) uses to refer to individuals' "striving for freedom, for autonomy and for personal interest" (p. 124). When individuals rebel against the ways a Discourse defines them (such as when a person resists being labeled a 'manager' in favor of 'leader'), a space is created between the hegemonic attempts of a Discourse to affix meaning and whatever meaning potentials constitute resistance (Fleming, 2005; Mumby, 2005). The presence of other meaning potentials, in effect, dislocates a subject's identities, which opens a space for contingency and choice (Holmer-Nadesan, 1996; Laclau, 1990). Following Laclau (1990), *dislocation* is possible when more than one Discourse pose alternative meanings around similar sets of objects or privileged signs.[7] As subjects experience something lacking in a Discourse to which they have been linked ("This is not me," "I don't see myself in that way," and so forth), they have room to resist within a competitively structured discursive field ("I see myself in *these* terms, not those."). Thus, the conditions that create an undecidable structure of Discourses within a discursive field also create and define *agency* as a space of action (Holmer-Nadesan, 1996; Laclau, 1990).[8] Although some scholars interpret Foucault and the work he inspires as weak on the subject of agency,[9] many agree with Gabriel (1999) that

> It is time to allow agency back into (D)iscourses of power at the workplace, not as a coherent transcendental subject, but as a struggling, interacting, feeling, thinking and suffering subject, one capable of obeying and disobeying, controlling and being controlled, losing control and escaping control, defining and redefining control for itself and others. (p. 199)[10]

The choices we embrace and those we abandon materialize in our self-interpretations, which discursively take shape in "seemingly endless personal narratives," what Holstein and Gubrium (2000) call *narrating the self* (p. 80). Similarly, Giddens (1991) and Alvesson and Willmott (2002) speak of a *self-identity,* which is a reflexively organized narrative drawn from an individual's involvement with competing Discourses and life experiences. Holstein and Gubrium's reference to "seemingly endless" self-narration targets one of Giddens's (1991) key points: Our ability to reflexively interpret and narrate our life's history by positioning ourselves within various Discourses brings continuity to our self-identity across time and space. Such continuity in self-interpretation does not presume an experiential center. It is instead subjectivity-in-the-making, or working subjectivity, in which the experience of the self as both an agential 'subject' and an 'object' of our self-consciousness produces self-identities that, ethnomethodologists would say, are practical everyday accomplishments as they become both medium and outcome of how we think, feel, and value (Alvesson & Willmott, 2002; Collinson, 2003; Hassard, Holliday, & Willmott, 2000).

But what does the notion of a narratively conceived, working subjectivity really mean for the study of leadership? To understand this fully, consider first how locating the self in multiple Discourses might be misunderstood in the case of leadership. Authentic leadership will again serve as a useful example.

MULTIPLE DISCOURSES AND LEADERSHIP

The June 2005 issue of *Leadership Quarterly* was devoted entirely to authentic leadership, deemed the root concept of all positive forms of leadership (Avolio & Gardner, 2005; Ilies et al., 2005; Shamir & Eilam, 2005). As mentioned earlier, a leader is authentic when truly able to 'know thyself' and act accordingly. When leaders' actions are less than transparent because they are acting only to please others or with hidden motives like ambition, avarice, or disdain, they are faking their leadership and hiding their true self. Such a view seems deeply ensconced in the conventional wisdom of writers and observers of American politics. Consider an editorial by the syndicated writer, Kathleen Parker (2005), on U.S. Senator and former First Lady Hillary Clinton that captures what authentic leadership researchers like Avolio and Gardner are trying to say:

> What's more concerning about the ever-evolving Hillary Clinton is that no one knows who she is. She's whoever you need her to be.
>
> Writing for the June 6 issue of *The Nation* magazine, Greg Sargent described Hillary during two speaking engagements in a single day. One was before an audience of Democratic activists, for whom she delivered a red-meat GOP-bashing speech. The other was to some 300 farmers, for whom she was jest a kuntry gal makin' fun of them city folks. They ate it up—both crowds—but which group saw the real Hillary?
>
> Neither and both. Obviously, some of this is just politics and common sense. You check the temperature of a room before entering and adjust your shtick accordingly. But with Hillary, there's something more, a something-else that puts people on edge, something they distrust without knowing its name. It is, I think, rage.
>
> It's a rage that comes from having to tamp herself down and play nursemaid all these years while Baby Bill swaddled himself in the raiment of public adoration.
>
> The real Hillary Clinton is one ticked-off mother, in other words, and she wants to be the most powerful person in the world. (p. B15)

Whether or not one agrees with Parker's sentiments, she is not alone in asking American political leaders to stand up and reveal their 'true' selves. On the surface, this example suggests that Senator Clinton is quite adept at deploying multiple Discourses to win over audiences filled with future voters, what Sparrowe (2005) might call "garden-variety flip-flopping" (p. 422). However, look closer and we see that Senator Clinton was and continues to be a political leader caught in a nexus of multiple and competing Discourses regardless of any authenticity issues. Any U.S. female politician, much less a former-first-lady-turned-senator, would be caught inter alia in the Discourses of a patriarchal society in which women are expected to know 'their place'; the professional and bureaucratic Discourses of the American presidency, government, law, and politics; the task-based Discourses of that which she helps to legislate (health care, tax reform, military spending, and so on); the interest-based Discourses of her many constituents—and, as discussed below, psychological Discourses that dichotomize the self as 'true and real' or 'fake and inauthentic.' The unfortunate inference that may come from observing chameleonic leaders is that they are unique in attending to multiple Discourses. Yet, as microcosms of society, organizations themselves are multi-discursive, "not only because of the complexity of task requirements, the multitude of centres of power and social identities, but also because increasingly complex dynamic operations—as in social life itself—demand adaptability and employee adoption of a variety of subject positions"

(Alvesson & Willmott, 2002, p. 637). Before addressing the idea of subject positioning in greater detail, consider first how authenticity assumes a discursive form.

MULTIPLE DISCOURSES AND AUTHENTIC LEADERSHIP

'Authenticity' is keenly tied to the business of self-construction. As Holstein and Gubrium (2000) assert, it has become a cottage industry in contemporary society with many players other than psychologists:

> Selves are now paraded and bandied about in diverse institutional sites, from pastoral counseling, self-help groups, and mental commitment hearings, to romance novels, television talk shows, and advice books. Much like Bentham's Panopticon, we have taken on board—within ourselves—the language games and associated subjectivities of Foucauldian 'guardians' of all kinds, inciting ourselves to display and communicate the selves expected of us and that we assume others, in turn, share with us. (p. 80)

One such Foucauldian guardian came to light in Chapter 4's discussion of the alpha male. To the degree the alpha subjects himself to executive coaching Discourses, he eventually becomes his own guardian as he learns to self-police and discipline his 'alpha-ness' for the (imagined) panoptic gaze of those with whom he works. As Deetz (1995) observes, modern corporate management (and its network of providers like consultants, business writers, academics, and so on) understands the need to manage the 'insides' of employees all too well, not just in terms of modern forms of control based in culture, norms, or ideology, but in the name of participation, empowerment, diversity, and other beneficent themes to which we could add executive coaching, authentic leadership, and others. In Chapter 4, Miller and Rose (1990) also reminded us of the subtle use of power with these various approaches for the enterprising subject where "'free' individuals and 'private' spaces can be 'ruled' without breaching their formal autonomy" (p. 18). The recent increase in their number has led many critical scholars to focus on identity regulation as a powerful form of organizational control, especially for new economy workers who are pushed to be more creative, adaptable, and flexible (Collinson, 2003; Deetz, 1995; S. J. Tracy & Tretheway, 2005)

New economy themes often forecast a growing list of conflicting professional and personal selves for organizational members,[11] but identities are rarely thought of by either leadership psychologists or practitioners in the fragmented, discursively-constituted terms of a working subjectivity (Collinson, 2006). S. J. Tracy and Tretheway (2005) argue that organizational members turn instead toward a more modernist and simplistic rendering of identity as either real or fake, much as we see with Kathleen Parker's editorializing of the 'real' Hillary Clinton.

Yet, Tracy and Tretheway (2005) assert that the real-self↔fake-self dichotomy is actually a set of powerful Discourses rooted in psychology, managerialism, and entrepreneurialism that, like all Discourses, produces its own truth effects.[12] In particular, it will normalize aspects of the self and pathologize others. How so in the case of authentic leadership? As mentioned earlier, authentic leadership draws heavily from *positive psychology* (Erickson, 1995; Kernis, 2003). Seligman and Csikzentmihalyi (2000) discuss how it differs from traditional psychology:

> Psychology has, since World War II, become a science largely about healing. It concentrates on repairing damage within a disease model of human functioning. This almost exclusive attention to pathology neglects the fulfilled individual and the thriving community. The aim of positive psychology is to begin to catalyze a change in the focus of psychology from preoccupation only with repairing the worst things in life to also building positive qualities . . . well-being, contentment, satisfaction (in the past); hope and optimism (for the future); and flow and happiness (in the present). (p. 5)

Because the keys to building life's positive qualities are thought to rest with authenticity, some leadership psychologists are applying positive psychology Discourses to leadership in works with the not unexpected titles of *Unlocking the Mask* (Avolio et al., 2004), *Can You See the Real Me?* (Gardner et al., 2005), and *Authentic Leadership and Eudaemonic Well-Being* (Ilies et al., 2005). However, in an attempt to create a body of power/knowledge that sees and normalizes leadership in positive terms, positive psychology Discourses legitimate portraying leader authenticity as the ego ideal. One's authentic self is equated with virtuosity, as the leader is encouraged to engage in self-regulating processes to assure that he or she meets high personal standards of conduct (Gardner et al., 2005). One's negative traits are thus deemed inauthentic or derivative, in some way, of other positive features (as when a scathing critic putatively masks a deep concern for eliciting others' best work). Such a view represents a clear break from psychology's traditional pathology Discourses of disease in which authenticity is implicitly equated with the display of negative traits. That is, when a person's bad mood overtakes them, the 'real' or 'true' person is thought to emerge, and the individual's positive traits must be inauthentic or derivative in some way.

Positive psychology Discourses suggest that in the presence of bad behavior or negative traits such as low self-esteem or weak emotional intelligence, leaders simply lack awareness of themselves (Gardner et al., 2005; Ilies et al., 2005). By contrast, the authentic (virtuous) leader possesses higher levels of self-awareness, implying that the core that lies beneath surface appearances must always be positive; it just awaits discovery. Yet, just which traits and behaviors are 'genuine' and which are 'inauthentic' depends upon the Discourse one chooses.

For example, a *Fortune* magazine article on "America's Toughest Bosses" profiled Linda Wachner, CEO of the corporate apparel maker Warnaco from

1986–2001, as one of seven toughest bosses in the United States at the time (Dumaine, 1993). She was described in the article by colleagues as "Smart, impatient . . . rewards employees but demands absolute fealty . . . a screamer who's not above swearing like a trooper" (p. 41). One time she reportedly lashed out at a meeting of executives from the women's clothing group. Angered by their performance, she declared, "You're eunuchs. How can your wives stand you? You've got nothing between your legs" (p. 41). At another meeting she suggested to a new executive that he start firing people for no other reason except to underscore how serious he would be about performance issues. When asked about these and other incidents for the *Fortune* article, Ms. Wachner replied,

> I've yelled at people, and I'm not ashamed of it. We have to run this company efficiently and without a bunch of babies who say, "Mommy yelled at me today." It's impossible to run a leveraged operation like camp. If you don't like it, leave. It's not prison. (p. 41)

Positive psychology Discourses would paint leaders like Linda Wachner as simply unaware of her true self. By contrast, pathology Discourses would suggest that Wachner may be lacking many things, but personal insight does not seem to be among them. The 'real' Linda Wachner surfaces in her display of negative traits.

Again, the key point here is that each Discourse produces its own truth effects by portraying certain traits and behaviors as authentic and others as inauthentic.[13] Indeed, a joint consideration of both Discourses calls to mind Grint's (2000) observation that leadership has more to do with invention than analysis. Wachner's authenticity is not out there in the world just waiting to be discovered through proper scientific methods and analysis. It is an attribution, one that may be contested by virtue of the space opened up by competing authenticity Discourses. Wachner herself can certainly claim authenticity, but only in the context of a particular Discourse, or language game as Wittgenstein would say. This does not mean that the door opens to 'anything goes' authenticity claims because a working subjectivity is practically grounded; that is, the subject is always locally accountable.[14] For this reason, we are dealing in 'authenticities' that are by necessity situated and plural (Holstein & Gubrium, 2000).

However, the case of Linda Wachner is instructive not just for self-identity issues in authentic leadership, but also because the multiple Discourses at play here are gendered.

GENDER AND IDENTITY WORK

With Linda Wachner's use of words and phrases like "eunuchs," "nothing between your legs," and "mommy," our discussion of authentic leadership also becomes steeped in gendered Discourses. While Foucault focused heavily on madness, illness, death, crime, and sexuality to interrogate the relationship between power/knowledge and subjectivity, gender is playing such a role in the organizational sciences today. This in no way suggests that gender alone is (or should be) of interest to organizational scholars because every identity is still partial (at a minimum, identity is also raced and classed). Rather, gender has emerged as a deeply rooted organizing principle, playing a particularly strong role in matters of control, resistance, and organizational identity. For example, Ashcraft and Mumby (2004) begin their book with the following four claims about gender in organizations:

> First, gender is constitutive of organizing; it is an omnipresent, defining feature of collective human activity, regardless of whether such activity appears to be about gender. Second, the gendering of organization involves a struggle over meaning, identity, and difference; this ongoing, discursive struggle occurs amid, and acts upon, gendered institutional structures. Third, such struggle (re)produces social realities that privilege certain interests. It follows that gender is inextricably linked with power; it is medium and out-come of the vested interests of organizational life. This implies, finally, that the struggle for gendered meaning is a deeply material matter, for it produces not only preferred truths, selves, and courses of action but also tangible systems of 'advantage and disadvantage, exploitation and coercion.' (p. xv)

Our discussion of the 'real' Linda Wachner and the previous chapter's discussion of coaching the alpha male exemplify these principles. Recall that in Chapter 4, Ludeman and Erlandson (2004) wrote that alpha males represent some 70% of all senior executives. Although alpha females rival the power of alpha males in the animal world, executive coaching Discourses argue against the notion of alpha females in business because they are not 'alpha' enough. Gender becomes an omnipresent feature of coaching Discourses with this dividing practice and rationales like the one Ludeman and Erlandson (2004) proffer: (1) women leaders place too much emphasis on harmonious relation-ships, collaboration, and diplomacy, although they may be as data-driven and opinionated as alpha males; (2) women leaders may be comfortable in control, but rarely do they seek to dominate or enjoy conflict and intimidation in the ways that alpha males do; (3) they are more inclined toward the 'velvet ham-mer' where they transform orders into polite suggestions; and (4) alpha males' compulsive desire to control creates special coaching challenges lest they be emasculated and turned into "unrecognizable powder puffs" with unsuitable feminine qualities (p. 60).

Women leaders like the Linda Wachners of the world need not be excluded from masculinity Discourses of rational control and instrumentalism (Collinson & Hearn, 1996a; Kerfoot & Knights, 1996), but by preempting alpha females, Ludeman and Erlandson (2004) succeed in making masculinity exclu-sive to men and exhaustive of what it means to be a senior leader. Executive coaching Discourses thus have the power to normalize by defining all female leaders, alphas or otherwise, as deviants. Should we challenge such a view in light of Linda Wachner's reported comments to her male colleagues, "You're eunuchs. How can your wives stand you? You've got nothing between your legs" (Dumaine, 1993, p. 41), and about her male colleagues, "I've yelled at people, and I'm not ashamed of it. We have to run this company efficiently and without a bunch of babies who say, 'Mommy yelled at me today'" (p. 41)?

Wachner makes an excellent case against the exclusion of females from the alpha category as she rather adeptly neuters her male colleagues in the first quote and in the second renders them powerless children as they seek adjudication from a 'mommy' positioned as the sole authority figure. Wachner too saw the organizational world in gendered terms. She opened up a space of resistance to patriarchy through a strategy of *emasculating matriarchy* that questions and negates others' masculinity—an adept deployment of a masculinity Discourse if there ever was one.

The poststructuralist literature on the gendering of organizations is replete with examples of struggles over meaning, identity, and difference (Ashcraft & Mumby, 2004).[15] That such struggles over meaning also reproduce social realities that privilege the powerful is evidenced by Eagly's (2005) discussion of the special problems that female leaders have with authenticity: "Finding . . . authenticity by knowing and being oneself is a luxury enjoyed by people from groups that have traditionally inhabited high-level leadership roles—in most contexts, white men from relatively privileged backgrounds" (p. 471). Eagly recommends that female leaders aim for a *relational authenticity*. She urges them to tone down the extremes of their femininity or their masculinity (to avoid labels like 'battle axe,' 'dragon lady,' 'bitch,' and so on) so as not to make the males around them uncomfortable and stymie identification processes. Two points are noteworthy in this regard.

First, Eagly's arguments are further testimony to the gendered nature of leadership Discourses. Recall Ashcraft and Mumby's (2004) assertion that gender is a defining feature of organizing, *regardless of whether such activity appears to be about gender*. Even though the issue of *Leadership Quarterly* devoted to authenticity is largely devoid of discussions of gender (in contrast to the explicitness of it in executive coaching), Eagly (2005) makes a strong case for its gendered nature in the privileging of white males and the advice to women only to calibrate their self-presentations. Thus, in addressing who the 'real' Linda Wachner is, there is an unavoidable intersection of gender and authenticity Discourses.

Second, Eagly's (2005) arguments suggest that female leaders ignore gendered Discourses at their peril. Linda Wachner's successful rise to the top notwithstanding, the material consequences of lower salaries, less challenging assignments, fewer promotions, and so on are real for many women leaders who have chosen similar paths. Yet, when power/knowledge conceptions of authenticity ground it in masculine Discourses, there is more than a little irony in concepts like relational authenticity. In short, is there no authenticity for women leaders unless it conforms to male expectations?

However, the constructed nature of gender, identity, and organizing is not just a women's issue. We must similarly speak of the variable constructions of men, managers, and masculinities (Collinson & Hearn, 1996b). For example, alpha males can be diversely constructed within masculine Discourses of rational control and instrumentalism. Yet, it is not the category of 'alpha male' per se that is important here. As Seidler (1989) suggests, it is the way that a "category normalises a distorted life experience" (p. 8).[16] For example, such distortions surface in *narcissistic alpha males,* who achieve their control through overpowering 'It's all about me' narratives, floor dominance, poor listening habits, and abrupt departures when the conversation at hand is no longer alpha-centered. Other alpha males are *good ol' boys* whose networking, counsel, and inclusiveness (in decision making) privileges other males while marginalizing women through exclusion, competitiveness, or back-channel politicking. Still other alpha males are *passive-aggressive* in that their need for control does not appear overt. Yet, their instrumentalism with respect to managing social relationships becomes all too apparent in how they suppress and regulate their emotions, keep their own counsel in information sharing, and lack inclusiveness in decision making.

In these and other possible enactments of masculinity Discourses, it is important to remember that identities are multilayered, fluid, and contingent (Collinson, 2006; Kerfoot & Knights, 1996). Especially for the *recovering alpha,* the self has acquired "the status of a project to be worked upon, policed for weaknesses, fought against, pushed and honed to meet the refinements of the ideal—this in spite of the often very real sensation of fear, weakness, or failure" (Kerfoot & Knights, 1996, p. 92). Kerfoot and Knights were not writing about executive coaching, but they may as well have been. At the start of the coaching process, the alpha male's subjectivity is likely to be *radically external* in the way it produces a disagreeing but willing subject (Fleming & Spicer, 2003). Yet, it remains a working subjectivity because, as time goes on, that which is radically external one moment may give way to full-blown dissent, a more disciplined subjectivity, or feigned progress and expert choreography the very next (Collinson, 2006). In dialectically managing the tension between control and resistance the subject is always, recalling Gabriel (1999), "a struggling, interacting, feeling, thinking and suffering subject, one capable of obeying and disobeying, controlling and being controlled, losing control and escaping control, defining and redefining control for itself and others" (p. 199).

The examples in this chapter are further testimony to the gendered turn in the poststructuralist literature on control, resistance, and organizational identity (Ashcraft & Mumby, 2004; Mumby, 2005). It is not just that leadership Discourses are either explicitly (executive coaching) or implicitly (authentic leadership) gendered, but also that male and female leaders often locate their identities in resistance to some type of management effort to control and surveil. Linda Wachner virtually emasculated her male colleagues so as to level, if not gain advantage on, a patriarchal playing field at Warnaco. Consider also the radically external subjectivity of the recovering alpha male who at any turn may deny his recovering status and return to familiar ground. Each in his or her own way uses discursive strategies to produce "resistant spaces" and "recalcitrant identities" within larger masculine, patriarchal, managerialist, coaching, or feminine Discourses (Gabriel, 1999).

Even as resistance becomes a kind of gendered identity work, working subjectivities are "not a straightforward reading of feminine resistance against patriarchal power" (Mumby, 2005, p. 17) nor, for that matter, are they simply masculine resistance against the more feminine Discourses of participation and inclusiveness that executive coaching promotes. To appreciate just how working subjectivities are complex, shifting, often contradictory, and insecure (Collinson, 2006; Kerfoot & Knights, 1996; Knights & McCabe, 2000), one must be willing to see leaders and leadership in terms of both dissent and resistance (Zoller & Fairhurst, 2006). While workers' resistance to management is neither uncommon nor unexpected even in an age of cultural control through ideology (Jermier, Knights, & Lord, 1994), leaders' resistance may be both. Perhaps it is because too many leadership theories within the mainstream literature just assume that leaders, especially senior ones, all 'drink the Kool-Aid,' and thus are of the same mind.[17]

Yet, as Fleming and Spicer (2003) argue, resistance occurs at all levels in the organization, and it is "not the sole prerogative of labour" (p. 433). Even if highly visible senior leaders are unlikely to assume the mantle of bomb-throwing dissidents, they are quite capable of everyday forms of resistance like developing hidden transcripts that weave tales of revenge, subtle tyranny, or hero-worship into gossip—trial *in absentia* (Morrill, Zald, & Hayagreeva, 2003; Tucker, 1993), indirect resistance through passive aggression or feigned ignorance (Prasad & Prasad, 2000), sabotage through circumvention by withholding information or keeping key people out of decision making (Morrill et al., 2003), disorganized coaction in which female managers both comply with and subvert the masculine order simultaneously (Martin & Meyerson, 1999), ambivalence that indirectly supports resistance to change (Larson & Tompkins, 2005), or cynicism that produces the disagreeing but willing managers (Fleming, 2005; Fleming & Spicer, 2003), to name a few. All such "subtle subversions" or "ambiguous accommodations" (Prasad & Prasad, 2000) may be dismissively relegated to playing politics. However, as Mumby (2005) argues, these complex, contradictory, situated attempts to affect oppositional meanings and identities are wrought by subjects who find themselves at the intersection of multiple Discourses and are willing to creatively, even artfully, engage them. This takes us directly to the notion of interpretative repertoires and subject positioning.

Interpretative Repertoires and Subject Positioning

Thus far, we have adopted Holstein and Gubrium's (2000) notion of a working subjectivity, in which the business of self-construction is grounded in discursive practices that locate subjects (leadership actors) in a nexus of Discourses as they experience the world. However, in order to understand what a working subjectivity really means for the study of leadership, we have to understand what phrases like "locating subjects in Discourse" and "at the intersection (nexus) of multiple Discourses" mean in practical terms. These phrasings remain fairly abstract until we can begin to see Discourse as an *interpretative repertoire* and 'locating' as *subject positioning* through (little 'd') discourse. For example, while discursive psychologists like Potter, Wetherell, Gill, and Edwards (1990) appreciate Foucault's view of Discourse as a powerful cultural force lying beyond social interaction while still shaping it, they are critical that it has become

> something akin to the geology of plate tectonics—great plates on the earth's crust circulate and clash together; some plates grind violently together; others slip quietly over [the] top of one another; volcanoes burst through while massive forces work unseen below. The limitation of this approach is that the (D)iscourses in this view become formed as coherent and carefully systematized . . . wholes which take on the status of causal agents for analytic purposes. (p. 209)

Potter and company prefer to look at Discourses from the bottom up, that is, how they are invoked at the level of conversation or text. They reason that if Discourses are resources for communicating actors, then we should be able to infer their presence from actors' linguistic choices. Discourses, in effect, become abstractions from practices in context (Potter et al., 1990). For this reason, the authors prefer the term *interpretative repertoire,* which they liken to moves within a dancer's repertoire, substituting instead terms, tropes, metaphors, themes, commonplaces, habitual forms of argument, and so on (Potter & Wetherell, 1987; Potter et al., 1990; Wetherell, 1998) (for a brief overview of discursive psychology, see Appendix A4). All such 'moves' are actors' methods or tools for sensemaking in context. As Wetherell (1998) notes, "they are the common sense which organizes accountability and serves as a back-cloth for the realization of locally managed positions in actual interaction" (pp. 400–401).

In Foucauldian terms, interpretative repertoires thus represent the conditions of possibility afforded by various Discourses, while their deployment in social interaction enables subjects to position themselves. *Subject positioning* thus refers to the specific linguistic terms used to characterize a subject within a Discourse (as in neo-charisma Discourses, which distinguish 'leaders' from 'managers') and the ways that individuals come to understand and cast themselves either in those terms ("I am a leader, not a manager.") or in opposition to those terms ("What a useless distinction. We are a team here.") in their personal narratives constituting little 'd' discourse. A working subjectivity thus amounts to subjects' continuous in situ positioning of themselves amid the possibilities or constraints afforded by their repertoires. Such a view captures the interplay between 'discourse' and 'Discourse,' which in this case is the complementary analytics of ethnomethodology (and usually conversation analysis) and the poststructuralist work of Foucault and others. In slightly different ways, both discursive psychologists Potter and Wetherell and postmodern self theorists Holstein and Gubrium argue the merits of this approach.

While ethnomethodological and poststructuralist views both shed light on the ways in which language practices work to structure reality, Holstein and Gubrium (2000) adopt an analytic stance that preserves the integrity of both theoretical traditions.[18] Unlike discursive psychology, they argue strongly against any sort of merger of discourse and Discourse into one theoretical or analytic frame because each brings different questions to the table. For example, ethnomethodology-informed conversation analyses would address '*how is leadership brought off?*' questions because the focus is on how leadership actors jointly use the tools of language and interaction to make sense of their worlds. By contrast, poststructuralist approaches address '*what kind of leadership are we talking about?*' because the focus is on powerful cultural and historical forces that form present-day systems of thought defining, in this case, leadership.

To properly understand the interplay between discourse and Discourse, Holstein and Gubrium (2000) recommend *analytic bracketing.* This is a takeoff on the notion of *ethnomethodological indifference,* which is the temporary suspension of belief in, or indifference toward, the real in order to highlight the means by which members construct what they *believe* to be real. Because *how* questions are fundamentally different from *what* questions, analysts must bracket or suspend one while studying the other: "analytic bracketing alternately orients to the activities of producing everyday realities (the *hows*), then to those realities as substantive resources that members use in these activities (the *whats*)" (Holstein & Gubrium, 2000, p. 97).

For example, recall the membership categorization example in Excerpt 3.4 from Chapter 3, in which two female leaders disagreed over whether to confront a male higher-up with an 'old style' management philosophy as it related to a Total Quality Management (TQM) issue. The women heard through a confidential source that this male leader was displeased because their plant was not sending a team to attend a TQM training session that he was promoting. Pat, the female leader in the following excerpt, wanted to send a team to the session or confront the male leader directly to explain their decision, thereby breaking the confidence of their source. When Jane, the more junior manager, showed herself to be against both courses of action, Pat strategically categorized the male higher-up as 'old style.' Along with the word 'traditional,' she projected five next actions for him to form the 'old style' category that, in turn, constituted the complaint and warrant for her proposed responses to the problem. Recall also from Chapter 3 that Pat's projections along with her reference to "very much the old style of it" (line 15) also suggested a *type categorization*, where the description of the traditional manager is really an ascription to a type, in this case 'old style.'

3.3 'Old Style' Management

1	Pat:	I guess I know ((higher up's name)), (1.3) and I know a little how he
2		he operates (2.2) and=
3	Jane:	=okay tell me about that.
4	Pat:	I just think [he's
5	Jane:	[How does he operate? What do you know?
6		(1.5)
7	Pat:	He is just uhm to me a good ol' boyish (1.8) kind of. Uhm (.8)
8		you know, he sat behind me at June meetings and was
9		very much in the old style of the division manager.
10		And (1.8) not like Skip at all ((Indistinguishable)) participative
11	Jane:	((Indistinguishable))
12	Pat:	No
13	Jane:	((Heh-huh-huh))
14	Pat:	Uhm (1.6) not like- he's not like Skip where he can work
15		through, I mean, he's very much in the old style of
16		it. (1.2) traditional.(1.0) So (2.0) you know he'll play the-
17		he'll play the game. He'll play the politics. He'll put the
18		pressure on. He'll put the fear in. He'll- he'll make
19		the comments and he's very much with the *comments*
20		and the jabs and things, and that will forever
21		be out in the system. And *we don't need that.* So
22		we have to either (1.2) have to go and solve it, or we need to
23		send someone to UT (for the training session).

Jayyusi's (1984) point that categorization work is not just descriptive but ascriptive to a 'type' foregrounds the interplay between 'discourse' and 'Discourse.' To paraphrase Wetherell (1998), we could ask, why this category here?[19] Why this typecasting here? To be sure, the ethnomethodology-informed conversation analyst has a ready answer: The more subordinate manager asks the leader to account for her claim, ("=okay tell me about that. . . . How does he operate? What do you know?" (lines 3, 5). Yet, the answer to the 'why this category here?' question restricts itself to what members specifically orient to within the interaction—how this leader skillfully elaborates and reconfigures this 'old style' category for the purposes of her argument. Without question, this is a key 'discourse' concern. However, analysts like Wetherell (1998) and Holstein and Gubrium (2000) do not dispute the validity of the conversation analysts' orientation to members' everyday methods, only the exclusivity of it.[20]

They suggest an answer to the 'why here?' question through a focus on Discourse (or interpretative repertoire) because there is something culturally familiar about the category-constitutive features of 'old style'—a nonparticipative (in decision making)[21] male manager, who within his ranks will play politics, apply pressure, and use fear with pointed comments and jabs. The déjà vu of the words 'old style' and 'traditional' (line 16) evokes two interwoven forms of organizational power deployed throughout United States and Western management history: management as hierarchically authority-based and masculine (Collinson & Hearn, 1996a) or patriarchal (Holmer-Nadesan, 1996). Shapiro (1992) would term the logic of an 'old style' categorization an *institutionalized form of intelligibility*, à la Foucault, because intelligible ways of thinking and talking are always culturally situated. They subsume a complex history of struggle in which certain ways of establishing context and preferences for context-meaning relations overcame others and sedimented over time. Such is the case with U.S. management as traditionally masculine and hierarchical, brought into relief by the 1970s influx of women into management (Kanter, 1977). The category 'old style' is testimony to the power struggles and alternative ways of thinking around gendered forms of management that have since ensued in Western management cultures.

This sense of cultural familiarity or institutionalized intelligibility signals a Foucauldian stance on Discourse and raises a number of *what* questions indicative of an interpretative repertoire in play. For example, *what* are the available configurations of this category? We could imagine alternative nouns and adjectives like autocrat, controlling, and tyrannical, or specific nicknames and pejoratives denoting authoritarianism such as 'Attila the Hun' or 'Hitler' for men and 'dragon lady,' 'bitch,' or 'queen bee' for women. *What* are the varied institutionalizations by industry or occupation? We could envision the god complex usually accorded to physicians, but rarely to managers. *What* are some practical or failed applications of 'old style' for specific situations, for example, a downsizing? Former General Electric Chairman Jack Welch was nicknamed 'Neutron Jack' for his ability to rid GE of people and jobs while leaving buildings intact (Byrne, 1998). Finally, *what* language games are made possible?

There are two interesting answers to this last question, the first of which concerns the management style of the leader, Pat, who invokes the 'old style' category and, by implication, a self-identity quite different from this category. In the above excerpt and continued 30-minute dialogue (not shown), Pat consistently persuades her more junior manager as to the merits of confronting this male higher-up directly (Wilhelm & Fairhurst, 1997). In Wittgenstein's terms, she plays an 'influence game' here, never an 'authority game,' because to mandate a course of action is to model the very masculine 'old style' management that she argues against. It is quite easy to imagine that if asked to describe her management style, a characterization antithetical to 'old style' would be included in her repertoire of structured narrations about herself (Holstein & Gubrium, 2000). Thus, we see how identity comes to be defined both by the way individuals act and what they say about themselves.

Interestingly, as Pat persuades, she adopts a second language game associated with the word 'fear' (line 18: "He'll put the fear in"). Because of the change taking place in their organization at the time, both leaders were well versed in Deming's (1982) TQM philosophy and his ubiquitous slogan, "Drive out fear."[22] Deming's TQM is an example of an organizational change initiative that supplies its own fairly elaborate *discursive template*, which Tsoukas and Chia (2002) define as "a set of new interpretive codes—which enables a novel way of talking and acting" (p. 579). In effect, new ways of talking initiate new ways to do the work. New work practices, in turn, elaborate the linguistic practices surrounding how the work might be done (Barrett, Thomas, & Hocevar, 1995). Most organizational change agents try to get members to embrace the discursive 'template du jour' so that it becomes a part of members' interpretative repertoires and thus the means by which they contingently organize, articulate, and act upon experience. As such, these templates usually contain *ultimate terms* like positively-charged *god terms* and negatively-charged *devil terms* that are emblematic of key values and arguments associated with the change at hand (Burke, 1962).[23] In this case, Deming's TQM god terms are 'customer' and 'quality,' and a key devil term is 'fear' (Fairhurst & Sarr, 1996).

Thus, Pat in Excerpt 3.4 would appear to be invoking both patriarchal and TQM Discourses in a mutually reinforcing fashion. These Discourses 'intersect' to produce a more diversified repertoire for her. While more diversified repertoires suggest better planning options and more target-adapted persuasive appeals (O'Keefe, Lambert, & Lambert, 1993; Wilson, 2002), leadership actors often can produce both faithful and ironic appropriations of a new discursive template. Indeed, there is something ironic about Pat's argumentative stance in this example because one of her proposed solutions to making things right with the male higher-up is not sending a team to the TQM training session and explaining this position to him. In the broader scheme of things, driving out fear (the spirit of her argument for approaching this male higher-up) could lead to driving out TQM, at least for the moment (DeSanctis & Poole, 1994).[24]

Barrett et al.'s (1995) observation that organizational change is not some outside force propelling the insides of an organization to change is most relevant here. In their investigation of the implementation of TQM within the U.S. Navy, the appropriation of a discursive template into a person's repertoire involves "a general project whose implementation involves the continual discovery of its own content, a discovery that accomplishes its own alteration" (p. 367). In other words, leadership actors always appropriate these templates into their repertoires more or less actively, critically, artfully (Alvesson & Willmott, 2002), and to this we might add somewhat promiscuously, as in the midst of argument over their interests they may care little as to whether the imported terms serve the immediate causes of the organization or not. When this occurs, leadership actors embody the very antithesis of a passive receptor or carrier of a Discourse (Holstein & Gubrium, 2000). Hence, we see that in discursive leadership, actors are considered to be both managers of meaning and its passive receptors.

A Backward Glance—Final Thoughts

The key aspects of this chapter on self-identities and interpretative repertoires include the following:

- Theories in leadership psychology tend to rest on a Western, humanist conception of the self as more or less an integrated whole and centered in knowledge and experience.
- Those who have been influenced by Foucault challenge a humanist conception of the self in favor of a poststructuralist view, which favors a *decentered self.*
- Because subjects attain their identities by being represented discursively, *identity* is thus a contingent identification with a subject position in a competitive discursive field. As the subject experiences a lack in a Discourse to which he or she has been linked, the subject has room to resist within this competitive field.
- We develop a sense of self across time and space through our *self-identities,* which are reflexively organized narratives derived from participation in multiple Discourses and various life experiences.
- Our self-interpretations are aided considerably by the identity regulation goals of many groups in society, including management. However, the self they capture is often simplistic, dichotomized as either 'real' or 'fake.' Such dichotomizing produces real-self ↔ fake-self Discourses with their own truth effects.
  - o Such truth effects are apparent in the authentic leadership movement. Authentic leadership rooted in a positive psychology Discourse equates

authenticity with virtuosity; while a pathology psychology Discourse equates authenticity with negative traits and behavior. Either Discourse may be resisted and contested by virtue of the space opened up by the presence of the other.

- The gendering of organizations also involves struggles over meaning, identity, and difference. Struggles over meaning (re)produce social realities that privilege certain interests. Gender and power are inexorably linked as demonstrated in the notion of *relational authenticity* and the construction of *masculinity* in alpha males.

- Discursive psychologists view Discourse as an overly rigid concept. They prefer the term *interpretative repertoire* to Discourse, which they liken to moves within a dancer's repertoire, substituting instead terms, tropes, metaphors, themes, commonplaces, or habitual forms of argument.

- One of the benefits of the interpretative repertoire is that it signals the interplay between *discourse* as language in use and *Discourse* as a system of thought; it potentially answers the 'why this (linguistic) resource here?' question in social interaction.

Capturing the interplay between discourse and Discourse in a working subjectivity suggests a number of directions for future research. For example, 'interpretative repertoire' is largely an unfamiliar term in the mainstream leadership literature. However, the burgeoning organizational discourse literature routinely reports on the linguistic devices that source a repertoire, including metaphors (Barrett et al., 1995), membership categories (Jayyusi, 1984), floating signifiers (Eisenberg, 1984; Laclau & Mouffe, 1985), framing devices (Fairhurst, 1993), habitual forms of argument (Wetherell, 1998), institutionalized forms of intelligibility (Shapiro, 1992), and sets of structured narrations (Holstein & Gubrium, 2000), among others. As this literature suggests, these forms easily lend themselves to expert choreography and multiple coherences depending upon the Discourses at play and the interactional conditions at hand. This is especially true during times of organizational change and conflict when the identity work of leadership actors can provoke a comparison of cultural codes or mark the boundaries of a cultural divide (Huspek, 2000).

It is perhaps during these trying times that actors' improvisation abilities and repertoire diversity matter the most. One cannot help but cite the skilled evasiveness of U.S. President Bill Clinton during the Monica Lewinsky scandal when in a court deposition he attempted to parse the meaning of the verb 'is' (as in "it depends on what the meaning of the word 'is' is"). Reflective of lawyering Discourses and a highly developed repertoire, it was such a skilled improvisation that it smacked of a 'manipulation game.' The transparency of his attempted evasion of the truth would later draw mocking rebukes in the press and nighttime talk shows.

Consider also the 'macho/cowboy language games' of George W. Bush through which he prematurely proclaimed victory in Iraq after the early invasion by coalition forces.[25] When Bush was asked by a reporter about the rising attacks on U.S. troops in Iraq some two months later, his improvised words, "Bring them on," would later come back to haunt him. At this writing in year three of the war in Iraq, the Islamic insurgency shows few signs of letting up, while Bush concedes that he may have gone too far in his blunt language of three years earlier (Wolffe & Bailey, 2006). Bush's cowboy language games as a sitting U.S. president suggest a limited repertoire and a weak ability to respond with the tact, subtlety, and discretion required of international politics. These examples with two U.S. presidents suggest how leadership reputations can hinge on their improvisation abilities, language games, and interpretative repertoires.[26]

However, there is still much to learn about ongoing improvisation by leadership actors, especially around authentic leadership. In the earlier discussion of Linda Wachner, former CEO of Warnaco, we noted that leadership actors could claim authenticity, but only in the context of a particular Discourse or language game. We thus have to speak of plural and situated authenticities. However, we have also established in this chapter that authenticity is a contestable term depending upon the Discourse one chooses. Does authenticity lie in one's virtuosity, negative traits, or in a relational sensitivity to gender? If leaders believe they are charged with developing and integrating followers' current goals and possible selves, as Lord and Brown (2004) suggest, what 'real self–fake self' language games must leaders and members improvise and play in leadership development discussions? How does the leader's 'self' or, more accurately, 'selves' become a resource for explanations of authenticity? When subject positioning can construct identities in various and contradictory ways, even within the same conversation (Antaki, Condor, & Levine, 1996), how do a 'real self' and a 'fake self' get constructed under these conditions? Finally, what are the language games of followers who seek to resist leaders' attempts to normalize authenticity in some fashion? These are important questions for future research to address.

In this chapter, we have discussed the interplay between the interactional realm of an ethnomethodology/conversation analysis and the cultural/historical realm of Foucault and poststructuralism. In doing so, we simultaneously address the tensions between structure and agency in the joint operation of discourse and Discourse. We will continue these themes in the ensuing discussion of dialectics and narrative identities in Chapter 6.

NOTES

1. Lord and colleagues draw from self theorists Kihlstrom and Klein (1994) and Markus and Wurf (1987).

2. For authenticity writers such as Avolio and Gardner (2005), this does not diminish how the self takes shape through reflexive interactions with others, much as in Mead (1934), Goffman (1959), and Cooley (1902).

3. See Holstein and Gubrium (2000) for an extensive discussion of the humanist self as centered in knowledge and experience and a Foucauldian view that suggests it is discursively formulated.

4. Holstein and Gubrium's (2000) notion of a working subjectivity invites a comparison with Lord and Brown's (2004) working self concept (WSC). Unlike the poststructuralist self of Holstein and Gubrium, the WSC appears to have humanist underpinnings in such notions as a core and peripheral self, and of many "compartmentalized selves" requiring integration. However, like a working subjectivity, Lord and Brown also cast the WSC as a *constantly shifting* combination of core and peripheral self-schemas made salient by the context.

5. For example, see Ashcraft and Mumby (2004), Holmer-Nadeson (1996), and Holstein and Gubrium (2000). These scholars diverge from Foucault in his tendency to single out only one knowledge regime in a given historical era to focus instead on the interplay and competitive struggle of multiple Discourses.

6. Based on a poststructuralist critique of the Saussurian tradition of structural linguistics, Laclau and Mouffe (1985) argue that the attempted fixation of signs occurs within a relational net in which the subject assumes an identity or meaning because it is contrasted with what it is not. A subject's positioning within a Discourse can always be destabilized by articulations that place signs in different contrasting relations to one another. For an extended discussion and critique, see Phillips and Jørgensen (2002).

7. Laclau and Mouffe (1985) term these "nodal points."

8. When discussing the work of Laclau and Mouffe (1985) and Laclau (1990), Holmer-Nadeson (1996) often uses the phrase "space of action/articulation," given Laclau's emphasis on articulation. However, the latter term has been dropped here for the sake of brevity.

9. Newton (1998) argues that Foucault's work and the research it spawns represses the subject and minimizes agency relative to disciplinary power. However, it must be acknowledged that Reed (2000, 2001) charges him with an 'anything goes' relativism that results in the complete subjugation of the material world to the discursive and a bias toward agency. Knights and McCabe (2000) also argue that if one is to understand Foucault's view of power as relational as Foucault intended, resistance can occur anywhere in a series of power/knowledge relations, and subjects always actively participate in their own self-discipline.

10. Gabriel is not alone, as many have argued similarly (Alvesson & Kärreman, 2000; Alvesson & Willmott, 2002; Ashcraft & Mumby, 2004; Holmer-Nadesan, 1996; Knights & McCabe, 2000; Mumby, 2005; Newton, 1998; S. J. Tracy & Tretheway, 2005; Weedon, 1997).

11. See, for example, Bennis and Thomas (2002) and Hill and Stephens (2005).

12. In managerialism, the interests of the organization are privileged over the individuals in matters of money, career, and relationships (Deetz, 1992). In entrepreneurialism, the self is a project to be worked on such that the enterprising individual increases his or her development, motivation, and sense of personal achievement (du Gay & Salaman, 1996; Miller & Rose, 1990).

13. All Discourses produce their own truth effects, including this author's poststructuralist Discourse from which she views theories and paradigms as alternative ways of talking (Deetz, 1996; Rorty, 1982).

14. As Holstein and Gubrium (2000) state, "Truth and authenticity are placed squarely within and spread between language games, not in the relation between a grand narrative and the objects or matters it references" (p. 70).

15. Several other sources might be cited here (Ashcraft, 2000; Buzzanell, 2000; Clair, 1998; Collinson, 1992, 2006; Collinson & Hearn, 1996a, 1996b; Hegde, 1998; Holmer-Nadesan, 1996; Jorgenson, 2002; Knights & McCabe, 2001; Kondo, 1990; Mumby, 1996).

16. Seidler (1989) was cited in Kerfoot & Knights (1996).

17. This idiom stems from the 1978 Jonestown massacre in Guyana in which followers of Peoples Temple cult leader, Jim Jones, were urged to drink Kool-Aid containing a fatal poison that led to a mass suicide.

18. Holsten and Gubrium (2000) term ethnonomethodology-informed conversation analysis *discursive practice* and the poststructuralist emphasis as *Discourses-in-practice*. Their dual orientation is termed as *interpretive practice,* which they define as "the constellation of procedures, conditions, and resources through which reality . . . is apprehended, understood, organized, and represented in the course of everyday life" (p. 94). Such an orientation encapsulates *discursive practice* and *Discourses in practice,* but with a particular emphasis on the technology of self construction.

19. Wetherell (1998) actually asked, "why this utterance here?", in considering the contributions of conversation analysis relative to poststructuralism in talk-in-interaction.

20. See debate over this issue in Schegloff (1997, 1998) and Wetherell (1998).

21. The rest of the transcript makes clear that the words "participative" and "non-participative" refer to decision-making style.

22. The meaning behind 'Drive out fear' suggests that team members must be encouraged to voice their opinions and counter-opinions without fear of retribution, lest some aspect of quality be overlooked.

23. Fairhurst and Sarr (1996) draw from Burke's (1954, 1957, 1962) work on ultimate terms to describe the nature of the symbols that leaders employ in an engaging vision. According to Burke, *ultimate terms* are little more than extreme good (god terms) or bad forms (devil terms) of a concept or theme. When the adoption of god terms transcends disagreement among people with opposing views by identifying values or principles to which nearly all can agree, Burke termed this *transcendence.*

24. Poole and DeSanctis (1992) use "spirit" terminology to refer to the intended use of a technology and how faithful those who appropriated it were to the original intent.

25. Shortly after the invasion of Iraq by U.S. forces, Bush stood on the USS Abraham Lincoln flight deck under a banner reading, "Mission Accomplished."

26. The question of whether both Clinton's and Bush's remarks were improvisations can certainly be raised.

6

Narrative Logics

W here to begin? So much has been written on the role of narrative in leadership and organizations that there are wide avenues of choices for a single chapter. However, this chapter will focus on the relevance of narrative for leader–member exchange theory and research (Graen & Scandura, 1987; Graen & Uhl-Bien, 1995). Its strong social-psychological emphasis in the leader–member relationship, early narrative history, and a 30-year track record of mostly survey research make it an ideal subject.[1] This chapter will also continue the previous chapter's efforts to examine intersecting views of discourse and Discourse; hence, the title "Narrative Logics" addresses itself to the use of narrative in social interaction as well as the narrative resources that various Discourses make available to communicating leaders and members (for a brief overview of narrative analyses, see Appendix A7).

Leader–Member Exchange Theory

Leader–member exchange (LMX) theory is based on a simple premise: leaders discriminate in their treatment of direct reports or 'members' in forming relationships. However, in the early days of LMX research, this premise was somewhat counterintuitive when stacked against leadership-style research, which typed leaders in terms of their initiating structure (task behavior) and consideration (relationship orientation). Such typing was made famous in the Ohio State studies and led to the unwarranted, yet understandable, conclusion that 'style' meant that leaders treated everyone pretty much the same (Bass, 1981). Thus, the individual differences among members that could impact the leader–member relationship were not seriously considered, and deviations in the average member perception of the leader were treated as error variance (Katerberg & Hom, 1981). By contrast, LMX asserted that leaders exchange their positional and personal resources for a member's performance

(Graen & Scandura, 1987; Graen & Uhl-Bien, 1995). In high quality LMXs, leaders and members exchange high levels of mutual influence, trust, and support and an internalization of common goals. There is extra-contractual behavior by the member—a willingness to exceed role expectations—that is duly recognized by the leader in social capital. Oftentimes, this takes the form of decision-making influence, inside information, valued task assignments, task autonomy, and leader support and attention (Graen & Scandura, 1987). In low quality LMXs, there is formal authority, contractual behavior exchange, role-bound relations, low trust and support, and economic rewards. High versus low LMX differences also mirror a host of relational outcomes in job satisfaction, performance, communication frequency, turnover, productivity, and job problems, to name just a few (Liden, Sparrowe, & Wayne, 1997).

There have been a number of reviews of the LMX literature, many of which point to measurement problems associated with the LMX scale.[2] In particular, scholars have raised questions about the ever-evolving nature of LMX measurement and its psychometric and theoretical soundness (Dienesch & Liden, 1986; Schriesheim, Neider, Scandura, & Tepper, 1992; Vecchio & Gobdel, 1984). Suffice it to say that the vast majority of LMX researchers use surveys and 7-point scales to retrospectively query, "What is the nature of this relationship?" Interestingly, Robert Liden (personal communication, April 2004), an LMX researcher who studied with George Graen in the early years of LMX research, indicates that initial LMX scale measurement was derived from stories told by leaders and especially members[3] in which they shared what life was like in the in- or out-group (Graen, Novak, & Sommerkamp, 1982).[4] How ironic that we return to the narrative roots of LMX after letting it lie dormant for some 30 years (Fairhurst & Hamlett, 2003).

NARRATIVE POSSIBILITIES

Because LMX is a social exchange theory, it operates on an information processing model for its actors that suggests a rational calculation of resources expended to resources received (Roloff, 1981).[5] LMX scale items are designed to elicit this rough calculation. However, according to Bruner (1986, 1990), there is an *information processing mode* of rational analysis and paradigmatic thinking (akin to the LMX scale judgment), but also a *narrative mode* in which actors continuously narrate experience in order to make sense of it.[6] Influenced by Bruner (1990), Weick (1995) underscores the ways in which sequence and temporal form are the source of sense for equivocal events:

> The requirements necessary to produce a good narrative provide a plausible frame for sensemaking. Stories posit a history for an outcome. They gather the strands of experience into a plot that produces that outcome. The plot follows either the sequence beginning-middle-end or the sequence situation-transformation-situation. But the sequence is the source of sense. (p. 128)

For Weick (1995), stories can (1) aid comprehension because they integrate the known and the speculative, (2) suggest a causal order for unorganized or unrelated events, (3) enable actors to call forth the absent to talk about the present in order to construct meaning, (4) serve as mnemonics that help people to reconstruct prior complex events, (5) guide action before routines are formed or reinforce existing routines, (6) contribute to a database of experience with which to form mental models of how the world works, and (7) convey shared values and meaning (p. 129). In short, through narrative we understand the world and remember it.

As mentioned at the start, there is already a narrative presence in the organizational sciences (Boje, 1991; Boje, Alvarez, & Schooling, 2001; Czarniawska-Joerges, 1997). Unlike more traditional studies of narrative in cognitive psychology or literary narratology that focus on generalized types and categories of narrative structure (Edwards, 1997), the organizational discourse literature focuses primarily on the ways that narrative performs social actions in-the-telling. It has moved well beyond the days of stories as mere artifacts of organizational cultures (Ouchi & Wilkins, 1985; Schein, 1985) to focus instead on narrating as organizing or as a means of control. We see this in research on narrative as *storytelling performances* in naturally occurring conversation, which can signal organizational subgroup differences, decision making, or turbulence and change (Boje, 1991; O'Connor, 1997; Orr, 1990); narrative as *ideological control* that (re)produces the interests of dominant groups by reinforcing key values and reifying privileged structures (Helmer, 1993; Mumby, 1987, 1988); and *narrative modes of knowing and organizing* through the episodic ordering of speech acts that nest and build into larger structures (Cooren, 2001; Fairhurst & Cooren, 2004; J. R. Taylor & Van Every, 2000). In the leadership literature, the role of life stories in organizational learning is fast emerging (Shamir & Eilam, 2005; Sparrowe, 2005) and is an area to which we shall return.

The Narrative Basis of LMX

According to Fairhurst and Hamlett (2003), the extant LMX literature underplays the experience of LMX, particularly as the leader–member relationship is forming. This is due partly to the use of survey methods where the format (as compared to interviews) precludes the ability to qualify answers, supply crucial details, or challenge questions. For example, elsewhere I have argued that the LMX literature assumes that successful relationships progress on a path that is unidirectional and cumulative, moving toward increasing levels of closeness or fusion, relational stability, and transformation beyond self-interests (Fairhurst, 2001). The three-stage process of the leadership-making model (Graen & Uhl-Bien, 1995; Uhl-Bien & Graen, 1992) is a case in point, but the same might be said of other LMX developmental models (Bauer & Green, 1996; Liden, Wayne, & Stilwell, 1993; Sparrowe & Liden, 1997). In the leadership-making model, participants progress through an initial 'stranger' stage of role-finding, which is formal and contractual. If both want to improve the relationship, they progress on to a second, 'acquaintance' stage of role-making where there is a lot of secret testing and feeling out of one another. If test results are mutually satisfactory, a select few make it to the 'mature partnership' stage where there is an in-kind exchange of resources, as described earlier for 'high quality' exchanges. Thus, in successful relationships there is a putatively simple progression to an increasingly close, stable, and mutually satisfying relationship.

However, this contradicts work in dialectical approaches to relationship development (Altman, Vinsel, & Brown, 1981; Baxter, 1990; Baxter & Montgomery, 1996). Such work questions the assumption that relationships are stable because even healthy relationships possess tensions in the form of dialectical oppositions that create simultaneous pulls to fuse with and differentiate from another. In other words, relational bonding implies fusion and separation, closeness and distance, interdependence and autonomy. Too much of either pole creates a need to shift toward the other. Moreover, Baxter's (1988, 1990) work suggests that it is the strategic responses to contradiction in message behavior that forms the basis for understanding how relationships are forged. Thus, when interviewed, a member whose leader leaves her alone might characterize it as 'isolation' (indicating a low quality LMX), or conversely, she might say it is 'autonomy' and reframe it as a form of connection with the leader (indicating a high quality LMX) (Fairhurst, 2001).

Unfortunately, few LMX studies focus on discourse (Fairhurst, 1993b; Fairhurst & Chandler, 1989; Sias, 1996), and except for Lee and Jablin (1995), even fewer question the assumption of relational stability. According to Fairhurst and Hamlett (2003)

> It follows that if relational stability is assumed, there is scant attention to tension, contradiction, dynamism, and flux in relationships-as-they-happen that serve as prompts for sensemaking. Narrative as a mode of knowing would be obscured because of a requested ratings judgment that takes a single snapshot of the relationship as effective or ineffective, trusting or untrusting, etc., the usual scale item indicators of high or low quality LMX. Just *what* is experienced as effective or ineffective, trustworthy or not, etc. is most likely to be narratively organized, but is not a subject for inquiry. (p. 123)

Compared to survey work, in-depth interviews give leadership actors a greater chance to discursively reflect upon their LMX experiences, thus taking advantage of the ways that sensemaking and meaning get worked out *in communication*. Also in contrast to survey work, studying the actual dialogue between leaders and members can reveal the ways in which narrative is used to construct LMXs as they happen. Consequently, in explicating the narrative basis of LMX, Fairhurst and Hamlett (2003) argue for three research agendas, which are extended in this chapter. The agendas include narrative reflection and the uniqueness paradox, constructing LMX through narratives and stories, and narrative resources for LMX.

NARRATIVE REFLECTION AND
THE UNIQUENESS PARADOX IN LMX STORIES

In the same way that storytelling in a cultural analysis is seen as reflective of an organization's culture (Ouchi & Wilkins, 1985; Schein, 1985), so too could the stories told about work relationships be seen as reflective of LMX quality. Yet, it is important to realize that storytelling is not just a *sensegiving* exercise (Gioia & Chittipeddi, 1991) in which leadership actors, when queried, simply relay the meanings that they have already assigned to their LMX. It is fundamentally a *sensemaking* exercise in which actor and interviewer work out meanings for LMX in communication with another. Leadership actors discover these meanings in the work of producing them (Boden, 1994; Cronen, 1995a), which is precisely Weick's (1979) point in his discussion of retrospective sense-making. In other words, how can I know what I think (about my LMX) until I see what I say? As White (1987) argues, "narrative discourse does not simply reflect or passively register a world already made; it works up the material in perception and reflection, fashions it, and creates something new" (p. 999).

Narrative becomes a distinct mode of knowing LMX and coping with the everyday world because of our ability to remember and reconstruct the past and project into the future. As interpretive devices, narratives tell us how one's LMX works today and how it is likely to work tomorrow. Precisely because they are so connected to the experience of LMX, narratives readily display commonsense wisdom based on unspoken premises that reinforce the tacit aspects of organizational knowledge (Patriotta, 2003). Consider the following examples, which demonstrate LMX as a type of knowledge structure known through narrative.

One of my graduate students, Elizabeth Prebles (2002), surveyed and interviewed leaders and members in a medium-sized manufacturing firm in the United States for her thesis. In the mostly male sample ranging in ages from 18 to 60, participants completed the LMX-7, one of the more commonly used LMX measurement devices (Gerstner & Day, 1997). The actual scaled items served as prompts for sensemaking in ensuing interviews in order to elicit narrated experiences behind the ratings judgment.[7] In the data set, several stories were told by those members deemed to have LMXs of medium quality,[8] a particularly interesting group to study because so little is known about them relative to high and low quality LMXs. In the narratives that follow, the italics signal an interview question or response.[9]

Narrative 6.1

1   I had a situation where people weren't backing up what they said . . . said

2   verbally over a time period, and it was forgotten. And if you couldn't prove it

3   [what they said] with paperwork, what can you do there? They're higher up

4   in rank than you. When you're in situations like that, it doesn't seem to be

5   good. But in the same regard, there are situations where they do stick up for

6   you regardless of whether you can show proof or not. I've had it both ways.

Narrative 6.2

1   Well, they understand your potential, but they don't show it. See what

2   I'm saying?

3   *What indicates to you that they know your potential but don't show it?*

4   Pay. Pay. Pay. Real quick, pay. Like when I first got hired on, I just got out

5   of the service and I come in here and they said they hired you because of your

6   knowledge and your skill, but that's not true. That's not true at all. I had my

7   experience when I got in here, but it took them a while to give me my

8   Leadman. Although I was doing a Leadman job, they didn't give me my

9   'Leadman' title for a while. It was not very fair.

Narrative 6.3

1   I don't think my leader is quite, you know what I mean, up to snuff on what

2   he's trying to get me to do.

3   *So he's not familiar with the job or . . . ?*

4   Job or . . . A good example is a job. You know, when they come out there and

5   they try and tell ya, 'We need to do this, we need to do that,' yet you can tell

6   the way that they're explaining it to you, they really aren't for sure

7   themselves. Or, there might be changes they aren't aware of. We have a lot

8   of that here.

Narrative 6.4

1   Of all the supervisors I think that [my leader] is probably the most

2   knowledgeable about what we do . . . because he took the time to self teach. He

3   seems to be in touch with what the job actually entails.

4   *Is he an electrician then?*

5   Um, no.

6   *So when you say that he took the time to learn, do you mean because it wasn't*

7   *necessarily his trade?*

8   And that happens a lot in this type of industry. I mean this is industry wide.

9   A lot of times you'll have a guy that's a supervisor and he has management

10   training and no skills training for those particular jobs. It's not always the

11   case, but a lot of times. And that makes a big difference. I mean, if they don't

12   know how to do the job, how can they manage properly?

Narrative 6.5

1   His experience in the field is minimum. He has a mechanical background and

2   he's the supervisor. It's hard for Jim to answer my questions.

Narrative 6.6

1   That's just to do with his experience versus my experience. I can't turn

2   toward Jim for advice.

3   *What kind of advice?*

4   Any kind of technical advice.

In this sampling, the first two narratives suggest mixed results in the exchange of members' performances for leaders' resources. Narrative 6.1 suggests uneven support of the member, and 6.2 reveals delayed recognition of the member. Because support and recognition are neither minimal nor unconditional, they logically calibrate at a medium level of exchange from the member's vantage point.

Narratives 6.3–6.6 all seem to be telling the same story. It is one in which the members' technical expertise exceeds that of their leaders. Thus, members cannot turn to their leaders for help and advice (6.5, 6.6), or leaders may appear unsure of what they are requesting of members (6.3), all of which raises questions about their ability to manage (6.4). Thus, in this second group of stories leaders have positional power, but insufficient expert power. This situation could place a ceiling on the resources at the leaders' disposal, or alternatively, dissuade them from dispersing key resources if they are discomfited over the lack of 'value added' that is supposed to derive from hierarchical level (Jacques, 1990). Particularly skilled members may be denied key resources if 'who is leader' and 'who is led' are in danger of a reversal because a leader feels threatened.

This second group of stories also suggests the possibility of a uniqueness paradox (Martin, Feldman, Hatch, & Sitkin, 1983). First written about when describing organizational cultures, the uniqueness paradox suggests that a culture's claim to uniqueness, as expressed in its stories and rituals, is quite the opposite. Martin et al. (1983) argue that this is because key tensions over equality, security, and control underlie all complex organizations, and quite often come into conflict with the values of individuals, organizations, or society. Actors must work through these tensions, and narrative is a means by which they do this (an argument reminiscent of relational dialectics). In the working out of these tensions, individuals will offer self-enhancing attributions for organizational successes and failures, and in their sensemaking, endow the organization with a uniqueness that is conveniently embraced or disparaged.

Although Martin et al. (1983) focus on culture, they reason that the uniqueness paradox should also be seen at individual, cultural, and societal levels. Fairhurst and Hamlett (2003) argue for its relational relevance based on three arguments. First, issues over equality, security, and control impact relationships in equal measure to culture. Equality tensions emerge in differential amounts of social distance in high versus low quality LMXs (Fairhurst & Chandler, 1989). Security versus insecurity may reflect the ontological status of high versus low quality LMXs respectively, especially in an age of corporate downsizing. Finally, control versus lack of control has been a distinguishing feature of high versus low LMXs from the start (Graen & Scandura, 1987).

Second, drawing from Schank and Abelson (1977), Martin et al. (1983) argue that stories can differ yet share a set of common scripts that "specify a set of characters or roles and a causally connected sequence of events, sometimes with oppositional branches for alternative story components and events" (p. 441). Clearly, common script elements concerning the role of hierarchy inform individual work relationships as much as they inform the culture because the former is nested within the latter. Indeed, many of Martin et al.'s cultural story types reflect hierarchical themes such as, "Is the big boss human?" "Can the little person rise to the top?", "Will I get fired?", and "How will the boss react to mistakes?"

Third, it also follows that if individuals embrace or disparage their organization's uniqueness to play into self-enhancing attributions for organizational successes or failures, a similar dynamic will work for the LMX relationship. As Fairhurst and Hamlett (2003) argue, "Idiosyncrasies surrounding the effectiveness or ineffectiveness of the relationship will likely be targeted positively or negatively as individuals engage in face saving and self-enhancing attributions as they explain their behavior" (p. 126). Indeed, the somewhat less than ideal level of effectiveness of the medium quality LMXs is displayed in Narratives 6.3–6.6 as members justify their ratings judgments with self-enhancing attributions based on their superior skill set relative to that of their leaders.

Thus, even in this small amount of data, we can see how the elicitation of narratives through interviews allows LMX actors to discursively reflect upon their relational experiences. In so doing, they reclaim the ways that sense-making and meanings for the relationship get worked out in communication and through discourse.

NARRATIVES AND STORIES: CONSTRUCTING LMX

Fairhurst and Hamlett (2003) propose a second narrative research agenda for LMX, based upon the study of talk-in-interaction in which leaders and members use narratives to construct their LMX. However, this research agenda requires that we make a distinction between 'narrative' and 'story,' unlike the previous agenda in which the terms are used interchangeably. According to Ochs (1997)

> the interactional production of narrative maintains and transforms persons and relationships. How we think about ourselves and others is influenced by both the message content of jointly told narratives and the experience of working together to construct a coherent narrative. (p. 185)

Ochs is making a distinction here between "jointly told narratives" and "working together to construct a coherent narrative." Others similarly distinguish between 'stories told' and 'stories lived' (Cronen, 1995a; Pearce, 1995), and 'story' and 'narrative' (Cunliffe, Luhman, & Boje, 2004). Despite the differences in language, all point to the fact that in living life, we become narrators of the unfolding nature of our relationships. Its rules and patterns of interaction are ongoing, unfinished, and subject to changes in meaning as we and others respond to the exigencies of the situation or context (Pearce, 1995). Narratives or 'stories lived' thus reflect the unfolding nature of relationships as story lines, wherein all discourse is in some way narrative (Alvesson & Skoldberg, 2000). As such, our ongoing narrative accounts may or may not include 'stories told,' or conventional storytelling, which actors are generally ready to do for strategic reasons or any time one's behavior comes into question (Boje, 1991; Cunliffe et al., 2004; Edwards, 1997).

For example, Shamir and Eilam (2005) argue that the most legitimate and convincing means by which leaders convey their authenticity is through their life stories, especially those life events that trigger growth and development. Such a process often focuses on the leaders' defining moments or crucibles in which actors try to relay what they have learned from the difficult choices they have been forced to make (Bennis & Thomas, 2002). Life stories are commonly used for identity management, coaching, or role modeling, but it also seems reasonable to expect that LMX would be one basis for their use. Telling one's biography can be a deeply personal act of self-disclosure. Leaders and members in high quality LMXs may feel freer to share more personal stories because their trust levels are high. Moreover, leaders and members may engage in greater amounts of storytelling the higher the quality of the relationship, based on communication frequency or the opportunities that the discriminatory use of the leader's resources provide (for example, in decision-making influence; providing inside information; allocating task assignments; or offering job autonomy, support, or attention in the form of coaching or career counseling).

The key point here is that stories used in the context of the LMX relationship help to construct those relationships as high or low quality *in their telling*. For further evidence of this, consider the following excerpt from an earlier study of the discourse of LMX with women leaders in a manufacturing firm (Fairhurst, 1993).[10] Storytelling is used quite strategically by the low LMX member (Herb Conly) who happens to be male, white, older, less educated, and more tenured than his supervisor (Lori) who is female, black, young, more educated, and less tenured.

Narrative 6.7: Great Big Yellow Pill[11]

1   **Herb:**   I almost ended up on disability *twice* this weekend.

2   **Lori:**   What *happened?*

3   (2.3)

4   **Herb:**   Goin' down the stairs my leg gave out, and I went

5   flying down the stairs.

6   **Lori:**   *Oh no:::* (.) *here* at work? (1.9) [let me *see.*

7   **Herb:**   [INDISTINGUISHABLE

8   **Lori:**   Your [hurt?.

9   **Herb:**   [INDISTINGUISHABLE

10   **Lori:**   Oh oh you hurt yourself at home?

11   **Herb:**   *Yeah* (.9) Just couldn't put any weight on the leg and

12   went down the stairs,

13   **Lori:**   Oh go:::d

14   **Herb:**   Grabbed onto the wall. Cut *that.*

15   **Lori:**   *Oh god,* I see. Let me *see* let me see this hand (1.4)

16   You say you cut that one. I don't I don't see, oh on your

17   finger?

18   (.7)

19	**Herb:**	I got a couple little [cuts
20	**Lori:**	[You have one on this hand too? Okay.
21		You're gonna have to be *careful.* You're gonna hurt
22		yourself *real bad.*
23		(1.4)
24	**Herb:**	Then I almost drowned.
25	**Lori:**	You almost *drowned?* (.6) Uh, wh-what happened?
26	**Herb:**	I (.5) went swimming (1.1), stayed in the pool until I gave out (1.0).
27	**Lori:**	Till you gave *out?*
28	**Herb:**	Yeah, I was swimmin' 80-80 foot length of the pool and gave
29		out when it was 9 feet deep.
30		(3.8)
31	**Lori:**	*What happened?* (2.8) How did you save yourself? What
32		happened?
33	**Herb:**	Just kept swimmin'
34		(.8)
35	**Lori:**	I'm glad you're okay, Herb. *God* you you scare me
36		sometimes.
37	**Herb:**	I almost drowned a *lotta* times (2.2). It doesn't stop me.
38	**Lori:**	You better take care of yourself (2.1). You should do that
39		cause you scare me with some of those stories you
40		tell me, I don't know.
41	**Herb:**	I got a pill from the V.A. now I could kill myself if I
42		wanted to
43		(1.0)
44	**Lori:**	You got a pill to kill yourself?
45	**Herb:**	Yeah, if I wanted to kill myself, I got a pill to do
46		it now.
47		(1.6)
48	**Lori:**	Well, I hope you don't take the thing.
49	**Herb:**	Great big (1.8) yellow pill. No markings on it

50   (3.4)

51   **Lori:**   ((Sigh)) Mr. Conly, (1.1) I don't know about you

52   sometimes. I wonder (1.2) Anyhow (2.6) let's get back

53   to this. As far as (.7) the associates with mechanical skills

54   working the *line* (1.8) who *else* can fill in?

Herb tells stories of falling down stairs (lines 4–5), bodily injury (lines 4–5, 11–12), near drowning (lines 24–37), and potential suicide (lines 41–49). Yet, these stories are a joint performance between leader and member (Boje, 1991). Lori coproduces these stories with each expression of strong interest or concern (lines 2, 6, 8, 10, 13, 15–17, 20–22, 25, 27, and so on) until the subject of suicide emerges (line 41), at which point she takes the unusual step of switching the subject back to more work-related concerns! Displaying more concern for a cut on the hand than talk of suicide makes sense only if Herb has exceeded the bounds of credulity (Fairhurst, 1993). Consider also the greater use of pauses toward the end of the excerpt (lines 51–54), which may indicate momentary reflection by Lori on the veracity of Herb's stories.

Clearly, this older, white male member is playing power games with his younger, black female leader as they *coconstruct* an interactional pattern of deceit, distrust, and resistance to authority (Fairhurst & Hamlett, 2003). This is evidenced by Herb's increasingly implausible string of narratives both prompted and unchallenged by Lori. Unless she intervenes, this pattern is likely to repeat itself in the future, as it has in the past (lines 38–40). Thus, we see how storytelling as an assisted control move constitutes, not merely reflects, this LMX. Story upon story become part of an unfolding lived narrative (or story line) of low LMX quality.

Contrast the low quality LMX of Narrative 6.7 with the high quality LMX of Narrative 6.8 (Fairhurst, 1993). In this example, the male member's (Paul) use of narrative opens an opportunity for the female leader (Jan) to back previous commitments she made to him.

Narrative 6.8: Romantic Interlude

1   **Jan:**   Even if we're not here, there oughta be a way to

2   cover it. (.3) So if someone from the day shift who was

3   at the morning meeting could cover what happened

4   at the next meeting (.6) or for third shift, [we'd be

5   **Paul:**   [You gonna do that?

6   **Jan:**   in real good shape. (1.0) Do you want me to

7		to ask somebody? Is that what you're sayin? (1.5)
8	**Paul:**	*Yeah.*
9	Jan:	*Yeah,* I can [ask Joanie or Shelby or somebody like that
10	**Paul:**	[My list my list is getting long.
11		My list is getting *longer*
12	Jan:	I know, I had a meeting with my boss[this morning
13	**Paul:**	[I'm supposed ta (1.5)
14		I'm supposed to get my list *shorter* (.2) if you *remember.*
15		(.6)
16	Jan:	*I know*
17	**Paul:**	And I'm not making any *progress.*
18	Jan:	So you can have a romantic interlude or [something
19	**Paul:**	[Right
20		I'm not- I don't have *time.*
21	Jan:	Heh-heh-heh-huh..I'll ask Shelby or Tony or the
22		both of them

Unlike the way in which we have come to think of stories with identifiable plots and progression toward some resolution, the abbreviated use of narrative in 6.8 is what Boje (1991) terms 'terse storytelling': "A terse telling is an abbreviated and succinct simplification of the story in which parts of the plot, some of the characters, and segments of the sequence of events are left to the hearer's imagination" (p. 115). Paul commences a terse telling at lines 10–11, 13–14 ("My list is getting long. . . . I'm supposed to get my list *shorter* (.) if you *remember*") immediately after he directly challenges Jan over shift coverage (line 5: "You gonna do that?"). Paul is using a story to legitimate his resistance to covering the shift.

Again we see a leader who actively coconstructs the story. Jan not only acknowledges the abbreviated narrative over the shortening of Paul's to-do list (lines 12 and 16), but adds to the story by humorously characterizing his motivation to reduce his workload (line 18: "So you can have a romantic interlude or something"). Boje (1991) argues that there may be strategic reasons for the chosen parts of stories in a terse telling, and in this instance, Lori's attempt at humor may be to diffuse the emotion behind Paul's rather direct threat to her face at line 5 ("You gonna do that?"). Fortunately, Paul responds in kind at lines 19–20 ("Right, I'm not. I don't have *time*."), effectively achieving Lori's goal. Importantly, this entire exchange is an opportunity for consistent follow-through by Lori in honoring previous her commitments, an indication of a high quality LMX (Graen & Uhl-Bien, 1995).

Boje (1991) also asserts that the more terse the storytelling, the more shared is the understanding of the social context because insiders know what can be left unsaid. Communication frequency is reportedly greater in high quality LMXs (Baker & Ganster, 1985) and may explain the more restricted code that enables a terse telling. In short, the 'romantic interlude' story was tersely told, actively coproduced by both leader and member, and marked by in-kind responses and the leader's consistent follow-through on a previous commitment to the member (Fairhurst & Hamlett, 2003). This is but one instance of an unfolding story line of a trusting, high quality LMX.

One final example of a high quality LMX from Fairhurst (1993) nicely demonstrates the distinction between narrative (stories lived) and story (stories told). It involves a case of insider joking by the male member (Jim) toward his female leader (Pam).

Narrative 6.9: Insider Joking

1	Jim:	((papers shuffling)) I wanted to talk *about* (.4) feasibility
2		(1.4) uhm ((papers shuffling)) (2.9) update on uh (.) making
3		operation, my perspective on that
4	Pam:	Oh good (2.6) Mm-hmm.
5	Jim:	Is this how you're gonna do this while we're on tape
6		keep sayin' "Oh good" to everything I mention?
7	Pam:	HAH-HEH-heh-[heh-heh-heh-huh
8	Jim:	[Heh-heh-huh-huh
9	Pam:	That's what I told Carol, I said, "*Hey,* I know you've
10		already had this uh (.4) session already so if you do anything
11		out of characteris- out of character, I'm going to call you
12		on it."

Pam's back-channel comments at line 4 ("Oh good. (2.6) Mm-hmm.") prompt Jim to humorously tease her by reflecting on her behavior in story-like fashion (lines 5–6: "Is this how you're gonna do this while we're on tape keep sayin' 'Oh good' to everything I mention?"). The telling of this story, albeit a brief one about the taping of their conversation, is done while living the story (narrative) of actually doing so.

In addition, the humor is face-threatening, but playful and indicative of a high quality of an LMX as Pam reacts favorably to the jab with a hearty laugh (line 7) and her own narrative that she aligns with Jim's sentiments (lines 9–12: "That's what I told Carol . . ."). Again, we see a coproduction of the narrative by the leader and member, and the way humor can disarm potentially face-threatening challenges. Unlike Narrative 6.8, the humor is directed upward here, which is significant because teasing is frequently a privilege of the powerful (Coser, 1960). In this example, it appears indicative of a lack of social distance within the relationship, again a high quality LMX marker (Fairhurst & Chandler, 1989).

As the above examples demonstrate, the narrative construction of LMX and its story performances are coproductions of leader and members' talk-in-interaction. Meanings are continuously negotiated, especially in 'terse tellings' in which the narrator's theatrical license to accentuate, abbreviate, or otherwise edit selected stories becomes apparent. However, there is still much to be said about the construction of the LMX relationship based upon the narrative resources available, a topic to which we must now turn.

NARRATIVE RESOURCES FOR THE LMX

Thus far we have focused on the role of stories and narratives in LMX discourse, specifically the language used in leader–member talk-in-interaction and member interviews. However, based on a more Foucauldian view of Discourse, we can also ask about the narrative resources available to LMX actors (Fairhurst & Hamlett, 2003). Recall that discursive psychologists prefer the term 'interpretative repertoire' to Discourse (see Appendix A4) because it focuses upon the linguistic resources that actors are using; they include terms, tropes, metaphors, themes, commonplaces, habitual forms of argument, and so forth (Potter & Wetherell, 1987; Potter et al., 1990; Wetherell, 1998). This discussion requires the use of *both* Discourse and interpretative repertoire.

Drawing from Foucault, Cronen (1995a) argues that certain stories of a special character rise to the level of a discursive formation:

> Foucault used the term *(D)iscourse* to describe stories of a particular character. In my use of this term, a story can be regarded as a (D)iscourse if it includes a formalized set of grammatical relationships among utterances that is well instantiated in a group of users. The formalizations include the kind of relationships persons have with each other. The relationships that make up the discourse are widely known and available, carrying great authority and strong feeling for certain people. (p. 47, emphasis original)

While one might debate the merits of equating story with Discourse for clarity purposes, Cronen's (1995a) point is that Discourses inform the stories that people tell, giving those stories and the repertoires they supply a kind of authority vis-à-vis other stories. As such, we should be able to discern other voices in LMX narratives, signaling the influence of society, the corporate community, the organization's culture, one or more professions, and so forth. Recall from Chapter 4 that the power of these Discourses is their ability to normalize, that is, define problems based upon what a discursive formation deems normal versus abnormal, reasonable versus unreasonable, and so on.

It will also be useful to adopt a poststructuralist view of the self, defined here as a repertoire of structured narrations (Holstein & Gubrium, 2000). Recall Chapter 5's discussion of subjectivity-in-the-making, or working subjectivity, in which the experience of the self as both an agential 'subject' and an 'object' of our self-consciousness produces self-identities that are practical everyday accomplishments, becoming both medium and outcome of how we think, feel, and value (Alvesson & Willmott, 2002; Collinson, 2003; Hassard, Holliday, & Willmott, 2000). These self-identities assume a narrative form in discourse as they respond to the contingencies of the interaction and context.

Consider the following example from Fairhurst (1993) in which a female leader (Barb) is coaching a female member (Sue) in a medium quality LMX. These women work in a manufacturing plant that had recently converted to a socio-technical systems philosophy.

Narrative 6.10: Coaching Tip

1	Barb:	One of the coaching tips that Bob gave me
2		today (.6) is that *I* tend (.4) and I and I do this *purposely*, not
3		to (.8) throw in my input
4	Sue:	Mm[-hmm
5	Barb:	[in the middle of a conversation (.8) when
6		maybe my perspective would let somebody else
7		know that I knew what was going on (.7) cause some
8		people are gonna interpret that like I don't know
9		what's going on. And (1.6) contract manufacturing?
10		when you when we give presentations to Smith or
11		whoever came through? (1.0) whoever was specifically
12		working on that *project*, whether (.3) my input was 50%
13		or *not*, if I thought they had ownership to the
14		*project*, I let them do the presentation because then:::

15		they felt more ownership to the end product. They
16		they could be more *proud* of what they were
17		doing (.3) and that's *my perspective*, but that's that's
18		why I I manage and I sit back a lotta times and let
19		somebody else *do* that. And some people *like* that
20		style (.) and some people say, "You're doing yourself
21		an injustice by not speaking up."
22	**Sue:**	Mm-hmm.
23	**Barb:**	So (1.4) understanding that (.) there are cases where your
24		presentation (.) I may be somewhat underlying and being
25		a *driving force* and stuff, but I would prefer to *tend* to
26		stay *out* of it. If I need to tell Goldberg my role, I can
27		do that another time. And I told Bob, I said, "Bob,
28		I think that's part of *your* role (.4) is to know what I'm
29		doing (.4) behind the scenes, to let other people know."
30		So I need to give him that (.5) *information* so he knows
31		those types of things. But *that's a bit of feedback*
32		that Bob gave *me* today that I just wanna share
33	**Sue:**	Okay
34	**Barb:**	Uhm, anyway, so that's *why I'm* giving an overall
35		perspective of the whole program.

As leaders grow more invisible with greater team self-management (Manz & Sims, 1987), Barb is told by her manager, Bob, that her selflessness in letting team members take credit for accomplishments was creating a problem in the current management structure. A visible, individual display of command appears necessary to be competitive even in this team environment. In the taped conversation above, Barb selects from her repertoire of self-narratives and begins 'telling her biography' around team ownership (Shamir & Eilam, 2005).

While framed as a coaching tip to Sue, Barb engages in a lot of identity work by justifying her actions, perhaps to a more sympathetic audience this time around (lines 1–3, 5–21). Self-justifications often emerge in post hoc reports of conflict, and in this scenario, there are several voices at play whose authority conflicts. Since Sue does little but listen and back-channel (lines 4, 22, and 33), we can discern these voices chiefly through the terminology and habitual forms of argument in Barb's interpretative repertoire as she speaks and also gives voice to her manager. For example, Barb's manager (reportedly) aligns himself with a masculinity Discourse, which is individualistic and competitive, and thus focused on a visible display of one's achievements and abilities (lines 1–3, 5–9). Masculinity Discourses also converge with neo-charisma Discourses here, equating leadership with a demonstration of agency. Both Discourses problematize the lack of Barb's visibility, making her selflessness ill advised. By contrast, both masculinity and neo-charisma Discourses conflict with a self-managing team Discourse in which leadership shifts and distributes itself within the team-based expertise, ownership, or time expended. Barb uses a self-managing team Discourse to justify putting team members in the spotlight, thus explaining her relative silence in the presence of visiting dignitaries (lines 9–21). Team Discourse also intersects with feminine management Discourses that feature inclusiveness and self-sacrifice as strong feminist values (Buzzanell, 1994, 2000). Thus, these latter two Discourses render this leader's selflessness as normal.

These multiple and conflicting Discourses appear to create a space of action for Barb. She reports that she challenged her manager by offering solutions that would require additional work for him and her, so as to increase her visibility without taking away from the team's time in the spotlight (lines 23–32). However, for the presentation they were planning, she negotiates the struggle between the Discourses by placing herself in a moderator's role in providing an overview of the project in the planned presentation to higher-ups (lines 34–35). While still doing what is best for the team, it remains unclear whether the moderator role ameliorates the presumed career consequences of a less visible leadership role from those who embrace masculine, neo-charisma Discourses in this management culture.

This telling of one's biography also hints at a teaching moment between Barb and her manager—and perhaps a change in her repertoire of self-narratives. Such moments usually occur when the circumstances of the member (in this case, Barb who is being coached by her manager) increase her receptivity to feedback and teaching (Tichy, 1997). However, in this instance, sensemaking and perhaps dissonance reduction seem to be more pressing concerns because of the putative weight Barb assigns to the feedback with which she disagrees. As demonstrated, Barb engages in considerable identity work as she accounts for her behavior, apparently not for the first time as she claims knowledge of others' views (lines 19–21: "And some people like that style and some people say, 'You're doing yourself an injustice by not speaking up'"). If true, these are additional examples of discovering meanings in the work of producing them, aided perhaps by new listeners and fresh insights. It also suggests that telling one's biography involves more than just crafting an inspirational story that will resonate with members (Shamir & Eilam, 2005). Leaders may story their unfinished business with members in search of meanings and self-justifications that elude them.

Finally, it appears that not only should the self be viewed as a repertoire of structured narrations, but so should LMX. Like self-narratives, leaders and members will construct their LMXs based upon the linguistic resources afforded by the Discourses to which they consistently lay claim. For example, low quality LMX members might be more subject to downsizing Discourses from the leader than high quality LMX members because the former are considered expendable. Conversely, high quality LMX leaders and members may share in a greater range of Discourses from the corporate community (e.g., globalization, technology, outsourcing Discourses, etc.) the more varied and challenging the members' task assignments. Low LMX members may seize upon those Discourses as well, although it may well be with irony and contradiction. A leader's reliance on more feminine management Discourses around inclusiveness may show that members with medium quality LMXs, in addition to high quality LMXs, will be coached and given more resources than a leader who subscribes to masculinity Discourses. Whatever the Discourses drawn upon, the investigation into narrative resources shows that the business conducted within the LMX is not just relational, but is also significantly impacted by cultural forces (Fairhurst & Hamlett, 2003). These cultural forces carry great authority as they are drawn upon to construct the relationship, complete tasks, and manage identities. With discursive analyses, we have the potential to see the interactive input of both culture and dyad (team), a subject long overlooked in this literature (Fairhurst, 2001).

A Backward Glance—Final Thoughts

In this chapter, the following points have been made:

- The study of narrative involves discourse as language in use and Discourses as sets of narrative resources.
  - o LMX is a theory of relationships between leaders and members whose narrative roots for high, medium, and low quality can be reclaimed.
- Narrative is a basis for sensemaking; it is a primary means by which we understand the world and make sense of it.
  - o The extant LMX literature may underplay the experience of LMX due to a heavy use of survey research. In-depth interviews give leadership actors a greater chance to narratively reflect upon their LMX experiences and project into the future.
- The uniqueness paradox, which challenges a culture's claim to distinctiveness, can also be applied to LMX.

- o   Individuals in an LMX relationship will embrace or disparage their relationship's uniqueness to play into self-enhancing attributions of personal success or failure.
- A distinction between narrative and story is necessary to understand the means by which LMX is constructed.
  - o   Narratives or 'stories lived' reflect the unfolding nature of LMX as story lines where all discourse is in some way narrative.
  - o   These narrative accounts may or may not include 'stories told' (conventional storytelling), which perform a number of actions in their telling.
- The storytelling between leaders and members in actual dialogue is often coconstructed and tersely told, that is, abbreviated and succinct. The more tersely told the story, the more shared the understanding of the social context because insiders know what can be said and left unsaid.
- Various Discourses of society, the corporate community, the organization's culture, various professions, and so on serve as linguistic resources for narratives and stories.
  - o   Both the self and LMX can be viewed as a repertoire of structured narrations that draws from these Discourses.

It is appropriate to end this chapter by again reiterating the complementarities of a discursive view of leadership with a psychological one. Indeed, it would be hypocritical to do otherwise because some 30 years of social-psychological LMX research serve as the foundation for this chapter. However, the concern here is that a psychological, empiricist orientation to LMX not be the only orientation. As we have seen in this chapter, discursive perspectives have the capacity to add nuance and detailed meaning to the character and quality of LMX. When the bird's-eye view of LMX scaled measurement comes in for a landing with a discursive's view from the ground, or 'below,'[12] LMX only benefits from this kind of cross-paradigmatic, multi-method thinking and analysis. Indeed, all three narrative approaches to LMX reviewed in this chapter took as their starting point the scaled judgments of the members. Finally, it is important to reinforce that a narrative research agenda is a diverse one, whether narrative reflection and the uniqueness paradox are used to make sense of LMX quality; narratives and stories in actual leader–member dialogue construct the LMX in elaborated or terse tellings; or the narrative resources used in dialogue or interviews reveal powerful cultural voices other than leaders and members. In short, the variety that characterizes the study of narrative awaits LMX and other mainstream leadership researchers.

NOTES

1. Much of the conceptual framework for this chapter draws from Fairhurst and Hamlett (2003).

2. At least 10 reviews of the literature were found (Barge & Schleuter, 1991; Dienesch & Liden, 1986; Fairhurst, 2001; Gerstner & Day, 1997; Graen & Uhl-Bien,

1995; House & Aditya, 1997; Keller & Dansereau, 1995; Liden et al., 1997; Schriesheim, Coglister, & Neider, 1995; Schriesheim, Castro, & Coglister, 1999).

3. Leaders were prone to socially desirable answers, while members tended to give more unvarnished accounts (Fairhurst, 1993).

4. The early LMX work used 'in group,' 'middle group,' and 'out group' (Graen et al., 1982), but changed to high, medium, and low quality respectively (Graen & Scandura, 1987; Graen & Uhl-Bien, 1995).

5. Based on Roloff's (1981) observation that individuals are active and self-aware calculators in social exchange theories, Fairhurst and Hamlett (2003) argue that the calculation may be situational, gradual, post hoc, or an individualized tendency, but it remains a resources in/resources out rational assessment nonetheless (p. 120).

6. Bruner's (1990) argument for a narrative psychology in which people organize their experiences, knowledge and transactions in the world corresponds to conceptions of *episodic memory*, which Lord and Brown (2004) highlight in their book on leadership processes and follower-self identity. Episodic memory provides a temporal organization to events because of our innate ability as humans to locate the self in time; we remember our 'selves' in the past and project them into the future (Tulving, 2002; Wheeler, Stuss, & Tulving, 1997). From a narrative perspective, however, *we reconstruct as we remember* our 'selves' and we project them into the future.

7. More specifically, "You indicated an answer of 2 out of 5 for the first survey question, 'Do you know where you stand with your leader?' (or Do you usually know how satisfied your leader is with what you do?' and so on). Can you give me a specific example to illustrate your answer?" or 'What experiences have you had that would lead you to give this specific rating?'"

8. Normative data for LMX placement was provided by Graen and Scandura (1985).

9. Reprinted with permission.

10. Fairhurst's (1993) original analysis does very little with narrative.

11. Narratives 6.7, 6.8, 6.9 and 6.10: From "Social structure in leader-member interaction" by T. Gail, et al., *Communication Monographs, 56*, 1989. Reprinted with permission of Taylor and Francis, www.tandf.co.uk.

12. Hosking (1988) characterizes the study of interaction as 'from below.'

7

Material Mediations[1]

S ince the early 1980s, charisma has weighed heavily in mainstream leadership theory.[2] With intellectual roots in Weber (1968) and Burns (1978), charismatic (Conger & Kanungo, 1987; House, 1977; Shamir, House, & Arthur, 1993) and transformational (Bass, 1985, 1990) leadership theories have emerged as the 'neo-charisma' approaches.[3] The differences among these theories are testimony to the enduring elusiveness of charisma as a phenomenon.[4] For example, Conger and Kanungo (1988, 1998) locate charisma in the attributions of extraordinary qualities by followers. In Bass's (1990) transformational leadership theory, charisma is roughly equivalent to possession of an organizational vision. Graham (1991) depicts House's (1977) view of charisma as "personal celebrity charisma" because of his focus on leaders' personality characteristics. Later versions by Shamir, House, and colleagues define charisma in terms of its effects on followers, increasing the social psychological emphasis by including followers' self needs and identification processes, but also its contextual influences (Shamir, Arthur, & House, 1994; Shamir et al., 1993; Shamir & Howell, 1999).

Yukl (1999) asserts that the theorizing around charismatic leadership (mostly) in a business context has actually moved it closer to the transformational theories, where 'transformational' increasingly refers to almost any form of effective leadership. Beyer (1999) argues that charisma has been 'tamed' in this regard, and is much less the rarity that Weber conceived it to be. However, Yukl also raises other key issues such as whether the primary influence processes underlying charismatic leadership involve personal identification (Conger & Kanungo, 1998) or internalization and collective identification (Shamir et al., 1994). There is disagreement about essential behaviors in charismatic leadership such that case studies of political and cult leaders are much more likely to focus on the dark and manipulative side of charisma (think Adolph Hitler, Benito Mussolini, Charles Manson, Jim Jones, and so on), while management theories espouse a distinct preference for socially acceptable behaviors.[5] Finally, the facilitating conditions necessary for attributions of charisma are ambiguous; crisis seems to be an important facilitating condition for Weber and others (House, Spangler & Woycke, 1991; Roberts & Bradley, 1988; Trice & Beyer, 1986), but not a necessary one for Shamir and Howell (1999). In turn, charismatic attributions are putatively more likely if followers are feeling psychic distress of some kind as a result of threats to physical safety or economic security. However, Yukl (1999) suggests that all such claims require more research.

Given this state of affairs, can discursive leadership add anything to the charisma theories of leadership? Can a focus on discourse address some of charisma's elusiveness? This chapter supplies a definitive "yes" to these questions, however, not by anchoring charisma in an extraordinary leader or even in relations with needy followers. With the help of actor-network theory (ANT) (Callon & Latour, 1981; Latour, 1994, 1999) and a group of discourse scholars at the University of Montreal (Cooren, 2001; J. R. Taylor & Van Every, 2000), we will take the unusual step of defining charisma as an attributed product of a distributed actor-network of human and nonhuman entities.[6]

Ironically, Shils (1958, 1965) made a similar argument decades ago, well before ANT's emergence on the scene. Shils (1965) argued that Weber (1968) focused on charisma in its most concentrated and intense forms and "did not consider the more widely dispersed, unintense operation of the charismatic element in corporate bodies governed by the rational-legal type of authority" (p. 202). Weber himself alluded to kinship charisma, hereditary charisma, and charisma of office, but it was Shils who took seriously the notion that charisma may be attributed to bloodlines, locality, social roles, institutions, and so forth (think the Kennedys, the Oval Office of the U.S. presidency, any country's highest office, and so on). He suggested that there is a *charismatic propensity* operating in the routine functioning of society brought on by any massive organization of authority. Charisma will be attributed to that which is sacred and central to authority, even if it is dispersed in institutions, collectivities, social roles, rituals, or cultural objects. Underlying these dynamics is society's need for order; however, charisma both disrupts and maintains it. According to Shils (1965), we can explain this seeming paradox because of the propensity to attribute charisma to the *central and sacred routines of authority*—as well as to extraordinary individuals, who may emerge during times of crisis because they mobilize or associate themselves with these routines. More about this will be said as the chapter unfolds.

If charisma is far more protean than the current crop of charisma leadership theories recognizes, then Shils may have been on to something. However, the application of ANT and the Montreal scholars' work really takes Shils's argument one step further by suggesting *hybrid agency* between humans and nonhumans and attributions of charisma as products of specific actor-networks. To take this step, we must first discuss the role played by material conditions in the discourse of leadership actors; thus, in the first part of this chapter we will explore the criticisms of discourse analysis vis-à-vis materialist concerns. Next we will discuss actor-network theory and its use by the Montreal school as a rejoinder to these criticisms. Finally, we will consider the suitability of all of this work for the study of charismatic leadership and use Rudy Giuliani's leadership during the events of September 11, 2001, as an example.

Materialist Critiques of Discourse Analysis

Just as leadership scholars continue to disagree about definitions of leadership, so too discourse analysts disagree about definitions of discourse/Discourse, especially regarding materialist concerns. These concerns can be *institutional* in the form of social or economic structures or *material objects* like guns, radios, and police cars (to draw from the police rescue example of Officer Conway used in Chapters 2 and 3; see also Appendix B). For example, post-structuralists Laclau and Mouffe (1985) believe that social structures and physical objects certainly exist, but our access to them is never direct; access is always mediated by systems of meaning in the form of Discourses, à la Foucault. Thus, whether guns are weapons, historical artifacts, or bartered goods is a function of the discursive context. Because of the workings of our language within systems of Discourse, Laclau and Mouffe stress that social reality eclipses the physical because meaning is not intrinsic to physical objects themselves. Yet, they avoid linguistic reductionism by asserting that Discourses are themselves material, which includes objects and structures as much as the words spoken (Laclau & Mouffe, 1985). Nevertheless, by subjugating the physical to the discursive in a continual search for meaning (because all meanings are temporary and contingent), critics see a kind of 'anything goes' relativism in which reality is just what we define it to be (Gergen, 1991). But a prisoner could no more socially construct him- or herself out of prison (assuming all legal remedies have been exhausted) than we could imagine away natural disasters. The material intervenes, and just how this occurs has been the subject of considerable debate in social constructionist thought.[7]

When organizations are cast as discursive constructions, as they often are,[8] this raises the specter of relativism for some discourse analysts who object on materialist grounds. For example, Reed (2004) argues for a 'realist' stance that would "develop *a much stronger structural and historical account* of pre-existing institutional forms and material conditions that inevitably constrain the discursive options available to corporate agents as they struggle to maintain and challenge the status quo" (p. 418, emphasis original). For Cloud (2005), "the descent into discourse can result in overoptimistic accounts of employees' symbolic agency in situations where they have little or no control over the material conditions of their labor" (p. 515). Agency is not precluded for these realists, but the odds of successful agency are significantly lowered than when 'discoursism' (that is, the collapse of the organizational into discourse) (Conrad, 2004; Gergen, 2003) and, by implication, relativism (the collapse of the material into discourse) are thought to prevail. In contrast to Laclau and Mouffe (1985), writers like Reed and Cloud recommend distinguishing between the discursive and nondiscursive to assure that the material, structural, and coercive forces that constrain actors are given their due. For example, in Fairclough's work (for a brief overview of critical discourse analysis, see Appendix A6) (Chouliaraki & Fairclough, 1999; Fairclough, 1993, 1995), the discursive possesses a unique logic, while intersecting with the logics of the economic, physical, psychological, or biological realms. Each logic represents a moment of every social practice that is in a dialectical relationship with other logics (Chouliaraki & Fairclough, 1999). Thus, to cast organizations solely as discursive constructions is to neglect the material conditions of production and very real differences between macro (ideological structures, relations of power, and material realities) and micro (discourse) levels of analysis (Fairclough, 1995; Reed, 2000).[9]

Ironically, the French sociologists Bruno Latour and Michel Callon and their proponents in the Montreal school would still see arguments by realists like Reed, Cloud, and Fairclough as lacking sufficient complexity because of the difficulties in bridging the macro–micro levels thus created. In the next section, Latour and Callon's actor-network theory (ANT) is reviewed as a rejoinder along with its implications for leadership.

Actor-Network Theory

If, for Shakespeare, "All the world's a stage," then the world is filled with actors for Latour and Callon (Callon & Latour, 1981; Latour, 1994, 1996, 1999). But their actors are not just humans, as Goffman's would be; they are nonhumans as well, like the radio, guns, and cars in the Officer Conway example of Chapters 2 and 3. Since the words 'actor' and 'agent' in the case of nonhumans are unconventional, Latour (1994) prefers the term *actant,* which is any entity that acts in a plot. Material objects qualify as actants because they come with their own scripts or affordances (Gibson, 1979),[10] thereby enabling them to enter into associations with human subjects. Stated otherwise, there is a *mediation,* or link, between the human subject and object that previously did not exist before and which modifies both actants. For example, consider the use of guns by Officer Conway and her assailant in the police rescue example, which plays nicely into Latour's (1994) often cited gun example:

> If I define you by what you have (the gun), and by the series of associations
> that you enter into when you use what you have (when you fire the gun), then

you are modified by the gun—more or less so, depending on the weight of the other associations that you carry. This translation is wholly symmetrical. You are different with the gun in hand; the gun is different with you holding it. You are another subject because you hold the gun; the gun is another object because it has entered into a relationship with you. The gun is no longer the gun-in-the-armory or the gun-in-the-drawer or the gun-in-the-pocket, but the gun-in-your-hand, aimed at someone who is screaming. What is true of the subject, of the gunman, is true of the object, of the gun that is held. A good citizen becomes a criminal, a bad guy becomes a worse guy; a silent gun becomes a fired gun, a new gun becomes a used gun, a sporting gun becomes a weapon. The twin mistake of the materialists and the sociologists is to start with essences, those of subjects *or* those of objects. That starting point renders impossible our measurement of the mediating role of techniques. Neither subject nor object (nor their goals) is fixed. (p. 33, emphasis original)

As in Chapter 1, we see an anti-essentialist position, taken this time by Latour (1994) who says, "Essence is existence and existence is action" (p. 33). For Latour, action is continuously distributed or *networked* in a string of *hybrid* associations between actants, namely human subjects and nonhuman objects. We can see this in the Officer Conway example, where the assailant shoots her four times with a .357 Magnum, forming the hybrid actor, assailant-gun. As indicated in the above quote, the assailant is a different assailant with the gun in his hand, and the gun is different because there is someone willing to discharge it. But the action does not stop there because the assailant pushes Conway's body to the passenger side and begins driving her cruiser, thus forming two more hybrids, assailant-body (of Conway),[11] and assailant-car. However, each of these hybrids has its own subroutines that achieve it, such as the individual steps necessary to drive a car, move a body, or pull a trigger.[12] Taken altogether, we see the beginnings of networked action: assailant-gun-assailant-body-assailant-car. We also see how hybridity and networking create the embedded nature of action via subroutines. Such action resists essentializing because "the prime mover of an action becomes a new, distributed, and nested series of practices whose sum might be made but only if we respect the mediating role of all the actants mobilized in the list" (Latour, 1994, p. 34). Importantly, action becomes a property of the associated networked entities, and not, in this case, the assailant alone. To ignore the mediating role of various actants is to *blackbox* them, a process that Latour (1994) suggests "makes the joint production of actors and artifacts entirely opaque" (p. 36).

However, let us return to one of the leaders of this situation discussed in Chapter 2, Police Supervisor 1080, who reportedly demonstrated command presence with the statement, "1080, I'll be there in five seconds. Blockin' it off with four cars." How would ANT explain 1080's actions? A key concept for ANT is *translation,* which occurs when the interests of one actant are successfully taken up by another (Callon & Latour, 1981).[13] In simple terms, this is a process by which a set of actants enroll, in a network, or are persuaded to enroll by a network organizer (Grint & Woolgar, 1997). In the mobilization of allies for this network, a series of intermediaries and equivalences between actants leads either to the designation of a spokesperson or *macroactor* or the network acting as a unit to represent an even larger network of absent entities. The latter occurred for all of the police networks mobilized for Conway's rescue, which is why the entire Cincinnati Police Department (CPD) is held accountable for any citizen death or officer shot in the line of duty. Conway putatively translated the interests of the CPD when she responded with the use of force to kill her assailant. Similarly, supervisors, like 1080, translated CPD's interests as they instantiated a hybrid network of supervisors and objects (radio, guns, protocol, and so forth) to rescue her and secure the crime scene. The networks formed could be traced all the way back to the training of Conway, particularly in the use of force, and the training of her supervisors, especially for distress calls, which is why they are viewed as CPD representatives. This complex network could be traced even further back to alliances formed with the local municipality that must provide funding and oversight, thus making police officers representatives of the city as well.

However, the process of representation is often fraught with controversy and sometimes *betrayal* by one or more actants. It is for this reason that Callon and Latour (1981) are quick to note that networks can be fragile. The behavior of one or more actants may betray the interests of another, thus blocking the translation and reversing the blackboxing of various actants. For example, if Conway shot the assailant without provocation, Conway's gun failed to discharge because of poor equipment, the crime scene was breached by another car accident because Supervisor 1080 failed to secure it properly, or protocol was violated by other responding police supervisors, all would block the translation of the interests of the CPD. The translations between actants must hold in order for one to successfully represent another.

As demonstrated in the case of Officer Conway, there is an analytic impartiality in ANT toward whatever human or nonhuman actors are involved in a situation. ANT analysts also adopt an abstract neutral vocabulary (for example, 'actant') toward actors, thus disavowing a priori distinctions between the social and the natural or the technological (Callon, 1986b). The uniqueness of ANT notwithstanding, we can see the resonances of ethnomethodology in the analyst's goal to provide explanations that are local, contingent, practical, and reflective of the character of the specific network under study (Michael, 1996). Like ethnomethodology, ANT analyzes what has already occurred because 'subjects' and 'objects' only emerge in networked action. Importantly, ANT analysts also routinely reflect on their own involvement in networks, "on their status as network-builders and enrollees, and on the way that their story telling constitutes others in particular ways" (Michael, 1996, p. 62). Thus, they reflexively focus on themselves as *authors,* just like any actor whose own interest-laced narrations depict the actors enrolled, the practices adopted, and the agency ascribed. There is still much to say about ANT, but the Montreal school must first be introduced.

THE MONTREAL SCHOOL

The Montreal school includes the organizational communication scholars James Taylor, François Cooren, and Daniel Robichaud, among others, at the University of Montreal. Cooren's work on the episodic ordering of speech acts, known as speech act schematics (SAS), was a subject in Chapter 2. SAS is typical of the agenda of the Montreal school, which is to focus on the organizing properties of discourse and communication as the building blocks of organizations.[14] As such, their research agenda is not an offshoot of actor-network theory per se. However, they use ANT to help flesh out the organizational relevance of Greimas's (1987, 1988; Greimas & Courtes, 1982) narrative theory, upon which they depend so heavily.

Greimas (1987, 1988) asserts that sequence is the source of sense, similar to Bruner (1986, 1990) and Weick (1995) in Chapter 6. However, Greimas posits a universal narrative structure underlying all goal-directed activity, which Chapter 2 depicted as having five phases: *Manipulation* (X has to or is requested/invited by Y to perform an action A—a having to do), *Commitment* (X decides or agrees to perform A—a wanting to do), *Competence* (X needs to know how to perform A—knowing how to do, and X needs to be able to perform—being able to do), *Performance* (X performs A—to do), and *Sanction* (X is assessed by Y regarding her performing A).

The Montreal scholars argue that because narrative is basic to sensemaking in goal-directed action, it is the general sequential template for all organizing—with both human and nonhuman agency (Cooren, 2001; J. R. Taylor & Van Every, 2000). What the Montreal school finds so appealing in Latour's conception of nonhuman agents is that objects come with built-in properties or scripts *inscribed* with the traces of past organizing. According to J. R. Taylor and Van Every (2000), "For Latour, every local world carries the actantial traces of a larger, more extended world—indeed, extending indefinitely back in time as well as in space—and it is in the mobilization of objects that the mobilization of humans—the emergence of organization—is made possible" (p. 162). The speed bump is Latour's (1994) quintessential example and a favorite of the Montreal school. The initial placement of the speed bump is the result of a hybrid of human and nonhuman actants, but once created, the speed bump is a translation that continues to act on its own as a "silent policeman." Importantly, it carries the traces of past organizing (for example, networked alliances between various members of city planning, police, work crews, ordinances, work orders, cement, tools, and so on) as it performs its envisioned enablements and constraints in slowing down traffic.

Despite Latour's reticence to deal with issues of language and communication, the Montreal school argues that language carries the traces of past organizing as much as objects do (Cooren, 2001, 2004; J. R. Taylor & Van Every, 2000). Specifically, they see *discursive objects* in the performative aspects of our language, otherwise known as speech acts. As Chapter 2 suggests, there are six categories of speech acts, including directives, commissives, accreditives, assertives, declaratives, and expressives (see also Appendix A3). Importantly, speech acts are not analyzed from the speaker's intentions, as they originally were,[15] but as text objects that circulate among agents and recipients. For example, in the Conway case, Supervisor 1080 issued a directive to the dispatcher to "Check on her safety" (line 27, Appendix B). At that moment, the spoken directive became a discursive object, or *text*, to which both 1080 and the dispatcher must orient. As J. R. Taylor and Van Every (2000) argue, the text object undergoes a change or transformation by virtue of the exchange because "co-orienting actors are affected by either giving up or acquiring a possession or quality" (p. 46). Stated otherwise, Supervisor 1080 *possessed* the authority to issue such orders, and the dispatcher *had* the responsibility to accept them (generally speaking) by virtue of their employment contract and their training in emergency response calls requiring authoritative, on-scene action. Thus, if accepted, the spoken directive (police supervisor-text object) carries with it the traces of past organizing, thereby grounding the organization in action.[16]

As we saw in Chapter 2, directives and assertives often open schemas by establishing the necessity of some action. Commissives, accreditives, and assertives all contribute to schema development, while expressives contribute to the closure of the schema through an evaluation or acknowledgment of the action performed. This view also helps to explain what can happen when schemas embed themselves within one another because there may be some secondary tasks to complete before a requested action can be performed. We saw this in the Officer Conway case in which help was delayed until her location could first be determined. However, the Conway case also revealed how embedded schemas reflect various *translations* in which the interests of one actor have been taken up by another, for example, in the translations of the Cincinnati Police Department by Conway and her supervisors. In this series of translations, there may be a number of narrative schemas or subroutines that perform as expected, which become easy to *blackbox* and drop from conscious view. When they do not perform as expected, they are subject to attention and redoubled organizing activity.

The Montreal scholars thus spotlight the organizational and linguistic relevance of Latour's work for material forms of agency, but they split from him in their focus on the reflexive and recursive nature of human communication (Cooren, 2004; J. R. Taylor & Van Every, 2000). They suggest a crucial difference between human and nonhuman agents; the latter cannot know what they are doing in the way that humans do.[17] Action becomes action only when it is constituted reflexively as action (J. R. Taylor, personal communication, May 2005). However, like Latour and others influenced by the ethnomethodological tradition, they believe that the macro–micro distinction is a false dichotomy; there is no organizational entity per se because *organizations are grounded in action* (Fairhurst & Putnam, 2004).[18] Thus, the Montreal scholars are social constructionists in that they never leave the terra firma of social interaction; they are realists in their focus on the role of nonhuman actants. Yet, in contrast to realists like Reed, Cloud, and Fairclough, the Montreal scholars view 'structures,' 'power,' and 'ideology' as analytic shortcuts that do not do justice to the complexity of the phenomena they study (Cooren, in press). According to Cooren and Fairhurst (2002), an organization thus becomes "a kind of daily miracle, since it consists of mobilizing a series of human and/or nonhuman actants who can at any moment fail to join in the narrative schemas of the organisation (i.e., the narrative schema as told and anticipated by the managers)" (pp. 90–91). In the next section, leadership itself becomes a kind of daily miracle.

LEADERSHIP AND ACTOR-NETWORK THEORY (REVISED)

If the Montreal school highlights the organizational relevance of ANT, Latour (1988) himself addresses several leadership issues in his elaboration of Machiavelli's (1984) treatise on power, *The Prince*. Latour's leaders, like Machiavelli's Italian princes, appear as calculative, goal-directed entities (for example, individuals, teams, or corporations) with one paramount concern: "how to maintain power for a little longer in spite of enemies and adverse fortunes" (Latour, 1988, p. 20). Latour argues that the judgments of immorality from which Machiavelli suffered were the result of duplicitous analysts, that is, historians who decided virtue and evil in arbitrary fashion.[19] Latour argues that Machiavelli's view of continuing power as the arbiter of action transcended dualities like moral and immoral action (Grint, 1997). Indeed, it was Machiavelli's concern to arm oneself with more than just a self-righteous sense of morality because one must also "enlist allies, fight enemies, and beware of all" to sustain power (Latour, 1988, p. 20). For Latour, the concerns of analysts must first be to understand 'user needs' in the parlance of today's technologies or, in other words, the methods of association irrespective of the morality claims laid upon one or the other strategy.

Following Latour's (1988) argument, today's leaders would be better served if we could examine both the human and nonhuman allies they must marshal to maintain power. Resistance to nonhumans as actors must be overcome because strategic behavior usually embodies both. As Grint (1977) observes, "naked, friendless, money-less, and technology-less leaders are unlikely to prove persuasive" (p. 17). To better understand this, consider that leaders do battle on many fronts—with employees, higher-ups, collaborators, peers, and customers/ clients, usually in turbulent environments. The more fronts on which leaders must battle, the greater the need to delegate responsibilities to human and nonhuman agents in order to extend their influence (Latour, 1988). To take a simple example, monitoring employees' work arrivals and departures could be delegated to lower level managers, but time clocks, computerized sign-ins, and so forth obviate the need to do so, freeing the hierarchy in the process. While the freedom of the leader is typically relative to the number of nonhuman resources he or she has enrolled in her cause, nonhuman agents often seem trivial and easily taken-for-granted in the exercise of control. Yet, as Dale (2005) observes, it is in this level of triviality and taken-for-grantedness that material mediations become both hidden and powerful—as a network betrayal makes known.

Leaders (or leadership entities) will thus engage in *heterogeneous engineering*, in which they seek to enroll in a "seamless web" a diverse array of humans, technologies, materials, and techniques into their networks, while also displacing them (or other competing actants) from previous associations (Law, 1987).[20] As Michael (1996) observes, the task of the ANT analyst is to "disassemble this 'cascade' of ever-simplified inscriptions that lead to harder and harder facts, and greater and greater costs for anyone aiming to dissect them" (p. 54).[21] Again, ANT and Montreal school (authored) explanations will always reflect the character of the (already formed) network under study and the means by which localized and contingent associations between human and nonhumans were formed, associations that transformed humans and nonhumans in equal measure. From this rather transformative view of agency, we are now in a place to tackle one of leadership's most elusive constructs—charisma. The example of Rudy Giuliani's leadership surrounding the events of September 11, 2001, should clarify.

Rudy Giuliani and September 11, 2001

The lessons of Giuliani's 9/11 leadership suggest an attribution of charisma based upon four components. First, Giuliani macroacted at a time of crisis and great personal risk when he would not have been faulted for acting otherwise. Second, in hybrid fashion he associated himself with the charismatic central and sacred—people and objects that represent larger social orders like 'God and country.' Third, from the start he deployed a continuous networking strategy that embodied the emotions of the moment and its temporal flow. Premised upon the mutual regulation of emotion between leader and led, his networking and authoring constructed an emotional scaffolding that in dialectical fashion simultaneously affirmed devastating emotions while deftly regulating them to promote future healing. Fourth, Giuliani's 'charisma' benefited enormously from the social shaping that was almost immediate, proclaiming him one of the heroes of 9/11.

In order to unpack these claims, background on the events of September 11, 2001, and the texts used in this analysis must first be presented.

BACKGROUND AND TEXT

Rudolph Giuliani was mayor of New York City at the time that the World Trade Center was destroyed in a terrorist attack on September 11, 2001. Prior to that day, Giuliani was thought of as a far more polarizing than charismatic leader, with a mixed record of accomplishments. Credited with making New York streets safe again and a reduction of the social welfare rolls of past administrations, he was also combative, domineering, and perhaps best known in his second term for the "epic bathos" of his divorce and extramarital affair, prostate cancer, and canceled U.S. Senate run against Hillary Clinton (Traub, 2001). However, the events of 9/11 not only earned him the accolade of New York's greatest among the big mayors, but he also became "America's Mayor" to national network audiences. Biographer Andrew Kirtzman (2001) wrote

> Gone, incredibly, was the most polarizing leader New York had ever known since Richard Nixon. Giuliani was now applauded wherever he traveled, venerated on television and in the newspapers. Old adversaries became new converts. "He moves about the stricken city like a god," wrote [New York] Times columnist Bob Herbert. "People wanted to be in his presence. They want to touch him. They want to praise him." (p. 305)

Attributions of heroism and charisma followed what many regarded as his singular leadership on 9/11 and the days thereafter. He was even made *Time* magazine's "Person of the Year," with a remarkable bit of hyperbole by *Time* writer Nancy Gibbs (2001), "for not sleeping and not quitting and not shrinking from the pain all around him, Rudy Giuliani, Mayor of the World" (p. 35).

How did the events of 9/11 effect such a transformation in the attributions surrounding Giuliani, if not in Giuliani himself? Consider two excerpts from Kirtzman's (2001) biographical account of Giuliani at the time of the World Trade Center towers' collapse.[22] Kirtzman was then a beat reporter for New York 1 News, the city's all-news television channel. He had covered the mayor for some eight years and was with him when the second tower collapsed.

(Note: The two excerpts below are quoted verbatim from Kirtzman, 2001. Reprinted by permission of SLL/Sterling Lord Literistic, Inc. Copyright by Andrew Kirtzman.)

7.1 Giuliani Tries to Go Live

1   As we started to walk north, a noise from behind alerted us that the

2   whole sickening spectacle of the tower collapse was starting to repeat

3   itself. A volcanic explosion erupted as Tower 1, with thousands of office

4   workers, fire-fighters, and rescue crews still inside, collapsed in an

5   instant. It was a terrifying spectacle. Tony Coles, the most buttoned-up of

6   Giuliani's aides, yelled "fuck." And then we started to run.

7   The collapse produced a huge, violent mushroom of smoke and

8   concrete dust, which rose up to the sky and grew larger until it threatened

9   to envelop us. John Huvane, a big red-headed plain-clothes detective, threw

10   his arm around the mayor and started running north with him. The rest of us

11   followed, worriedly looking back over our shoulders to see if the tornado was

12   gaining on us.

13   "Just keep going north!" Giuliani shouted.

14   Our run finally slowed to a trot. I was sweating under the hot sun, and

15   my heart was palpitating from heat, smoke, and fear.

16   Giuliani fell back into line with the rest of us. "How the hell did they

17   get the Pentagon?" he asked (Police Commissioner, Bernard) Kerik.

18   He kept turning to me and imploring me to get my news station on

19   the phone, which was turning out to be impossible. "Andrew, get your station

20   to tell people to stay away from lower Manhattan," Giuliani said. "I can't get a

21   cell phone signal," I told him. He repeated his request to me twice more as we

22   walked up the avenue.

23   It was at about that moment that it occurred to me that Giuliani was the calmest one

24   in the bunch. The city—the country—was under a cataclysmic attack and he'd been

25   reduced to a wandering refugee. I watched him. He was thinking practically,

26   methodically. Keep the traffic away from the emergency vehicles.

27   I had an idea. "Would you take my cell phone and tell the people of New

28   York yourself what to do?" I asked Giuliani. He thought for a second. He'd been

29   out of touch with the people of the city, who were surely frantic for some

30   reassurance. "Sure," he said.

31   I tried dialing New York 1 again, and, miraculously, got through this

32   time. "Put me on the air!" I screamed. "I'm with Giuliani! He wants to go

33   live!"

34   The assignment desk editor didn't skip a beat. He transferred me to

35   the control room. Sharon Raifer, an executive producer, was at the helm.

36   "I've got Giuliani! Get us on the air now!" I got ready to hand him my

37   tiny StarTAC (cell phone).

38   "Okay," she said. "Let's do it." And at that, my connection went

39   dead. My cell phone didn't pick up another signal for twenty-four hours.

40   We were on our own. (p. 300)

7.2 Giuliani and Governor Pataki

41   At 2:35 p.m., the mayor of New York City held his first televised press

42   conference. It was held at the city's Police Academy, which for the next six days

43   would serve as New York's makeshift City Hall. He appeared on a dais with

44   Governor George Pataki.

45   Giuliani spoke slowly and deliberately. The gravity of the moment hung in

46   the air.

47   "Today is obviously one of the most difficult days in the history of the city

48   and the country," he began. "The tragedy that we're all undergoing right now is

49   something we've had nightmares about—probably thought wouldn't happen. My

50   heart goes out to all of the innocent victims of this horrible and vicious act of

51   terrorism."

52   Fire Commissioner Tom Von Essen, looking ashen, walked on stage and

53   slipped behind the mayor.

54   "Our focus now has to be on saving as many lives as possible," Giuliani

55   said. "We have hundreds of police officers and firefighters who are engaging in

56   rescue efforts in lower Manhattan."

57   "We will strive now very hard to save as many people as possible. And to

58   send a message that the city of New York and the United States of America is

59   much stronger than any group of barbaric terrorists. That our democracy, that

60   our rule of law, that our strength and our willingness to defend ourselves will

61   ultimately prevail."

62   "I'd ask the people of New York City to do everything they can to

63   cooperate, not to be frightened, to go about their lives as normal. Everything

64   is safe right now in the city."

65   When it was his turn to talk, Pataki could not match the power of

66   Giuliani's words. Never a noted speaker to begin with, he fell back on some

67   platitudes about freedom and the American way of life and then, almost

68   reflexively, started doling out thank-you's to fellow politicians, as if this were

69   just another press conference. ". . . And I want to thank my colleagues from

70   Connecticut, New Jersey, and Pennsylvania, and the federal government . . ."

71   For the remainder of the crisis, the governor would play second fiddle to the

72   mayor.

73   Giuliani proceeded to take questions about subjects great and small. . . .

74   He moved effortlessly from the smallest, most prosaic details to the broad

75   sweep of the calamity, playing military leader and chief psychologist. "The

76   number of casualities," he said, "will be more than any of us can bear ultimately."

Kirtzman is an author in a double sense. First, he is the author of Giuliani's biography. Second, from an ANT perspective, he is the *author* or narrator of specific actor-networks depicting the actants enrolled, practices adopted, and agency ascribed when the second tower collapses (Excerpt 7.1) and during Giuliani's first televised press conference (Excerpt 7.2). Kirtzman's own interests notwithstanding, he offers a first-person account in both instances.

GIULIANI MACROACTED AT A TIME OF GREAT PERSONAL RISK

Excerpt 7.1 opens as the second tower collapses and a "huge violent mushroom of smoke and dust . . . threatened to envelope us" (lines 7–9), and "The rest of us followed, worriedly looking back over our shoulders to see if the tornado was gaining on us" (lines 10–12). It is interesting to see Kirtzman's *actantial* use of language here, as he rather strikingly attributes agency to the cloud of smoke and dust that "threatened to envelope" and, like a tornado, might be "gaining on us." The experience of it forces the actors to align their interests to escape this scene of action or otherwise perish.

We then see *hybrids* and *networks* begin to form, first with Detective Huvane who treats Giuliani as precious cargo to be safeguarded (lines 9–10: "Huvane . . . threw his arm around the mayor and started running north with him") with the rest of the actors in tow. Specifically, John Huvane, the person, forms a hybrid with his (objectified) police role, prescribing protection for the mayor (Huvane-detective role) to which the mayor complies (mayor as object to be safeguarded-Giuliani). However, further role differentiation begins as Giuliani *translates* the interests of New York and its citizens by issuing three directives (Giuliani-text objects) to reporter Andrew Kirtzman to get the word out, through his television station, to stay away from Lower Manhattan (lines 18–22). Giuliani effectively enrolls Kirtzman in his network here as Kirtzman attempts to comply (text objects-Kirtzman), thereby donning his reporter role. It is at this time that Kirtzman is struck by the fact that Giuliani is *macroacting* here (that is, acting chiefly out of concern for the citizens of New York)—when Giuliani had every reason to remain the "wandering refugee" in pursuit of his own interests at least until they were out of harm's way (lines 23–26). This begins Kirtzman's attributions of extraordinariness accorded to Giuliani on 9/11.

Kirtzman then issues a directive, in the form of a request to Giuliani, to speak to the people of New York directly (lines 27–30). Giuliani accepts, thereby enrolling himself in Kirtzman's network, which involves hybrids between people and technology. For example, Kirtzman partners with his cell phone and the satellite technology that make it possible to reach his television station (lines 31–32). He then issues a directive (Kirtzman-text object) to "go live" with the mayor that, upon acceptance, enrolls the assignment desk editor and the technology that makes transfer to the control room possible (lines 32–34). With another directive by Kirtzman and subsequent acceptance by executive producer Sharon Raifer, now enrolled, the technology abruptly fails (lines 34–40). It is precisely this failure that causes ANT analysts like Callon and Latour (1981) to note how fragile networks can be because the actions of one or more actants (in this case, the technology) *betray* the interests of others (in this case, the mayor, reporter, and television station operators), effectively blocking the translation in the process. Suddenly, nonhuman objects had become not just full, but very visible actors (Cooren, 2001). How interesting, then, that by 2:35 that same afternoon, Giuliani holds his first televised press conference with nary a mention by Kirtzman of the technology that made it possible to do so (Excerpt 7.2).[23] The technology was functioning as it was supposed to and thus was effectively *blackboxed.*

At the press conference, Giuliani's first order of business was to reestablish for the public the durability of the networks of government so violated by the events of 9/11. After all, New York's City Hall was also in Lower Manhattan, just blocks away from the toppled towers. It was under a cloud of dust and debris, while Giuliani's prized new command center located at 7 World Trade Center fell victim to the destruction. The Police Academy became a command post after a Marriott Hotel, an initial site, became endangered. It was crucial that the mayor stage his first televised press conference with a narration of the actor-networks he had earlier activated behind the scenes. These included the Police Academy, an *architectural actant*; police and fire commissioners and representatives of all of the city's emergencies agencies, *macroactors all*; and Giuliani's executive assistant. However, *technological actants* like telephones were also necessary for contact with New York Governor Pataki and Washington, while GIS (geographic information systems) and related spatial technologies supplied highly detailed base maps needed to coordinate the response and recovery effort and guarantee critical infrastructure assurance in unaffected parts of the city (Cahan & Ball, 2002). Interestingly, Kirtzman's account of the press conference in 7.2 blackboxes most of these actants, save for the dramatic license supplied by the presence of the governor and the fire commissioner who, "looking ashen . . . slipped behind the mayor" on stage (lines 52–53). However, the earlier behind-the-scenes networking was the source of Giuliani's narrative ability to reconstruct this network for the public and his commitment to the rescue (lines 54–57), resolve to defend the city and country (57–61), request to citizens to remain calm (lines 62–63), and reassurance of the city's safety (lines 63–64). This combination of commissive and directive speech acts (text objects) would not have been possible had Giuliani not earlier enrolled, inter alia, the city, state, and federal government macroactors, a location in which to coordinate these activities, and various technologies into his network—all designed to produce the commitments necessary to keep the city running during this crisis.

IN HYBRID FASHION, GIULIANI ASSOCIATED
HIMSELF WITH THE CHARISMATIC CENTRAL AND SACRED

At the press conference, Kirtzman again reveals the source of attributions of extraordinariness accorded to Giuliani by comparing "the power of his words" to Governor Pataki's "platitudes" (lines 65–72). A deeper understanding of this comparison comes from Callon (1986a) and recent research into regulatory emotion. For Callon, a network is never situated within an 'outside' environment the way a system is. Instead, the environment *becomes* the organism vis-à-vis the network because, according to Hughes (1988), "The organizers of networks leave nothing outside, or to chance, that would affect the network" (p. 17). Playing off of Weick's (1979) terminology, the network doesn't so much possess the *requisite variety* found within the environment, as it embodies it. Thus, the network is never a mere assemblage of human and nonhuman elements. Instead, it represents their transformation through a network organizer's ability to translate their interests and features such that, through their interaction, the social and material components lose their categorical integrity (Law, 1987). The quality of that transformation is captured nicely in earlier references to the "seamless web" of heterogeneous allies that leaders as network organizers must weave.[24] Latour's (1986) overtures to Machiavelli are also relevant here because both authors' and network organizers' only task is to decide "which tie is weaker and which one stronger in a given encounter" (p. 33).

Kirtzman's account renders that Machiavellian comparison, although ironically on a surface level Giuliani and Pataki were saying similar kinds of things. Indeed, who could miss how "The gravity of the moment hung in the air" (lines 45–46)? What U.S. leader—at any level of government—would not desperately want to rise to this occasion, the worst attack on U.S. soil since Pearl Harbor? Yet, in Pataki's resorting to platitudes, Kirtzman (and most others) felt that there was something missing in his text objects, likely because clichés and tired expressions of gratitude are voiced as a matter of routine at most public gatherings.

By contrast, there was something more in Giuliani's remarks as he spoke "slowly and deliberately," befitting the enormity and seriousness associated with the massive loss of life (line 45); in his demonstrations of heartfelt compassion for the victims and their families and affirmations of almost unbearable pain (lines 47–51, 75–76); in his high-level disaster management skills intensively focused on rescue and recovery of the victims (lines 54–57, 62–64); and in his steadfast resolve that democracy will ultimately triumph over terrorism (lines 57–61). This 'something more' was not just the usual conduct of government in disaster management, but the recognition by Giuliani of the emotionally charged nature of the towers' collapse and the need to connect with New Yorkers immediately on an emotional level. In the words of Frost (2003), Giuliani became a "toxin handler" of the emotions that New Yorkers and the rest of America were feeling: shock, disbelief, horror, anger, grief, compassion, sadness, and loss.

While the leadership literature is no stranger to talk of emotions (Frost, 2003; George, 2000; Goleman, 1995), even for charismatics (Connelly, Gaddis, & Helton-Fauth, 2002; Emrich, Brower, Feldman, & Garland, 2001; Wasielewski, 1985), and even in the aftermath of 9/11 (Bligh, Kohles, & Meindl, 2004), there is little hard research on the *temporal quality* associated with the *mutual* regulation of emotion between charismatic leaders and followers.[25] For example, through the emotional pitch and tone in this televised press conference, Giuliani put into words the shock and disbelief that New York and the rest of America were feeling: "Today is obviously one of the most difficult days in the history of the city and the country. . . . The tragedy that we're all undergoing right now is something we've had nightmares about—probably thought wouldn't happen" (lines 47–49). However, registering this disbelief comes amid discharging his disaster management duties. Many commentators, including Kirtzman (lines 75–76), suggested that Giuliani effortlessly alternated between "military leader," as the chief strategist in directing the rescue, detailing subway reroutings, chronicling the body count, and so on, to "chief psychologist" in dealing with a traumatized populace.

Nowhere was the latter more evident than in the days immediately following 9/11. Critically, Giuliani recognized how shock gives way to grief as the dead are buried. He made it his business to attend the private funerals of some 200 fallen firefighters and other rescue workers. Unannounced to the press, Giuliani was seen (and photographed) standing at attention with rows of uniformed officers as caskets were loaded onto and unloaded from fire trucks cum hearses for church services amid tolling bells. He was seen embracing grief-stricken families with unabashed gestural displays, delivering eulogies of heroism and hope at funeral masses, and speaking to the children of the fallen as they clutched their fathers' helmets in their hands. Kirtzman depicts Giuliani's public face and emotional tone as increasingly one of firm resolve, hope for the future, and tolerance for Arab Americans, whom he feared might be subject to reprisal due to the anger that many Americans felt.

Giuliani's own authoring and networking progressively embodied the emotions of the moment: first shock and disbelief, then public and private grief, followed by a growing resolve.[26] In a very human way, he affirmed what the public was feeling as New Yorkers and Americans. At every turn, Giuliani also asked that they see themselves as a part of something larger, that is, a democratic society whose "rule of law . . . will ultimately prevail" (lines 57–61). It is within this latter context that Giuliani rendered the "barbaric terrorists" and the massive loss of life meaningful for most Americans. Who else but enemies to a capitalist free society and American values would strike such a symbolic blow that the towers represented? Shils (1965) observes that it is exactly these tie-ins to larger orders that "calm the mind" and "gratify by putting the individual into the 'right relationship' to what is important," thus satisfying a need for order through sensemaking (p. 204). As a result, that which is centrally connected or sacred to these larger orders becomes the object of charismatic attributions, and so it was with the adulation surrounding Giuliani as the public face of New York and American democratic values.

However, Shils would also likely assert the disposition to attribute charisma to objectifications like the funeral rites accorded to fallen heroes where the larger orders of 'God and country' converge. Indeed, few rituals are more sacred to either, and yet it is ANT with its associations between humans and non-humans that best explains the operation of this charismatic component and why pictures of Giuliani at these funerals are so very powerful. Mayor Giuliani could have restricted himself to less emotion-ridden public gatherings such as press conferences, public memorials, and behind-the-scenes action—much as Pataki did as governor. Instead, Giuliani networked with emotion-laden people and objects—funeral rites, the 'fallen' and their remains, caskets covered by the American flag, fire trucks as hearses, uniformed officers as pallbearers, churches with bells tolling, children clutching their fathers' helmets, and so forth. When not attending funerals, Giuliani was repeatedly seen at the site of the towers' collapse; Ground Zero had become hallowed ground, and he was its holy overseer.

Giuliani thus repeatedly associated himself with the charismatic central and sacred, which was about the business of profound grieving. Is it any wonder that *New York Times* columnist Bob Herbert observed, "He moves about the stricken city like a god. . . . People wanted to be in his presence" (p. 305)?

GIULIANI'S AUTHORING AND NETWORKING CONSTRUCTED AN EMOTIONAL SCAFFOLDING

Neither Kirtzman's (2001) analysis nor that of others affords us the ability to understand all of the specific networking and authoring in which Giuliani engaged; only an ethnography could provide such detail. However, what is available strongly suggests that Giuliani constructed what Tronick and colleagues (1998) calls *emotional scaffolding*.[27] Gleaned from the observations of mother–infant interactions and extrapolated to therapeutic relationships, emotional scaffolding occurs when one member of a relationship, such as a caregiver or therapist, provides emotional support to another that also helps to regulate or channel such emotion. Importantly, this scaffolding is premised on the mutual regulation of emotion over time. Applied to leadership, it in no way suggests that a leader like Giuliani carried the weight of the world on his shoulders during the events of 9/11 or that he in any way orchestrated the emotions of the moment; such interpretations give way to individualism. It is to suggest that when New Yorkers felt shock and disbelief, he affirmed their shock and disbelief—but also offered them reassurance. When they grieved their loss, he grieved right along with them—but each time asked that their loss be seen as fulfilling a higher purpose. When New Yorkers became angry and confused, he understood—but showed resolve and restraint toward those who would be unfairly charged. It was a dance of the dialectic that he would lead and be led simultaneously. Each step of the way, his authoring and networking embodied the emotions of the moment, but offered the kind of regulatory support that would best promote New York's healing. This emotional scaffolding was the 'something more' that differentiated Giuliani from Pataki.[28]

It is through Kirtzman's account, then, that we see how both Giuliani and Pataki are themselves authors who chose to construct their stories of 9/11 in very different ways. This is because their stories were as much about their leadership as about the towers' collapse; it could not be otherwise. Does the ability to author depend on the networks one mobilizes and in which one participates? Even though vicarious experience can certainly be the basis for authoring, it would seem that the heightened sensitivity to the environment, risk taking, and unconventional methods accorded to charismatic leaders (Conger & Kanungo, 1987) suggest an intimate knowledge of the environment (and the constraints and opportunities it affords) that only network organizers/participants could discern. Such knowledge includes the distributed nature of charisma and its imputation to institutions, collectivities, social roles, rituals, or cultural objects (Shils, 1958, 1965), a fact that Giuliani seemed to appreciate more than Pataki. Giuliani would many times tell the poignant story of his executive assistant, who worked tirelessly with him even in the early hours of the disaster although her firefighter husband had been lost. That she later found hope and consolation in discovering that she was pregnant would symbolize for Giuliani and his audiences that from the ashes, rebirth was possible.

GIULIANI'S CHARISMA BENEFITED
ENORMOUSLY FROM IMMEDIATE SOCIAL SHAPING

ANT's concern for authoring alerts us once again to the social and constructed nature of leadership vis-à-vis the attributions of others. Whether it is the work of Kirtzman (2001), other 9/11 writers (Bligh et al., 2004; Cahan & Ball, 2002; Gibbs, 2001; Traub, 2001), or this author, authoring can generate persuasive interpretations of leaders and their messages. In writing about the impact of Martin Luther King as a powerhouse rhetor, Grint (2000) observes that "speeches are the product not of gifted individuals, but of an entire corpus of supporters, human and nonhuman, who between them render oppositional accounts of the speech illegitimate or at least less legitimate than their own version" (p. 379). The media must be counted among them; their dramatized event narratives play a major role in the construction of celebrity, designed to garner positive emotional responses from the public (Rindova, Pollock, & Hayward, 2006). Like King, the social shaping of Giuliani into hero, charismatic leader, and celebrity was almost immediate. Just two days after the crisis, the print media led with stories of Giuliani's strength as a leader (Kirtzman, 2001). The *New York Post* deemed him "A Mayor for a Crisis," while the *New York Times* followed with "Mayor of the Moment." This was quickly followed by national media interviews with the likes of Barbara Walters, Tom Brokaw, Peter Jennings, and Larry King, where he was frequently introduced as "America's Mayor." More in-depth analyses like biographies, "Person of the Year" profiles, and congressional investigations would follow. Where did Giuliani's behavior stop and where did the social begin? As Grint (2000) so astutely observes, there is no separate section marked 'social shaping'; it is wrought throughout.

To summarize, the lessons of Giuliani's 9/11 leadership suggest an attribution of charisma based on his macroacting at a time of crisis and great personal risk; associating himself in hybrid fashion with the charismatic central and sacred; deploying a continuous networking strategy that constructed an emotional scaffolding, which dialectically affirmed devastating emotions while deftly regulating them to promote future healing; and the social shaping that was almost immediate, proclaiming him one of the heroes of 9/11.

Is this a recipe for charismatic leadership generally? No, because ANT always restricts itself to the character of the network under study and the means by which localized, contingent, and practical human and nonhuman associations are formed. Is this a recipe for charismatic leadership for Giuliani? Again, no, because prior to 9/11 Giuliani was hardly considered a charismatic leader, and an ANT analysis makes no claims as to his future leadership, in crisis or otherwise. In these ways, ANT is consistent with the discursive approaches in this book, which draw from theoretical frames that are not specifically about leadership per se, unlike the mainstream leadership literature.

It is also noteworthy that the case of Giuliani's 9/11 leadership reflects the metaphor of war that currently runs through ANT. As Michael (1996) suggests, "certainly, it often seems as if these accounts are structured by magnificent victories and disastrous defeats . . . a dramatic world of meteoric rises and tragic failures" (p. 63). For this reason, ANT may be particularly well suited for the study of charismatic leaders whose career trajectories may be so described.[29] With ANT's emphasis on nonhuman objects and hybrids with human subjects, charisma also appears as a much less elusive phenomenon in a dramatic rise and fall. Charismatic 'presence' can now be seen to be textual, scenic, technological, cultural, and embodied, ultimately networked and distributed into human and nonhuman hybrid forms. Most importantly, charisma remains an effect, never a cause. As such, it is an attributional phenomenon very much akin to Latour's (1986) view of power as "a *composition* made by many people . . . and *attributed* to one of them" (p. 265, emphasis original).[30] Charisma, like power, is that which is to be explained by the mobilized.

However, the Montreal school's work is also instructive here because they call our attention to the story structure of a Greimasian narrative, which hinges on a breach—a tear in the fabric of social existence that sources problematization and around which activity organizes to achieve a repair. Greimas (1987, 1988) argues that a narrative logic has a certain economy to it in the sense that any story is really the intersection of two conflicting paths around a contested object of value. One path is that of a protagonist or socially mandated actant. While charisma is embodied in a protagonist, the magnitude of his or her greatness is in direct proportion to the stature of an antagonist and the alternative path chosen. When, on September 11, 2001, the actions of Osama bin Laden and his terrorist allies took on bold, cataclysmic proportions, it set the stage for a great protagonist to emerge. Giuliani did not disappoint because he understood more than most that a hero must incarnate the emotion-laden hearts and minds of the people that he is mobilizing.

However, recall again the Montreal scholars' emphasis on the reflexive and recursive nature of human communication and the capacity of humans, unlike nonhumans, to understand and know what they are doing when they are doing it (J. R. Taylor, personal communication, May 2005). As Gilbert and Mulkay (1984) also observe, "Actors continually reinterpret given actions as their biography unfolds and as changing circumstances lead them to fit these activities into new social configurations" (p. 9). Indeed, this reflexivity not only explains Giuliani's 9/11 leadership that took him into the stratosphere of popularity, but also his rocky return to earth post 9/11 in a clumsy, failed attempt to extend his term of office as mayor, quite reminiscent of the "old Rudy" (Kirtzman, 2001). Perhaps he too had been influenced by others' social shaping of him as a bona fide hero (Hayward, Rindova, & Pollock, 2004).

How useful is ANT for the study of leadership that is not charismatic or transformational? This is a more difficult question to answer, especially when leadership networks involve ambiguous associations, multiple identities, and ambivalent discourse. Although analysts such as Singleton and Michael (1993) offer a modest elaboration of ANT in this regard, the means by which problems get defined (around which networks organize) such as "un-black-boxing, dis-enrolling, marginalization, extrication, ambivalence and multiplication," remain unsatisfactory without an articulated theory of discourse and communication (p. 228). This is a problem that runs throughout ANT, which the Montreal scholars have tried valiantly to correct with their attention to speech acts, Greimas's universal narrative template, and more recent forays into conversation analysis. Inattention to discursive matters results in critiques such as the one levied by Grint and Woolgar (1997):

> [I]t is not always clear where the boundaries of a network lie, nor which account of the network is to be taken as definitive. The spirit of actor-network theory suggests that competing accounts of the network are part of the process of network formation, yet the analyst's story seems to depend on a description of the actual network, as if this was objectively available to observers at the scene. (p. 30)

If, as Singleton and Michael (1993) suggest, there is an uneasy relationship between ANT and social constructionism, the relative inattention to discursive matters, including the possibility of a latent representational view of language and meaning, may be the greater sticking point than the realist or agency debates over the materiality of objects. ANT analysts like Latour, Michael, and others seem wary of discursive issues lest they give analytic priority to social interaction while diminishing nonhuman kinds of interaction. However, they must first explain how analysis and authoring can be conducted outside of them.

A Backward Glance—Final Thoughts

In this chapter, the following points have been made:

- Despite decades of research, charismatic leadership remains an elusive concept.
- When actor-network theory is applied to the study of charismatic leadership, charisma becomes the product of a distributed actor-network of human and nonhuman entities. However, Shils earlier proposed a similar argument by

suggesting that charisma adheres to the central and sacred routines associated with any massive organization of authority.

- The materialist critique of organizational discourse analysis suggests that the material does not collapse into discourse (relativism), and organizations do not collapse into discourse (discoursism). Materialist concerns include the *institutional* in the form of social or economic structures or *material objects* like guns, radios, and police cars.
- ANT considers both human and nonhuman agency. Both are types of *actants* that enter into associations with one another, such that a mediation or link forms between human subjects and nonhuman objects, transforming both in the process.
- In ANT, action is distributed or networked in a string of *hybrid* associations between human subjects and nonhuman objects. Thus, action is a property of the associated networked entities, not the subject alone.
- When objects function as they are supposed to, we pay them scant attention by *blackboxing* them. Yet, blackboxing is a reversible process when malfunctioning objects must be repaired or substituted.
- *Translation* occurs when the interests of one actant are taken up by another such that actor networks act as a unit or designate a spokesperson. Networks are fragile because the behavior of one or more actants may *betray* the interests of another, thus blocking the translation.
- Whereas network organizers create networks, authors narrate them by depicting the actors enrolled, the practices adopted, and the agency ascribed.
- The Montreal school focuses on the organization properties of discourse and communication as the building blocks of organizations. They are not an offshoot of ANT per se, but they make great use of it.
  - o They use ANT to flesh out the organizational implications of Greimas's narrative theory, which stipulates that all goal-directed action is organized by a basic schema.
  - o They spotlight the organizational relevance of Latour's work, noting that objects come with built-in properties or scripts inscribed with the traces of past organizing.
  - o They move past Latour's reticence to deal with language issues by arguing that our language carries the traces of past organizing as much as objects do. They see discursive objects in the performative aspects of language, otherwise known as *speech acts*. Discursive objects become *text objects* capable of hybridity and networking with human subjects.
- ANT and the Montreal school apply well to leadership study. For example, the freedom of a leader is only relative to the number of nonhuman resources the leader has enrolled in his or her cause.
- Rudolph Giuliani's actions during 9/11 exemplify charismatic leadership based on his macroacting at a time of crisis, hybrids formed with charismatic objects, networking and authoring that embodied the emotions of the moment, and social shaping that proclaimed him one of the heroes of 9/11.

The work of the Montreal school around ANT represents a significant attempt to consider the ways in which the material aspects of organizational life mediate social interaction. Such an approach resists the individualism bias in the mainstream leadership literature and points the way toward more distributed action beyond leader and led to include nonhumans as well. Although this chapter restricted itself to charismatic leadership, there is enormous potential here to study leadership and the heterogeneous engineering of its actors. The ever-evolving technological transformation of the workplace can be recast as the ever-evolving hybridization of leadership actants as various technologies mesh with their human users. As Grint (1997) has observed, "If the word 'leader' means to move in a new direction, then . . . don't trace the leader, don't even trace the followers; trace the mobilization" (p. 17).

NOTES

1. Credit for this chapter title must be given to Holstein and Gubrium (2000), although theirs is not an actor-network theory approach.

2. Several reviews of the leadership literature make this point (Bryman, 1992, 1996; Fairhurst, 2001; House & Aditya, 1997).

3. House and Aditya (1997) use the term "neo-charisma" to refer to the genre of charismatic and transformational theories of leadership. Frequently, *leaders* differ from *managers* in this genre because leaders possess organizational visions, unlike managers (Hickman, 1990; Kotter, 1990; Zaleznik, 1977). While managers are technical and process oriented, leaders are capable of sweeping organizational transformation (Bennis & Nanus, 1985; Kotter, 1990; Kouzes & Posner, 1995). Using Weber's (1968) terminology, managers operate from rational-legal authority, while leaders operate from the charismatic. As such, leaders understand their role as coconstructors of reality and managers of meanings, starting with a powerful vision that energizes, aligns, and mobilizes an organization's culture and its followers. Of course, vision and the ability to articulate it hinges on a clear mission and a set of core values.

4. Several articles discuss these differences (Avolio & Yammarino, 2002; Bryman, 1992; Yukl, 1999).

5. Manipulative behaviors include such things as misinterpreting events or inciting incidents to create the appearance of a crisis; exaggerating the leader's positive achievements and taking undue credit for others' work; using deference rituals and status symbols; and creating barriers to isolate members from contacts with outsiders (Yukl, 1999, p. 296).

6. Beyer (1999) has observed that, in contrast to the psychological emphasis on traits and behaviors of leaders, as measured by followers reports of same, "Sociologists . . . see charisma as a social structure that emerges from complex interactions of multiple factors that cannot be separated neatly into causes, moderators, and effects" (p. 309). ANT is certainly consistent with this sociological tradition.

7. Such debate can be found in a number of recent publications (Astley, 1985; Chia, 2000; Deetz, 1992; Foucault, 1972, 1980, 1995; Gergen, 2001; Gioia, 2003; Hacking, 1999; Parker, 1998; Pearce, 1995; Potter, 1996; Reed, 2000, 2001, 2004; Shotter, 1993; Tsoukas, 2000).

8. In one fashion or another, several discourse scholars treat organizations as discursive constructions (Boden, 1994; Deetz, 1992; Fairhurst & Putnam, 2004; Mumby & Clair, 1997; J. R. Taylor & Cooren, 1997).

9. Yet, even as this stance positions agency amid sociocultural and historical constraints, it is not without its own weaknesses. As Alvesson and Kärreman (2000b) argue, concern for the "discursive macro order" can lead analysts to neglect the details of language in use and thus downplay the formative power of discourse (p. 1145). Also, see Phillips and Jørgenson (2002) for a critique of Fairclough (1995).

10. For example, the script for a car usually focuses on it as a mode of transportation; however, it certainly has other affordances such as a weapon, a shield, or even a domicile.

11. It is unclear at what point Conway begins to fight back once she is shot. Thus, the presumption here is that the assailant treats Conway's body as an object to be moved.

12. For example, to drive a car that is already turned on, one must shift into the right gear, put a foot to the gas pedal, apply pressure, steer the car, and so forth.

13. Callon (1986b) posits four moments in the general process of *translation* including *problematization,* which occurs when a network organizer identifies a problem or obstacle in which a set of actants is needed to help solve it; *interessement,* which involves all of the actions of a network organizer to impose and stabilize the identity of the actants; *enrolment,* which is achieved if interessement is successful; and finally, *representation,* which occurs in the mobilization of allies to act as a unit or designate a spokesperson.

14. There is much to recommend in the voluminous work of the Montreal school (Cooren, 1999, 2001, in press; Cooren & Fairhurst, 2004, in press; Cooren & Taylor, 1997, 1998; Cooren, Taylor, & Van Every, 2006; Robichaud, 2003; J. R. Taylor & Cooren, 1997; J. R. Taylor & Robichaud, 2006; J. R. Taylor & Van Every, 2000).

15. See the work of Cooren and Taylor (Cooren, 2001; Cooren & Taylor, 1997; J. R. Taylor & Cooren, 1997) for a discussion of speech acts and intentionality.

16. It is the mutual orientation of 'A' and 'B' to an object 'X' that Taylor argues is the most basic unit of organizational communication. The presence of an 'X' takes the exchange from merely interactional to transactional, and hence *organizational* communication (J. R. Taylor, 2006).

17. The Montreal scholars draw from Greimas (1987) certainly, but also Giddens (1979, 1984) and Weick (1979).

18. See Fairhurst and Putnam (2004) for a comparison of entitative, becoming, and grounded-in-action views of the organization.

19. ANT adopts an analytic impartiality as to whatever actors are involved in a controversy. For this reason, Latour (1988) condemns historians who praise leaders for their accomplishments and denounces them for their methods. The choices of strategies or actions by leaders is neither inherently virtuous nor evil; they are simply alternative approaches for achieving a particular goal.

20. However, the enrollment process should be understood as an "arrangement of assent," which captures Latour's (1986) view of power. Through persuasion or other means, enrollees give up their consent to leader-enrollers who must weave a "seamless web" of heterogeneous allies to be successful (Hughes, 1988; Law, 1987). Indeed, leaders never stop weaving because, "what he weaves together is sometimes soft, sometimes hard, sometimes human, sometimes nonhuman. His only concern is to decide which tie is weaker and which one stronger in a given encounter" (Latour, 1986, p. 33). The goal of the seamless web is a durable actor-network. Specifically, there should be a number of narrative schemas or subroutines that can be blackboxed, made invisible and unproblematic. This is because only their input and output count, regardless of their

history, controversy, complexity, or size of the networks that hold them in place (Latour, 1987). In organizations, blackboxing is facilitated by the fact that what leader-enrollers mobilize is often textual, with the translation of organizational life into numbers, figures, and graphs in logs, charts, diagrams, models, surveys, and so on. These textual agents possess great resiliency, always ready for hybridization with other interests whose paths they may cross (Cooren, 2001, 2004; Taylor & Van Every, 2000).

21.   However, this is an interesting point at which to ask whether or not ANT is just so much more redescription of extant sociological theory. Michael (1996) argues that a key distinguishing feature of ANT is the role played by heterogeneous entities (nonhumans and humans) in stabilizing the relationships that make up institutions and groups and being indifferent toward the source(s) of agency of such hybrids.

22.   See Gronn (2005) for a discussion of the merits of biographical versus auto-biographical data for the study of leadership.

23.   Giuliani's televised press conference was actually his second contact with New Yorkers that day. His first contact was at 10:54 AM by telephone to two television news anchors; however, Kirtzman (2001) depicts both contacts in quite similar terms.

24.   We could also borrow a theater metaphor to depict 'seamlessness' by noting that the director's hand is never visible; that which is staged does not appear so. I am indebted to Bill Jennings for making this observation.

25.   A chapter by Connelly et al. (2002) comes closest. Their chapter hypothesizes specific emotions to be targeted by transformational and charismatic leaders (socialized and personalized) at different points in the strategic visioning process. However, in varying degrees the leaders come off as orchestrating the emotion of followers. There is little recognition of the leaders' emotions and complex interactions in which they take their emotional cues from followers as much as they attempt to channel followers' emotions. The psychological literature on emotion is somewhat more forthcoming on this point (Keltner & Haidt, 1999; Keltner & Kring, 1998), as are conceptual treatments of affect in the workplace (Brief & Weiss, 2002; Rafaeli & Sutton, 1987).

26.   The flow of emotions should not be interpreted as strictly linear.

27.   Studying the mutually regulated behavior of mothers and infants on video-tape, Tronick and colleagues (1998) observed caregivers giving support or "scaffolding" to infants regarding the regulation of their emotions that enables them to achieve a more complex level of brain organization. Moreover, they also suggest that the force for real change in therapy generally stems from the mutual regulation of emotion and the expanded states of consciousness that therapist and client produce.

28.   An argument was made that the attributions of leadership accorded to George W. Bush in the days following 9/11 hinged on how he dealt with the emotions of the American public (Bligh et al., 2004).

29.   Beyer (1999) also observed that the metaphors used to describe senior business leaders in the U.S. business press are frequently war-like.

30.   I am greatly indebted to James Taylor for drawing my attention to this quote and the ensuing relevance of Greimas's story structure to this discussion.

8

Praxis and More Conversation

A s I contemplated ending this book, two different directions for future work became increasingly clear to me. The first involves the practical implications of discursive leadership. Generally speaking, leadership psychologists do a much better job of drawing out these implications than discursive leadership scholars to date.[1] However, because discourse analysts open up the processes of social construction, they can play a key role in helping leadership actors understand how they create the realities to which they must then respond. Thus, the first half of this chapter examines the implications of discursive leadership for praxis.

Regarding the rest of the chapter, what I have written thus far is one turn in what I hope will be an ongoing conversation with leadership psychologists. To further this conversation, I invited several leadership psychologists and discourse scholars to respond to the contents of Chapter 1 and any other chapters that they wished to read. Each provides his or her own unique insights on the relationship between discursive leadership and leadership psychology to provide a fitting conclusion for this book.

Discursive Leadership and Praxis

From Aristotle we learned of the importance of *praxis,* or the process of putting theoretical knowledge into practice. Such an orientation is critical for discursive leadership because of the role played by discourse/Discourse in the social construction of meaning. When focusing on a meaning-centered model of communication, the implications for practice are different from those based on a transmissional model. As Barge and Oliver (2003) observe

> Historically, managerial communication skills have been associated with
> encoding and decoding skills—a model of communication that is based on
> an approach to language in which it is assumed that meaning is fixed and that

> the point of communication is to clearly convey one's point to another. . . .
> Viewing conversation as sites where various (D)iscourses intersect and mean-
> ing is continually unfolding requires managers to develop the ability to pick
> up the flow of conversation and to develop a sensibility for when and where
> to shape the conversation in new directions. (p. 138)

To discern conversational flow and where best to intervene depends upon an understanding of the constructed nature of the conversation—and that scaffolding is exactly what the outcomes of discourse analyses can impart.

For example, where are the 'teaching moments' (Tichy, 1997) in learning about the sequencing and temporal forms of interaction? In Chapter 2, Sanders (2006) called our attention to "a certain artfulness in the way speakers sequen-tially place and phrase what they say for the sake of being responsive to what has gone before, and at the same time anticipatory of fostering desired conse-quences for the ensuing interaction and for their presentation of self" (p. 169). Putting aside whether one person's 'artfulness' is another's 'manipulation' for the time being,[2] one's interactional competence rests partly on the ability to produce and manage constraints in successive turns at talk so as to shape what can be meaningfully said in the ensuing dialogue (Sanders, 1995, 2006).

We saw an excellent example of this kind of competence in Chapter 3's Excerpt 3.4 when Jack Levine, the vice president of Steinberg's, challenged his boss, Mr. Sam, through a series of rather pointed questions on whether Mr. Sam was (acting like) a manager or company president. While Levine was setting the problem of the kind of company leader Mr. Sam was going to be, he introduced certain constraints around organizational structure that the only right solution—acting presidential—could satisfy. Those constraints did not include micromanaging, which is putatively what a lowly manager would do. Thus Levine registered a complaint against Mr. Sam using a question–answer format to contrast 'manager' with 'company president' roles and then prefig-ured Mr. Sam's answer as the latter because of the constraints he had earlier associated with each role.

In examples such as these, Levine's problem setting easily becomes open to critique in a learning environment. An inquirer can ask, How was the problem set through the constraints introduced to prefigure a particular solution? What are the ethics guiding this kind of problem setting over possible others? How might a shift or removal of a constraint set reconfigure problem setting and pre-ferred solutions? How is reason and rationality usurped by persuasion through the introduction of constraint sets? Schön (1983) told us that, in problem setting, "we select what we will treat as the 'things' of the situation, we set the boundaries of our attention to it, and we impose upon it a coherence which allows us to say what is wrong and in what directions the situation needs to be changed" (p. 40). The notion of a *constraint set* gives a discernable form and function to the 'things,' 'boundaries,' and 'coherence' in problem setting to which Schön refers.

Yet another teachable linguistic device occurs with Chapter 3's membership categories and Hacking's (1999) notion of an *interactive kind*. What he suggests with this terminology is that actors experience themselves in the world as being persons of various kinds. They act "under descriptions," which is to say categories and their characterizations (p. 3). One of the ways in which leadership actors can interact with a category is by rejecting it, as demonstrated in Cooperrider, Barrett and Srivastva's (1995) study of appreciative inquiry at the Cleveland Clinic. The Cleveland Clinic had been involved in a shared governance model and a group practice democracy when the authors were invited in to strengthen this practice. One author trained the medical division in Vroom's well-known participative decision-making model, which outlines a number of decision rules regarding when subordinates should be brought into the decision making. However, the author/trainer was shocked when a young physician said the following to him:

8.1a 'Subordinate' Versus 'Partner'

1 You know this is all bullshit don't you! . . . I bet if you counted in both

2 the article and your lecture the number of times the word subordinate

3 was used, it would be close to fifty times. . . . The problem is that these

4 ideas may be all right for the business world, but they won't do here . . .

5 we are a partnership of physicians. I'm not a subordinate. I'm not just

6 an employee here. I resent what your training is trying to do to us. (p. 185)

Note the categories 'subordinate' and 'employee' and the physicality of the word count of 'subordinate' to which the physician reacts. The author/trainer made sense of this remark by unpacking the matrix in which the category 'subordinates' likely resides for this physician:

8.1b 'Subordinate' in Its Matrix

7 [T]he word subordinates was not just some neutral descriptive

8 term. There is no such thing as a subordinate out there somewhere

9 in reality that can be pointed to and objectively described. The

10 word subordinate is virtually nothing . . . until it is seen as a key

11 link in a broader theory of bureaucracy, a theory that says that

12 organizations work and work best when there is a hierarchy of

13 offices, and a clear chain-of-command. In such a system, orders

14   are to be issued by those above and those below have the duty

15   to carry them out . . . What is so memorable, then, was the author's

16   virtual lack of awareness that he, himself, had time and again

17   helped to support and reproduce, in interaction with others, a

18   powerful bureaucratic theory and ideology . . . 'I'm not a

19   subordinate,' he (the physician) said, 'I'm a partner.'

The interactive kind, the category 'subordinate,' influenced the young physician to outright reject it (line 1: "You know this is all bullshit don't you!") because, unlike the category 'partner,' it lacked the egalitarianism in the group practice democracy that was Cleveland Clinic's culture at the time. Hacking (1999) terms this a *looping effect* because what is known about people of a kind (in this case, 'subordinates') becomes "false because people of that kind have changed in virtue of how they have been classified, what they believe about themselves, or because of how they have been treated as so classified" (p. 104). Thus, new knowledge changes the behavior of the classified that, in turn, loops back to force changes in the original classifications. The author/trainer manifests this looping effect as he unearths the matrix in which 'subordinate' is located and confronts his own blanket use of this term—now with the awareness of the "powerful bureaucratic theory and ideology" (line 18) he unwittingly perpetuated while teaching a democratic form of decision making. Interactive kinds and looping effects suggest many opportunities to develop leadership actors' reflexivity around the ways in which they deploy categories.

From Chapter 4, Foucault's view of Discourse and discipline may at first seem too abstract to use in a training environment. However, consider once again Bennis and Thomas's (2002) *Geeks & Geezers: How Era, Values, and Defining Moments Shape Leaders,* a book written for practicing managers. They define *era* as shared history and culture and "a specific arena in which to act" (p. 10)—not far off the mark from Foucault. As discussed in earlier chapters, *geeks* are products of the era of the Internet and the end of the Cold War, while *geezers* are products of the Depression and World War II era. Bennis and Thomas contrast geeks and geezers in a host of ways, including how leaders from these two eras made sense of the world and formed their organizations.

If the shaping influences of a generational divide can be discussed and understood in the business press, so too can Foucault's notion of *disciplinary power* be utilized in a training environment. It may even strike an intuitive chord. As Whyte's (1956) classic portrayal of *The Organization Man* demonstrates, there are myriad ways in which organizational actors "have left home, spiritually as well as physically, to take the vows of organization life" (p. 3). Indeed, how can actors not be aware of the sacrifices they have made for their careers—long work hours, limited social life, time spent away from family, unhealthy lifestyles, or other means by which they fulfill their vows?

Ironically, leadership actors are perhaps most aware of their own self-discipline during what Bennis and Thomas (2002) call *crucibles*. A crucible is a defining, life-changing moment for leaders that is "both opportunity and a test . . . that unleashes ability, forces crucial choices, and sharpens focus . . . [and is] seen by the individual as a turning point" (p. 16). Crucibles can be as varied as experiencing a tragedy, going to war, going to prison, being mentored, serving an apprenticeship, mastering a martial art, climbing a mountain, losing an election, and so on. Sometimes the crucibles that set leaders apart revolve around a heightened reflexivity regarding one or more management Discourses that now no longer feels right. John Delorean's time at General Motors (GM) comes to mind here as he famously resisted the deference to authority that was a big part of GM's culture at the time, and later struck out on his own (Martin & Siehl, 1983). However, reflexivity also entails a perceived space of action that becomes apparent when considering other Discourses through which chosen actions can, in retrospect, be seen as bold, leader-making moves.

From Chapter 5, both *discursive template* and *interpretative repertoire* are useful concepts to explore during times of organizational change. Recall that a discursive template is the language and grammar of an organizational change initiative, typically including both *god* and *devil* terms (Burke, 1962). A repertoire is what actors appropriate for their own use. As training initiatives seek to communicate the discursive template to organizational members, an inquirer can ask or observe how faithful they have been to the spirit of the template and the framing devices they are using (or failing to use) to communicate it (Fairhurst, 1993). However, key points to consider go well beyond issues of fidelity and framing to include reflexivity around the source(s) of infidelity when appropriations stray. For example, Fairhurst and Sarr (1996) reported an ironic appropriation of Deming's "Drive out fear" slogan by the workforce of a U.S.-based manufacturing firm, whose orientations toward authority were deemed excessive by TQM standards. When "Drive out fear" became "Drive out fear, and if you can't we'll find someone who will!" the old culture reared its ugly head, albeit in amusing fashion. Nevertheless, such occurrences can provide further opportunity for reflection, discussion, criticism, and even dissent associated with competing values in an organization's culture.

Narrative, from Chapter 6, has become a popular subject in the leadership training and development literature (Barge, 2004; Conger, 1991; Gargiulo, 2005). However, the role of narrative in LMX, particularly medium quality LMXs, deserves special attention in a development context. In early LMX research, Graen, Novak, and Sommerkamp's (1982) experimental work suggested that leaders could be trained to enroll more medium quality LMX members into high quality relationships if leaders' awareness of their discretionary resources could be expanded. It is a worthy goal, no doubt, but only a partial fix if the training focuses solely on leaders. The *stories told* by medium quality LMX members and the cultural scripts of *stories lived* would seem to be instrumental to knowing how to intervene with one or both parties. The medium quality LMX script involving a member with greater technical expertise than the leader is a case in point; the status inconsistency between leader and member must be carefully navigated to ensure organizational effectiveness and relational bonding.

Finally, perhaps the most interesting implication for practice lies with Chapter 7's emphasis on material mediations. Recalling Grint's (1997) enjoinder, "If the word 'leader' means to move in a new direction, then . . . don't trace the leader, don't even trace the followers; trace the mobilization" (p. 17), we should look for the ways in which leadership actors form *hybrids* and *networks* with other human and nonhuman entities. A classic demonstration of the utility of this approach surfaced in New Orleans after Hurricane Katrina hit in 2005. As 12-foot high water surged into the city from levee breaks, technology failures like broken generators, downed cell phone towers, and unusable land lines forced city leaders out of their command center and into the Hyatt Hotel (Rhoads, 2005). In the hotel, city leaders were forced into "human chains of communication," according to George Meffert, the city's chief technology officer (Rhoads, 2005). They had to evacuate their families, break into an Office Depot to get computer equipment, and stave off the advances of some 200 gang members intent on raiding the hotel for food, water, and power. There was no communication with the outside world for two days until emergency power was returned to the hotel and a member of Mr. Meffert's technology team remembered that he had recently set up an Internet phone account. He found a working socket in a conference room and linked his laptop to the Internet connection.

This incident and several others constituted city leaders' attempts to cope with the enormity of this disaster. However, after-incident reviews could be greatly informed by the language and concepts of actor-network theory. For example, consider the *macroactors* from state and federal government organizations, who more often than not *betrayed* the networks in which they were enrolled. How might these betrayals have been reversed through networked action? Development efforts should also involve getting leadership actors to think of themselves not as individuals, but as *hybrids* and *networks* so they can reflect critically upon *how* they interfaced with humans and nonhumans given the constraints and enablements such partnering produced. Such an analysis of *heterogeneous engineering* would highlight leadership actors' abilities (or lack thereof) to improvise under difficult conditions and impart lessons learned for future crisis management.

Looking back over the pragmatic implications of these chapters, we can see a *practical discursive grammar* emerging with terms like constraint sets and problem setting; categories, interactive kinds, and looping effects; Discourse(s), era, discipline, and crucibles; discursive templates and linguistic repertoires; stories lived and stories told; and networks, betrayals, hybrids, and heterogeneous engineering. Although the language may need tweaking, the concepts appear translatable to leadership actors in need of greater reflexivity around their identities, relationships, and organizations as the examples provided suggest.

However, any emerging discursive grammar requires a *grammar of practice*, and at least three come to mind: practical theory, dialogue, and appreciative inquiry. All are natural partners for a practical discursive grammar because they too depend on opening up the processes of social construction, but with heightened ethical concerns. For example, in *grounded practical theory*, communication's moral and technical aspects are jointly considered within a critical inquiry that involves reflexive, dialectical movement between theory and practice (Barge & Craig, in press; Craig, 1989).[3] According to Craig and Tracy (1995), once a problematic situation is identified, grounded practical theory attempts to normatively reconstruct key situated practices to stimulate further reflection and future use of these practices. One can well imagine that in a leadership context, a rational reconstruction of key practices—such as problem and constraint setting in decision-making situations, interactive kinds and looping effects in diversity discussions, and discursive templates and interpretative repertoires in organizational change encounters—would easily suggest alternative formulations and moral consequences to consider.

Dialogue approaches drawing from Martin Buber and Mikhail Bakhtin focus upon the dynamic, unfolding, and emergent nature of communication in organizations.[4] For example, in Barge's (2004) work on reflexivity in managerial practice, "managers are encouraged to acknowledge their role in creating the situation that they are simultaneously reading and to recognize that the situations they create are dynamic as changes in the way they respond to others create different situations." (p. 74). Managers are encouraged to foster polyvocality and an appreciation for different moral orders; develop linguistic forms like story grammars to enable action and sensemaking; invite others into the process of meaning-making by unpacking their 'key words'; and invite the cocreation of meaning, to name just a few. Much of this kind of effort depends upon an appreciation for the use of linguistic devices to promote reflexivity.

For example, while Barge is explicit about story grammars, the 'key word' exercise is all about membership categorization and could benefit greatly from the depth of discourse knowledge in this area, especially around the morally organized character of categorization work (Jayyusi, 1984). Understanding the cocreation of meaning would benefit from an understanding of the temporal nature of human interaction because often meaning coheres sequentially just like action does (Boden, 1994). Finally, understanding various meaning potentials is made possible through a consideration of actors' interpretative repertoires and the multiple Discourses that produce them. All represent potentially rich, yet unexplored avenues for leadership actors' reflexivity development.

Finally, *appreciative inquiry* draws from the positive psychology Discourses (of Chapter 5) to interrogate that which is life-affirming to human systems and strengthens such systems' abilities to discern and promote positive potential (Cooperrider et al., 1995). Appreciative inquiry is also based on the social construction of organizations through language and stories as it promotes inquiry and intervention oriented to the positive human systems. We saw this demonstrated in the Cleveland Clinic physician's example earlier in this chapter. However, Barge and Oliver (2003) offer an alternative reading of appreciative inquiry based in poststructuralist Discourses that promote a more situated sensibility; the complexity of meaning rooted in multiple Discourses that may be at play; and the need to explore weaknesses, criticism, and concerns, as well as moments of excellence. Thus, the same applications drawn for dialogue approaches are relevant here as well.

Importantly, the teaching moments to be gleaned from combining the study of discourse/Discourse with these grammars of practice generally work toward the goal of promoting a climate of open and honest communication directed toward task accomplishment. By necessity, the learnings would inform the actions of all relevant interests groups, not just those who emerge as leaders (Watson, 1994). Such an orientation is in keeping with the growing democratization of the workplace, which values shared decision making and encourages employees to think and act like owners (Deetz, 1995). It is also in keeping with the spirit of critical management studies and education, which reflexively challenges the alignment between knowledge, truth, and organizational efficiency (Fournier & Grey, 2000) and reframes "managerial work as a social, political and economic practice . . . full of moral dilemmas" (Watson, 2001, p. 395).

As can be seen with all three grammars of practice, there is a conversation to continue with a practical discursive grammar. Of course, leadership actors are going to vary in their appreciation for linguistic forms and the reflexive thinking that will be required of them. However, many are already linguistically attuned and represent an important population for further development (Fairhurst, 2005). I now turn to a second important conversation with leadership psychologists.

Discursive Leadership and Leadership Psychology

As mentioned in Chapter 1, Rorty (1979) argues that conversation across diverse theories and paradigms is "the ultimate context within which knowledge is to be understood" (p. 389). Hopefully, by now the reader understands that discursive leadership and leadership psychology are two different lenses for studying leadership that are in many ways quite complementary. However, I thought that a fitting end to this book would be to ask five leadership psychologists and three discourse scholars what they thought of this issue. Thus, after asking them to first read Chapter 1, I suggested some topics to consider as they formulated their responses: (1) How can discursive leadership and leadership psychology inform each other? (2) How can both be held in a tension with one another? (3) What aspects of leadership require a *psychological* lens? (4) What aspects of leadership require a *discursive* lens? and (5) What other issues matter? Much to my delight, the invited scholars provided incisive and thoughtful responses that sometimes challenge discursive leadership, sometimes favor it, and in several instances, point to genuine cross-disciplinary opportunities.

Leadership Psychologists

Name:	Boas Shamir, PhD
Title:	Professor, Department of Sociology and Anthropology;
	Dean, Faculty of Social Sciences
Institution:	Hebrew University of Jerusalem
Major Area of Research:	Leaders' life stories, leadership as management of meanings, followers' roles in the leadership process

Leadership psychology is 'essentialized' in this book by characterizing it as relying on laboratory experiments and questionnaires with 7-point scales, imposing preconceived constructs on the study of leadership, ignoring processes, ignoring contexts, and focusing mechanistically on relationships between variables. While these are certainly dominant tendencies in leadership psychology, they should not be seen as necessary characteristics, and there are many actual and possible exceptions to these tendencies within leadership psychology. Therefore, I do not see a necessary contradiction between leadership psychology and discursive leadership, and the question for me is, how can discursive approaches complement the leadership psychology approach to enrich the study and understanding of leadership?

Fairhurst distinguishes between two broad definitions of discourse. The term discourse (little 'd' discourse) refers to the study of talk and text in social practices. By contrast, the term Discourses (big 'D' Discourse) refers to general and enduring systems for the formation and articulation of ideas in a historically situated time. The first term is fully consistent with leadership psychology. To a large extent, I believe, leadership is enacted in the social construction arena. One of my favorite definitions of leadership is "the guidance and facilitation of the social construction of a reality that enables the group to achieve its goals." Yet leadership psychology has not focused on the ways by which leaders guide and facilitate the social construction of reality. The discursive approach not only draws attention to the centrality of communication in leadership processes, an aspect which, surprisingly, has been 'blackboxed' by leadership psychology, it also provides us with conceptual and methodological tools with which to understand the social construction of reality process.

Discursive leadership with a big D represents a challenge to leadership psychology because it views it as a historically situated system of thought and language that imposes its concepts and terms on a reality that can be experienced and understood in many other ways. From this perspective, even the concept of leadership cannot be taken for granted. It is, of course, a legitimate critical perspective, which is particularly useful for understanding the political implications of certain Discourses. However, it is not very useful for those of us who wish to understand how leadership is achieved in the dyads, groups, organizations, and societies we study. While in principle, it may be true that leadership need not have existed, or need not be at all as it is, the fact is that the basic leadership Discourse, as demonstrated, for instance, in leadership myths, is rather similar across societies and historical periods. To the extent that, despite variations, the basic construction of leadership has been similar in many societies for thousands of years, and to the extent it has real consequences, it seems to me legitimate and useful to study leadership within this Discourse without worrying too much about its socially constructed nature.

Name:	Stephen G. Green, PhD
Title:	Basil F. Turner Professor of Management
Institution:	Purdue University
Major Area of Research:	Leadership, management of technological innovation

Having read several chapters and skimmed others, I have several reactions to this work. First, I have been studying and doing research on leadership for 30 years now. It is hard for me to be challenged or provoked by new treatments of the subject. Gail Fairhurst's reflections on the isolation and intersection of psychology and communication views of leadership create both reactions within me. She has always had this capacity to see "into" those things that I tend to look "at." Her observations and questions could provide a platform for new directions in leadership theory and research. I hope so. Second, it is so very hard for our two disciplines to truly understand each other; concepts, language, even the very entities that we "think" we are studying tend to slip away from me as I try to see where and how we speak to each other. Therein, however, lies the value of Fairhurst's discourse.

I am convinced that discursive leadership and leadership psychology can inform each other, and should. In my mind, psychological approaches often are aimed at trying to understand the engines for leadership action and reaction. Given humans are (or appear to be!) sentient and feeling beings, leadership must in some way arise within those thoughts and feelings and must eventually be embodied in the thoughts and feelings of those being led. The receptors/interpreters of experience that guide the decisions to lead or to follow thus have a significant psychological component for me. I sometimes think of leadership as a process that connects the leader's state of being with the follower's state of being in the pursuit of goals. Having said that, communication is widely acknowledged as the milieu within which this process transpires. Certainly, I think the content and structure of communication results from these actors' states of being (psychology). It is clearly more than that, however. Communication is not "subsidiary" to psychology. What happens in communication between leaders and followers creates psychological structures within both parties; states of being of both leader and follower are expressed, constructed, deconstructed, and reconstructed within communication processes. Moreover, I think communication can create structures that exist only in the relationship between these parties and are unique, new psychological structures; i.e., the psychology of the leader and of the follower is being constructed within the communication process. As Fairhurst says in the first chapter, "discursive approaches tend to focus on how leadership is achieved or 'brought off' in discourse." I'd go further and say discursive approaches help us understand how the psychology of leadership processes is created between sentient and feeling beings.

How can both be held in a tension with one another? The arguments above lead me to believe that discursive leadership and psychological leadership are not held in tension with each other (even though there are tense moments). Rather, I think that the two traditions can cradle each other. "Mental work and social processes" both are equally important. In reality, they are inseparable even though our disciplines have managed to ignore each other. I think this is more a matter of training than a necessary separation. The cradle exists; we just have trouble seeing it. Maybe Gail Fairhurst's book will help us.

What aspects of leadership require a psychological lens? Several aspects of leadership "require" a psychological lens from my perspective and I allude to them above. The thinking and feeling that surely is part of leading resides within the "psyche" of the actors. Fairhurst refers to "mental work" and this is an important aspect of leading. Nevertheless, one must not lose sight of emotions as part of this process too. To deny these psychological processes leaves us with some uncomfortable questions. How can leaders or followers act? How can they react? Why would they? Why would any utterance or interaction occur? A "psychology" of the leader and follower is necessary to understand the most fundamental questions of why a party engages in any action and how they choose. Thus, I think constructs such as beliefs, feelings and emotions, physiological responses, drives, and so forth are necessary and require a psychological lens for theorizing.

What aspects of leadership require a discursive lens? The discursive lens is required if we are really to begin to understand the intersection of the leader's and the follower's states of being. Psychology has studied this question often by looking at "behaviors" or "beliefs" about the relationship, but this work is really quite molar and leaves large gaps in our understanding of leadership as a process. Psychologists are often satisfied if they can find systematic covariance between what are seen as key states of being. Understanding the mechanisms of that covariance requires more fine-grained theory and analysis. Thus, I think issues such as creation and definition of the leadership relationship (e.g., LMX), the exercise of power and influence, creation and evolution of leadership strategies for change, and so on absolutely require a discursive approach if we are to understand leading in depth. As Fairhurst noted (drawing from Schegloff, 2001), discursive approaches can provide the "cellular biology" that is needed.

Name:	Robert C. Liden, PhD
Title:	Professor of Managerial Studies
Institution:	University of Illinois at Chicago
Major Area of Research:	Interpersonal processes within leadership, groups, career progression, and employment interviews

I concur with the conclusion of Chapter 6, which stresses that the discursive and psychological approaches to the study of leadership complement one another. Indeed, there do not seem to be inconsistencies between leader–member exchange (LMX) quality assessed in surveys and the manifestations of LMX quality captured through discourse analysis. This may be due to the in-depth interviews that were conducted in early LMX (then vertical dyad linkage) research (Dansereau, Graen, & Haga, 1975), as well as the critical incident interviews performed in the early stages of scale development for the multidimensional measure of LMX (LMX-MDM, Liden & Maslyn, 1998). Indeed, discourse analyses have *not* revealed that LMX survey measures lack validity. Rather, discourse analyses provide detail about the nature of LMX relationships. But whereas discourse analysis excels in illuminating the specific nature of interactions between leaders and members, it has tended to ignore the outcomes of LMX relationships. Conversely, the psychological approach has thoroughly examined outcomes associated with LMX quality. Recently, the psychological approach has also begun to learn about the larger context in which LMX relationships are embedded (e.g., Erdogan & Liden, 2006; Erodogan, Liden, & Kraimer, in press; Sparrowe & Liden, 2005), an issue largely ignored by the discourse approach.

Although there remain many research topics that may best be explored separately by discourse and psychological researchers, other research questions beg the integration of these methods. First, much needed refinement in relationships between LMX and outcomes could be gleaned through an examination of the way in which interactions between leaders and members revealed through discourse analysis translate into salient and frequently studied outcomes, such as job performance, organizational citizenship behavior, commitment, and job satisfaction. Henderson, Dulac, and Liden (in press) have attempted to link the two approaches by developing a theoretical model in which leader–member communications mediate the relations between LMX and goal understanding and between LMX and self-efficacy. Discourse analyses could play an integral role in the assessment of leader–member communications in tests of this theoretical model. Second, the emerging literature examining LMX across different cultures (Wang, Law, Hackett, Wang, & Chen, 2005) could benefit greatly from the integration of discourse methods. For example, due to varying levels across cultures on such variables as power distance and collectivism, how would communication exchanges between leaders and members differ, and how might they relate differently to outcomes?

Finally, both the psychological and discursive approaches to LMX need to consider the substantial variability *within* LMX "exchange groups." It appears that researchers working within both of these approaches to LMX have made the questionable assumption that all high (or low) LMX relationships can be characterized in the same way. However, I argue that substantial differences within each LMX status group may exist. Specifically, the same leader may form dramatically different high LMX relationships with a corresponding difference in the nature of communications. For example, the leader may simply empower and "set loose" one high LMX member, whereas with another high LMX member, the leader may provide substantial guidance and mentoring. Similarly, communication patterns within high quality LMX relationships may vary considerably. Some may be characterized by polite, respectful interactions, whereas others may involve off-color jokes and teasing. In sum, both the discursive and psychological approaches need to consider the many forms that good (or bad) relationships can take.

REFERENCES

Dansereau, F., Graen, G., & Haga, W. J. (1975). A vertical dyad approach to leadership within formal organizations. *Organizational Behavior and Human Performance, 13,* 46–78.

Erdogan, B., & Liden, R. C. (2006). Collectivism as a moderator of responses to organizational justice: Implications for leader–member exchange and ingratiation. *Journal of Organizational Behavior, 27,* 1–17.

Erdogan, B., Liden, R. C., & Kraimer, M. L. (in press). Justice and leader–member exchange: The moderating role of organization culture. *Academy of Management Journal.*

Henderson, D. J., Dulac, T., & Liden, R. C. (in press). The role of LMX and communication in the goal setting process. In G. B. Graen (Ed.), *LMX: The Series, IV.* Greenwich, CT: Information Age Publishing.

Liden, R. C., & Maslyn, J. M. (1998). Multidimensionality of leader–member exchange: An empirical assessment through scale development. *Journal of Management, 24,* 43–72.

Sparrowe, R. T., & Liden, R. C. (2005). Two routes to influence: Integrating leader–member exchange and network perspectives. *Administrative Science Quarterly, 50,* 505–535.

Wang, H.; Law, K. S.; Hackett, R. D.; Wang, D., & Chen, Z. X. (2005). Leader–member exchange as a mediator of the relationship between transformational leadership and followers' performance and organizational citizenship behavior. *Academy of Management Journal, 48,* 420–432.

Name: James G. (Jerry) Hunt

Title: Paul Whitfield Horn Professor of Management

Institution: Texas Tech University

Major Area   Aspects of complexity theory and leadership, dynamic and
of Research: processual approaches to leadership, and sociology of the
                science of management

I found it refreshing that Gail Fairhurst encourages leadership psychology and discursive approaches to be used in a complementary fashion. As I have done in my own research (Hunt, 2004), she argues that leadership's purpose and definition for the work at hand helps determine their role.

Some might consider me a defrocked defender of leadership psychology. Basically, though I received such training under Fred Fiedler, I am a PhD business school product, with a psychology minor, and have always worked in a B-school. One aspect of this is that I consider what is now termed "context" as very important, along with temporality and processual aspects of leadership. I respect the rigor involved in much of leadership psychology but am less and less convinced that an extreme Newtonian position is called for and strongly support a six-position objectivist/subjectivist, ontological/epistemological continuum (Hunt, 1991, 2004; Morgan & Smircich, 1980).

The two continuum extremes are "leadership reality as a concrete, static structure position" with a machine metaphor and a quest for predictable, deterministic underlying laws to explain and predict an orderly world, versus the most radical subjectivist position viewing reality as a "projection of human imagination" with a transcendental metaphor. I am a scientific realist described by a mid-continuum, "reality as a contextual field of information" position using a hologram, cybernetic metaphor that emphasizes understanding contexts in a holistic fashion.

Thus, I am a strong advocate of the underlying assumptions of what some have called the "third scientific discipline" consisting of perspectives focusing on complex adaptive systems (CAS), chaos/complexity, system dynamics, computational modeling, and qualitative and quantitative processual approaches. These works go beyond experimentation and regression-based works of the earlier disciplines (Hunt & Ropo, 2003). The common denominator here is context accompanied by nonlinearity, process, and dynamism. While there are some leadership psychology approaches that move toward such orientations, most are closer to the extreme machine metaphor position.

I have strongly emphasized context, which here reflects environmental and organizational factors, illustrated by those such as Osborn, Hunt, and Jauch (2002), along with the much more micro thrusts often treated in the various discursive approaches. Thus, for me, context and discursive treatments share a kinship. Context is similar to the leadership psychology "contingency," but differs in that it is a boundary condition that influences understanding of how phenomena emerge and not simply the extent to which or how contingencies may affect the strength of relations (Antonakis et al., 2004, p. 61).

Discursive leadership can be located along the earlier mentioned continuum and appears to straddle or perhaps occupy two positions, "reality as symbolic discourse" and "reality as a social construction," located between my midrange cybernetic position and the extreme subjectivist transcendental end of the continuum. Paraphrasing Morgan and Smircich (1980, p. 494), symbolic discourse stresses the social world as a pattern of symbolic relationships and meanings sustained through a process of human action and interaction. Reality as a social construction focuses on individuals imposing themselves on their world to establish a realm of meaningful definition through the use of language, labels, actions, and routines constituting symbolic notions of being in the world. Symbolic action and hermeneutics are respective research examples.

In summary, location along the objectivist/subjectivist continuum best summarizes my comparative stance.

REFERENCES

Antonakis, J., Schriesheim, C. A., Donovan, J. A., Gopalakrishna-Pillai, K., Pellegrini, E., & Rossomme, J. L. (2004). Methods for studying leadership. In J. Antonakis, A. T. Cianciolo, & R. J. Sternberg (Eds.), *The nature of leadership* (pp. 48–70). Thousand Oaks, CA: Sage.

Hunt, J. G. (1991). *Leadership: A new synthesis.* Newbury Park, CA: Sage.

Hunt, J. G. (2004). What is leadership? In J. Antonakis, A. T. Cianciolo, & R. J. Sternberg (Eds.), *The nature of leadership* (pp. 19–47). Thousand Oaks, CA: Sage.

Hunt, J. G., & Ropo, A. (2003). Longitudinal research and the third scientific discipline. *Group and Organization Management, 23*(3), 315–340.

Morgan, G., & Smircich, L. (1980). The case for qualitative research. *Academy of Management Review, 5*(4), 491–500.

Osborn, R. N., Hunt, J. G., & Jauch, L. R. (2002). Toward a contextual theory of leadership. *The Leadership Quarterly, 13*(6), 797–837.

Name:	Donna Chrobot-Mason, PhD
Title:	Assistant Professor
Institution:	University of Cincinnati
Major Area of Research:	Organizational diversity, climate, and training; leading across differences

As the study of leadership psychology has grown and matured in recent years, it has become increasingly evident that the models and theories of leadership we have historically relied upon are limited and overly simplistic. Indeed, what has become clearer over time is the fact that leadership is a highly complex, dynamic phenomenon, involving many actors and variables. A variety of disciplines have taken interest in studying leadership from multiple perspectives and lenses, which has certainly contributed greatly to our current understanding of leadership. However, I predict that the study of leadership will grow and mature much faster and more completely if disciplines can begin to speak to and collaborate with each other. This book is an excellent forum to begin such collaborative endeavors. It is only through discussion and collaboration that we may begin to view leadership through multiple lenses and begin to put the various pieces of leadership together to construct a more complete puzzle.

In my own work in the area of leadership psychology and diversity, I see many opportunities for collaboration across disciplines and approaches. As the workforce becomes increasingly diverse and the market increasingly global, leaders are becoming more diverse and assuming leadership positions in which they must manage more diverse teams. These changes require alternative leadership models and theories that seek to explain complex interactions between diverse leaders and followers.

Chapter 3 on membership categorization argues that while leadership psychologists view categorization processes as an automatic phenomenon, discursive theorists view categorization as a social practice and have attempted to study *how* categories are invoked. Leadership psychologists may be able to better explain the "black box" in many leadership theories by collaborating with discursive theorists and attempting to view leadership through multiple lenses. For example, social identity theory suggests that identification with social groups fulfills important psychological needs that all human beings desire such as the need for affiliation and uniqueness. Social identity theory has also been used to help explain in-group bias and its role in perpetuating discrimination and prejudice in the workplace. Social identity theorists have proposed strategies (e.g., recategorization, decategorization, subcategorization—see Brewer & Brown, 1998) to minimize or change group boundaries such that in-group/out-group distinctions are altered to create greater harmony.

In the work I am doing with the Center for Creative Leadership (CCL), we have recently attempted to apply these categorization strategies for potential use with leaders working in diverse organizations and with diverse teams. The theories and strategies proposed in the social psychology literature provide leaders with some possible remedies to alter group categorizations that inhibit work effectiveness, but offer little guidance as to how leaders may accomplish this in practice. By examining membership categorization as a discursive activity and understanding its role in leadership processes to "manage meaning," we may be better equipped to offer leaders who must manage differences guidance not only on what they can do to alter group categorization, but also *how* they may alter group boundaries to minimize conflict and maximize organizational effectiveness.

REFERENCES

Brewer, M. B., & Brown, R. J. (1998). Intergroup relations. In D. T. Gilbert, S. T. Fiske, & G. Lindzey (Eds.), *The handbook of social psychology, Vol. 2* (4th ed.) (pp. 554–595). New York: McGraw-Hill.

Discursive Scholars

Name:	J. Kevin Barge, PhD
Title:	Associate Professor of Speech Communication
Institution:	University of Georgia
Major Areas of Research:	Organizational communication, systemic leadership approaches, dialogue, appreciative inquiry

Gail Fairhurst's contention that psychological and discursive approaches can be used in a complementary fashion to enrich each other is an exciting proposition. The notion of complementary holism is reminiscent of Bateson's (1972) idea of binocular vision, where one's view of a phenomenon becomes deeper and richer when viewed simultaneously through two lenses versus one. The question is how psychological and discursive lenses can be positioned in relation to each other to take advantage of both their strengths and to create deeply textured, complex, and nuanced explorations of leadership.

One approach would be to position a discursive leadership approach as opening up the "black box" in psychology regarding leadership performance and context. As highlighted in Chapter 1, leadership psychologists have been concerned primarily with articulating the cognitive and affective variables that are believed to capture experience and subsequently correlating them to statements of behavioral intention (what leaders will do) and summary judgments (what leaders have done and how they evaluate it). Behavior is typically operationalized at a molar level and reflects the general behavioral style or orientation a leader performs. A discursive approach, with its emphasis on little 'd' discourse—the study of talk and text in social practices—builds on a psychological approach by adding detail to how various thoughts, feelings, and emotions are lived out in communicative practice, move-by-move during interaction. The emphasis on the sequencing of specific conversational and textual moves adopts a micro-level approach toward interaction that nicely complements the more molar orientation leadership psychologists typically adopt.

Similarly, a discursive approach with its emphasis on big 'D' discourse—the "general and enduring systems for the formation and articulation of ideas in a historically situated time" (Foucault, 1972, 1980, quoted in Chapter 1 of this volume)—elaborates the importance of context. Alvesson (1996; Alvesson & Sveningsson, 2003) has observed that most leadership studies that adopt a more objectivist and psychological stance background the influence of context on the enactment of leadership. A discursive approach recognizes that a variety of Discourses circulate within societies, organizations, and groups—each with a particular moral logic that creates opportunities and constraints for action—and that these different Discourses intersect in unique ways at particular moments, creating a distinctive discursive constellation that constitutes the context for leadership. A discursive approach provides leadership researchers and leaders a set of tools for making sense of the unique context leaders engage and how the way they have made sense of the situations offers opportunities and constraints for the way individuals respond to the situation.

The perspective I have just outlined places psychology in a more dominant position in relation to a discursive approach as psychological constructs are conceived as the drivers of communicative behavior. I could have just as easily constructed the relationship with an emphasis on a discursive approach by positioning Discourse/discourse as the driver of psychological structures such as thoughts, feelings, and emotions. However, if one views leadership as a reflexive activity—an activity that recognizes the mutual influence among communication, action, meaning, and context—then communicative practice generates psychological structures such as schemas that help individuals make sense of situations and act, and these psychological structures provide guides for individuals to subsequently make sense of and act into situations (Barge, 2004). The only way we can begin to capture this dynamic complexity is to treat psychological and discursive processes as coevolutionary. An illustrative example of this kind of coevolutionary perspective is hinted at in the work of Holman (2000), who conceptualizes skill as a dialogical process. Individuals come to conversation with a set of tools such as cognitive scripts that they use to guide their interaction, but the way the interaction unfolds (i.e., what membership categorization devices are invoked) influences what cognitive resources are appropriated, which influences how people respond to the evolving situation, and so on. To understand how leadership plays out within interaction requires theorists and researchers to tack back and forth between the psychological structures and communicative practices of leaders over time. An emphasis on one perspective and not the other prevents the kind of binocular vision that is required to account for leadership's evolutionary openness and dynamism.

REFERENCES

Alvesson, M. (1996). Leadership studies: From procedure and abstraction to reflexivity and situation. *Leadership Quarterly, 7,* 455–485.

Alvesson, M., & Sveningsson, S. (2003). The great disappearing act: Difficulties in doing "leadership." *Leadership Quarterly, 14,* 359–381.

Barge, J. K. (2004). Reflexivity and managerial practice. *Communication Monographs, 71,* 70–96.

Bateson, G. (1972). *Steps to an ecology of the mind.* New York: Ballentine.

Holman, D. (2000). A dialogical approach to skill and skilled activity. *Human Relations, 53,* 957–980.

Name:	Linda Putnam
Title:	George T. and Gladys H. Abell Professor of Communication
Institution:	Texas A&M University
Major Area of Research:	Negotiation and organizational conflict and language analysis in organizations

The discursive approach to leadership seems closely aligned with organizational culture, typically defined as an organization's values and ideology. Yet, for both the psychological and the discursive views of leadership, culture is often shortchanged. That is, both approaches often lack the richness of treating culture and leadership as mutually enacted processes, rooted in historical and situational parameters, and bridging micro and macro levels of organizing.

In the psychological perspective, culture typically surfaces as a variable that impinges on leadership effectiveness or as a contingency that interacts with situational factors of leadership. Studies of leadership and organizational culture typically focus on the symbols that charismatic leaders employ, strong founders as change agents, or managerial control strategies that constrain organizational actors (Knights & Willmott, 1987, 1992; Witmer, 1997; Wright, 1979). But founders are not necessarily the captains of organizational culture (Alvesson, 2002).

In the discursive approaches, culture appears as local knowledge, texts of action, and systems of meaning. Cultural studies of leadership often examine subordinate sensemaking or interpretations of CEO actions (Oswick, Keenoy, & Grant, 1997; Sharpe, 1997; Smircich, 1983), managers as orchestrators of meaning (Schein, 1991; Shamir, Arthur, & House, 1994), and cultural clashes between managers (Kleinberg, 1989). In this perspective, culture is socially constructed through discursive practices that shape leadership performances. Thus, in both the psychological and the discursive approaches, culture is often taken for granted as a backdrop for leadership.

This brief essay contends that three types of approaches are needed to capture leadership as a situated, enacted process at both the micro and macro levels. That is, scholars need to overlay cultural perspectives with psychological and discursive views of leadership. Culture captures both the local discursive processes of organizing as well as global societal forms of interaction through a dynamic process in which boundaries are permeable and negotiable. In this overlay, culture would function as sensemaking and cognitive systems in the psychological approach and as layered texts in the discursive view of leadership. This interplay would also reveal how organizational culture enacts leaders and how leaders as agents shape culture. Through this intersection, culture might demonstrate how leadership becomes symbolic and how these symbols, in turn, constitute systems of meaning. Composed of texts of discursive practices, this interplay might also reveal how networks of relationships form leadership and how agents employ these networks as local and global resources.

Overall, juxtaposing culture with both the psychological and discursive views of leadership provides a framework for embracing a process, meaning-centered view of leadership that might preserve the tension between agency and structure and unite the person as leader with the organization as leadership.

REFERENCES

Alvesson, M. (2002). *Understanding organizational culture.* London: Sage.

Kleinberg, J. (1989). Cultural clash between managers: America's Japanese firms. In S. Prasad (Ed.), *Advances in international comparative management* (Vol. 4, pp. 221–244). Greenwich, CT: JAI.

Knights, D., & Willmott, H. (1987). Organizational culture as a management strategy: A critique and illustration from the financial services industry. *International Studies of Management and Organization, 17*(3), 40–63.

Knights, D., & Willmott, H. (1992). Conceptualizing leaderships processes: A study of senior managers in a financial services company. *Journal of Management Studies, 29,* 761–782.

Oswick, C., Keenoy, T., & Grant, D. (1997). Managerial discourses: Words speak louder than actions? *Journal of Applied Management Studies, 6,* 5–12.

Schein, E. (1991). The role of the founder in creating organizational culture. In P. Frost, L. Moore, M. Louis, C. Lundberg, & J. Martin (Eds.), *Reframing organizational culture* (pp. 14–25). Newbury Park, CA: Sage.

Shamir, B., House, R. J., & Arthur, M. B. (1993). The motivational effects of charismatic leadership: A self-concept based theory. *Organization Science, 4,* 577–594.

Sharpe, D. (1997). Managerial control strategies and subcultural processes: On the shop floor in Japanese manufacturing organizations in the United Kingdom. In S. Sackman (Ed.), *Cultural complexity in organizations* (pp. 228–251). Thousand Oaks, CA: Sage.

Smircich, L. (1983). Organizations as shared meanings. In L. Pondy, P. Frost, G. Morgan, & T. Danridge (Eds.), *Organizational symbolism* (pp. 55–65). Greenwich, CT: JAI Press.

Witmer, D. F. (1997). Communication and recovery: Structuration as an ontological approach to organizational culture. *Communication Monographs, 64,* 324–349.

Wright, J. (1979). *On a clear day you can see General Motors.* Grosse Point, MI: Wright Enterprises.

Name:	François Cooren
Title:	Professor
Institution:	Université de Montréal
Major Area of Research:	Organizational communication, analyses of interactions, actor-network theory, pragmatics, and semiotics

As we learned from Gail Fairhurst's book, especially Chapters 6 and 7, a very interesting way to compare the respective contributions of leadership psychology and discursive leadership is to address the question of narrativity and its role in the construction and enactment of leadership. Boje (1995), Czarniawska-Joerges (1997), J. R. Taylor and Van Every (2000), and several others have convincingly shown that narratives are important sensemaking and sensegiving resources precisely because they are about sequences of action that get articulated within each other in order to constitute a plausible whole, what Weick (1979, 1995) basically identifies as organizing. As Weick, Sutcliffe, and Obstfeld (2005) remind us, "sensemaking is not about truth and getting it right. Instead, it is about continued redrafting of an emerging story so that it becomes more comprehensive, incorporates more of the observed data, and is more resilient in the face of criticism" (p. 415). If Calder (1977) as well as Meindl, Ehrlich, and Dukerich (1985) are right when they claim that leadership mainly is an attributional phenomenon, one interesting avenue to explore might be to study how these romanticized and heroic views of leadership are structured. Whether we like it or not, accounting for a given situation always consists of reconstructing a chain of causalities that identify what for us constitute the different sources of what is happening (Potter & Wetherell, 1987). By focusing on actors' leadership accounts, we might therefore be able to reconstruct not only how these narratives are organized, but also what specific sources of agency are typically selected, whether actors explain it in terms of the leaders' psychology, acts, or environment. It may also represent a way in which to pursue the connectionist architecture of implicit leadership theories from a very different direction from the usual scaled judgments (Hanges, Lord, & Dickson, 2000). Indeed, narrative accounts should display both the constancy and situational variability that connectionist architectures putatively embody.

In this regard, Greimasian semiotics might be extremely relevant, since it precisely consists of focusing on what or who is attributed agency in a given account and how these different sources of agency are organized to produce a plausible and meaningful narrative while simultaneously acknowledging the existence of universal narrative structures (Greimas, 1987). Whether people speak of a leader's passions or actions or what this person might represent for them (trust, integrity, honor), leadership accounts consist of selecting what happens to make a difference within a chain of agencies (for some illustration, although not applied to leadership, see Castor & Cooren, 2006; Cooren, 2006; as well as Cooren, Thompson, Canestraro, & Bodor, 2006). By chain of agencies, we mean that action has no absolute point of origin and that any contribution can always be reframed by what makes it possible (going upstream) and what follows it (going downstream) (Cooren, 2006; Latour, 2005). Paraphrasing Bateson (1979, p. 99), we could say that the attribution of leadership therefore implies that actors singularize specific differences that for them happen to make a difference in a given situation, a selection that will lead them to downplay other aspects that might be less romantic or heroic. These differences might be specific psychological traits, actions, or circumstances, but they all constitute ways in which actors can speak of leadership in plausible and meaningful ways. Surveys and scaled judgments certainly are valid ways to access people's attributions, but a more processual and constructive approach might also lead us to explore how such attributions function, narratively speaking.

REFERENCES

Bateson, G. (1979). *Mind and nature: A necessary unity*. San Francisco: Chandler.

Boje, D. M. (1995). Stories of the storytelling organization: A postmodern analysis of Disney as "Tamara-Land." *Academy of Management Journal, 38*(4), 997–1035.

Calder, B. J. (1977). An attribution theory of leadership. In B. Staw & R. Salancik (Eds.), *New directions in organizational behavior* (pp. 179–204). Chicago: St Clair Press.

Castor, T., & Cooren, F. (2006). Organizations as hybrid forms of life: The implications of the selection of agency in problem formulation. *Management Communication Quarterly, 16*.

Cooren, F. (2006). The organizational world as a plenum of agencies. In F. Cooren, J. R. Taylor, & E. J. Van Every (Eds.), *Communication as organizing: Empirical and theoretical explorations in the dynamic of text and conversation*. Mahwah, NJ: Erlbaum.

Cooren, F., Thompson, F., Canestraro, D., & Bodor, T. (2006). From agency to structure: Analysis of an episode in a facilitation process. *Human Relations, 59*(4), 533–565.

Czarniawska-Joerges, B. (1997). *Narrating the organization: Dramas of institutional identity*. Chicago/London: The University of Chicago Press.

Greimas, A. J. (1987). *On meaning. Selected writings in semiotic theory* (P. J. Perron & F. H. Collins, Trans.). London: Frances Pinter.

Hanges, P. J., Lord, R. G., & Dickson, M. W. (2000). An information-processing perspective on leadership and culture: A case for connectionist architecture. *Applied Psychology: An International Review, 49*, 133–161.

Latour, B. (2005). *Reassembling the social: An introduction to actor-network theory*. London: Oxford University Press.

Meindl, J. R., Ehrlich, S. B., & Dukerich, J. M. (1985). The romance of leadership. *Administrative Science Quarterly, 30*, 78–102.

Potter, J., & Wetherell, M. (1987). *Discourse and social psychology*. London: Sage.

Taylor, J. R., & Van Every, E. J. (2000). *The emergent organization. Communication as its site and surface*. Mahwah, NJ: Erlbaum.

Weick, K. E. (1979). *The social psychology of organizing*. New York: Random House.

Weick, K. E. (1995). *Sensemaking in organizations*. Thousand Oaks, CA: Sage.

Weick, K. E., Sutcliffe, K. M., & Obstfeld, D. (2005). Organizing and the process of sensemaking. *Organization Science, 16*(4), 409–421.

Conclusion

I conclude this book with three wishes in mind. First, as mentioned in the Preface, this book was less of a literature review and more of an exploration of key discourse/Discourse concepts and what they could mean for leadership. It is my sincere wish that leadership discourse research continues apace for these concepts, and that the promise of this book is fulfilled.

Second, I cannot underscore enough the practical implications to be drawn from discursive leadership research. The challenge, of course, is translating this material into a consumable form for organizational participants. As I learned when I wrote and lectured on *The Art of Framing: Managing the*

Language of Leadership with Bob Sarr (Fairhurst & Sarr, 1996), skills derived from a transmissional model of communication are much more easily comprehended than those from a meaning-centered model. Even with skills as basic as *framing,* some leaders will quickly catch on while others will flounder because of the seeming abstractness of the concept and differential sensitivities to language (Fairhurst, 2005). Thus, my second wish is that the pairing of discursive grammars with grammars of practice such as practical theory and dialogue approaches better confronts these obstacles while addressing the ethical components along the way.

Finally, as the invited scholars in this chapter have made clear, there is tremendous possibility for cross-disciplinary work between discursive leadership and leadership psychology—providing, of course, that discursive approaches are not cast as methodologies, as Hammersley (2003a) recommends. Thus, my third and final wish is for more cross-disciplinary work between the two. I rather like Steve Green's cradle metaphor here because it perfectly captures how discursive leadership and leadership psychology can offer each other both a support structure and an embrace.

NOTES

1. While critical theorists would argue that management scholars are too oriented to organizational interests, that does not obviate the general point made here.

2. This is not to diminish this as an issue. It is simply to suggest that constraint is built into the nature of the turn taking.

3. There are other perspectives on practical theory. For Shotter (1993), practical theory is a toolbox of ideas for praxis, while Cronen (1995b, 2001) treats practical theory as overtly heuristic "formalizations aiding inquirers' efforts to join with human systems to improve them" (2001, p. 14).

4. Eisenberg and Goodall (2004) have identified three *dialogue* approaches: dialogue as *equitable transaction* concerns itself with matters of voice and the sharedness of participation in dialogue; dialogue as *empathic conversation* involves efforts to understand others' positions as expanded upon by the MIT dialogue project (Isaacs, 1999; Senge, 1990); while dialogue as *real meeting* is the dynamic, unfolding, and emergent nature of communication in organizations. Only the third approach is the focus of discussion in this chapter.

Appendixes

Appendix A1: Conversation Analysis

Definition:	Conversation analysis (CA) is a type of discourse analysis that focuses on the detailed organization of talk-in-interaction. Its main purpose is to discern how people use various interactional methods and procedures to produce their activities and make sense of their worlds.
Focus:	Turn taking, membership categorization, adjacency pairs, insertion sequences, accounting practices, topic shifts, conversational openings and closings, agenda setting, decision making, and so on.
Theory Base:	Ethnomethodology (Boden, 1990, 1994; Garfinkel, 1967).
Advantages:	CA captures the inherent richness and complexity of social interaction better than most other discourse analyses. The macro–micro distinction dissolves because of an emphasis on social practices and the primacy of text. It is studying 'the world-as-it-happens' without researcher-imposed levels of analysis (Boden, 1994). Also, the interpretive practices and competencies of actors in their talk-in-interaction reveal how the organization is literally 'talked into being' (Heritage, 1997).
Criticisms:	CA has been criticized for a restricted view of the context; questions emerge as to what belongs to the text itself and what resides beyond the text, given that so much within a text is implied or presupposed. There is a greater role for analyst-assigned meanings than is typically acknowledged (Haslett, 1987). Hammersley (2003a) argues that CA deploys a rather 'thin' model of the human actor because it is not conducive to examining psychosocial features that are relatively stable across time or context.
Resources:	Atkinson and Heritage (1984), Boden (1994), Drew and Heritage (1992), Garfinkel (1967), Heritage (1997), Pomerantz and Fehr (1997), Psathas (1995)

Transcript Notation System:	A:	The [plant is	Brackets indicate overlapping speech.
	B:	[Oh goo:d	
	A:	Is the *structure* wrong?	Italics indicates emphasis in delivery.
	A:	Wait=	Equal signs indicate no audible gap
	B:	=Okay.	between one utterance and the next.
	A:	Let's (.) you know, go	Period in parentheses indicates a very short pause (less than a tenth of a second).
	A:	The manager said	Number in parentheses indicates elapsed
		(.3)	time in tenths of seconds.
	B:	said what? Tell me.	
	A:	He opera-	A hyphens indicates that the prior syllable
	B:	I know.	was cut off.
	A:	My findings	Double parentheses indicate an action
	B:	((sigh))	that characterizes the talk or scene.
	A:	So:::	Colons indicate that the prior syllable was stretched. The number of colons signals how long the syllable was stretched.
	A:	Heh-heh-huh-huh	Laughter particles.
	A:	Think about(hhh)	An 'h' in parentheses denotes breathiness in delivery.
	A:	On (game) day	Words enclosed in single parentheses indicate transcriber's doubt in hearing.
	A: >	Let's go forward<	Arrows designate speeded up speech.

Resources: The transcription notation system for CA was developed by Gail Jefferson. For more in-depth information, see Atkinson and Heritage (1984).

Appendix A2: Interaction Analysis

Definition: Interaction analysis (IA) is a genre of discourse analysis that focuses exclusively on language in use, interaction process, and the coding of behavior according to a predefined set of codes. It includes a host of quantitative and empiricist approaches that draw from studies of message functions and language structures to assess the frequency and types of coded verbal behavior in organizational interaction.

Focus: The sequences and stages of interaction, their redundancy and predictability, and the link between interactional structures and the organizational context (Putnam & Fairhurst, 2001).

Theory Base: Various theories including systems theory, behaviorist theory, and structuration theory. No common intellectual tradition anchors interaction analysis (Fairhurst, 2004).

Variations: Interaction process analysis (Bales, 1950); behaviorist studies
(Coding schemes) (Gioia & Sims, 1986; Komaki, 1998); systems interaction (Fairhurst, Green, & Courtright, 1995); negotiation (Putnam & Wilson, 1989; Weingart, Hyder, & Prietula, 1996); adaptive structuration theory (DeSanctis & Poole, 1994); group time studies (Gersick, 1988)

Advantages: IA maps longer chains of behavior than conversation analysis or speech act schematics, examines more inclusive levels of temporal form, and usually characterizes the general shape of an interaction in terms of patterns or phases (Holmes & Rogers, 1995).

Criticisms: Meanings are more ephemeral, malleable, and negotiable than coding schemes can capture (Firth, 1995). The constructs of interest (for example, control) that form the basis of the coding schemes may not always be relevant to actors (Boden, 1994).

Resources: Bakeman and Gottman (1986), DeSanctis & Poole (1994), Fairhurst (2004), Fairhurst and Cooren (2004), Komaki (1998), Putnam and Fairhurst (2001), Rogers and Escudero (2004a)

Appendix A3: Speech Act Schematics

Definition: Speech act schematics (SAS) is a genre of discourse analysis that focuses on language in use and episodic interaction processes. Drawing from the speech act tradition, which examines the performative character of language, SAS focuses on the larger episodic or schematic forms that arise from stringing speech acts together. Specific categories of speech acts constitute the opening, enactment, and closure of episodes. Through closure, episodes are able to embed themselves within one another.

Focus: Categorizations of speech acts as *assertives* (representing an actual state of affairs: "It is raining."); *commissives* (committing to a future course of action: "I'll be right there."); *directives* (attempting to get the hearer to do something: "Check on her safety."); *declaratives* (bring a state of affairs into existence by representing oneself as performing that action: "I baptize you."); *expressives* (express the attitudes of the speaker about a state of affairs: "Thank you."); *accreditives* (transfer permission or authorization from one agent to a recipient: "You have my permission to leave."). Also, the ordering of speech acts within episodes and episodic embedding.

Theory Base: Speech act theory (Austin, 1962, 1975; Searle, 1969, 1979, 1989; Vanderveken, 1990–1991); Greimas's narratology (Greimas, 1987, 1988; Greimas & Courtes, 1982); actor-network theory (Callon & Latour, 1981; Latour, 1986, 1994, 1996)

Advantages: SAS shows how organizations are built through speech agency, whether through speech acts performed by human agents or text-objects. SAS incorporates the mediating role of objects and the way the organization inscribes itself in them.

Criticisms: SAS relies on speech act theory, which has been criticized for an intentionality bias and lack of empirical grounding (Schegloff, 1988). Also, organizations cannot solely be built through speech agency because order or pattern in interaction does not beget the complex social form 'organization.' Organizing can always take place in the absence of 'organization,' an entity with formal properties (McPhee & Zaug, 2002).

Resources: Cooren (2001); Cooren and Taylor (1997, 1998); Cooren, Taylor, and Van Every (2006); Robichaud (2003); Taylor and Van Every (2000)

Appendix A4: Discursive Psychology

Definition: Discursive psychology (DP) is a genre of discourse analysis with a social constructionist focus. It explores the way psychological, material, and social objects are formed and transformed through interaction. DP combines a conversation analysis focus on talk-in-interaction with a Foucauldian view of Discourse as systems of thought. However, DP scholars recast Discourse as *interpretative repertoire*, which they liken to a dancer's repertoire, substituting instead terms, tropes, metaphors, themes, commonplaces, or habitual forms of argument. DP examines how people draw from their repertoires (Discourses) to form identities and representations of the world in talk-in-interaction.

Focus: Descriptions of psychological, material, or social objects (for example, attitudes, categories, memory, attributions, and so on) are examined for the ways in which they surface in talk-in-interaction, a clear departure from a psychology based in cognitivism. Accountability is also key for the ways in which individuals (or other social units) are constructed as sites of agency and responsibility in everyday and institutional settings (Potter, 2005).

Theory Base: Primarily constructionism from the tradition in sociology of scientific knowledge (Ashmore, 1989), but also conversation analysis (Sacks, 1992), ethnomethodology (Garfinkel, 1967), and poststructuralism (Foucault, 1972).

Advantages: DP answers the question, 'Why this utterance here?' in social interaction by going beyond the interaction to focus on interpretative repertoires that source communicating actors (Wetherell, 1998). As such, it nicely signals the interplay between discourse as language in use and Discourse as systems of thought.

Criticisms: Hammersley (2003) argues that DP deploys a rather 'thin' model of the human actor that is not conducive to examining psychosocial features that are relatively stable across time or context. See also Potter's (2003) response.

Resources: Edwards (1997, 2005), Edwards and Potter (1992), Potter (1996, 1997, 2003, 2005), Potter and Wetherell (1987), Wetherell (1998)

Appendix A5: Foucauldian Analyses

Definition: Foucault's *archeology* is the study of specific and shaping historical influences through which statements are combined and regulated to form and define a distinct field of knowledge/objects. *Genealogy* analyzes the way in which Discourse develops and gets deployed through situated technologies of power (C. Barker, 2003). Foucault prioritizes genealogy over archeology.

Focus: For *archeology*, the focus is a specific set of concepts that produce their own 'truth effects' or what counts as truth. Emphasis is given to the ways in which discursive formations emerge, often with discontinuous breaks with Discourses from previous eras. For *genealogy*, the focus is on relations of power, knowledge, and the body and how they are brought into play in modern society. Emphasis is given to the material and institutional conditions of Discourse (C. Barker, 2003; Dreyfus & Rabinow, 1983).

Theory Base: Foucault (1972, 1973, 1979, 1980, 1983, 1990, 1995)

Advantages: Foucault's work corrects for the underdeveloped role of cultural and historical influences on human actors and the bias toward agency this may produce. Also, his work has inspired many critical, poststructuralist, and feminist analyses to move beyond single Discourses to focus on the interplay and competitive struggle of multiple Discourses vying for dominance.

Criticisms: Discursive psychology views Discourse as an overly rigid concept, akin to 'plate tectonics' (Potter et al., 1990). Foucault's work reflects too little emphasis on the competition among Discourses within a given historical period (Holstein & Gubrium, 2000). Foucault's work has also been criticized on matters of agency, including charges of relativism (Reed, 2000, 2001) and repression of the subject (Newton, 1998).

Resources: C. Barker (2003), Dreyfus and Rabinow (1983), Foucault (1972, 1973, 1979, 1980, 1983, 1990, 1995), Shapiro (1992)

Appendix A6: Critical Discourse Analysis

Definition: Fairclough (1993) defines critical discourse analysis (CDA) as "analysis which aims to systematically explore often opaque relationships of causality and determination between (a) discursive practices, events, and texts, and (b) wider social and cultural structures, relations, and processes; to investigate how such practices, events, and texts arise out of and are ideologically shaped by relations of power and struggles over power; and to explore how the opacity of these relationships between (D)iscourse and society is itself a factor securing power and hegemony" (p. 135).

Focus: Emphasis is given to the triadic relationship between Discourse, ideology, and power, especially power exercised by consent or *hegemony*. For example, the way Discourse simultaneously produces and hides deep structure relations of power and inequality; how organizations are sites of struggle where different groups (for example, based on gender) compete to shape a reality vested with their own interests; and how conflicts are resolved through the control of symbolic, discursive, or material resources (Mumby & Clair, 1997).

Theory Base: Bakhtin (1981a, 1981b), Chouliaraki and Fairclough (1999), Fairclough (1992, 1993, 1995, 2003), Fairclough and Thomas (2004) Foucault (1972), Giddens (1979, 1984), Gramsci (1971), and Habermas (1984)

Variations: French Discourse analysis, critical linguistics, social semiotics, sociocultural change and change in Discourse, sociocognitive studies, Discourse-historical methods, reading analysis, and the Duisburg school. For a review, see Fairclough and Wodak (1997).

Advantages: CDA addresses socially relevant concerns; demonstrates how power relations are discursive and material; shows how Discourse performs ideological work; and reveals a dialectical relationship between Discourse and culture (Fairclough & Wodak, 1997).

Criticisms: Analyses are often limited to single texts. There is also a theoretically weak understanding of group formation processes, the subject, and agency (Phillips & Jørgensen, 2002). Other criticism suggests an elitism and impracticality associated with critical research (Alvesson & Deetz, 1996).

Resources: van Dijk (1985, 1991, 1997), Fairclough (1995, 2003), Fairclough and Wodak (1997), Mumby and Clair (1997), Phillips and Jørgenson (2002)

Appendix A7: Narrative Analyses

Definition: Narrative analyses (NA) is a huge area of study that generally distinguishes between narrative and story, although not consistently across authors. Gabriel (2004) sees *narrative* as a particular type of text, involving temporal chains of interrelated events or actions undertaken by actors, wherein all discourse is in some way narrative. *Story* requires 'emplotment' (characters, sequencing, predicaments, action, and so on) or the weaving together of events in some meaningful way. However, characters and events in stories can be real or imagined (Czarniawska-Joerges, 1997). Stories may be viewed as 'poetic elaborations' of narrative material (Gabriel, 2004).

Focus: Narrative focus may be sensemaking, identity or relationship management, information sharing, socialization, organizing processes, change, ideological control, and so on.

Theory Base: Varies depending upon the type of narrative analysis. It may include Boje (2001), Bruner (1986, 1990), Czarniawska-Joerges (1997), Fisher (1984), or Greimas (1987, 1988), among others.

Variations: Deconstruction, grand narrative, microstoria, story network, intertextuality, causality, and plot. For a review, see Boje (2001).

Advantages: Narrative is an alternative mode of knowing and organizing relative to an information-processing mode (Bruner, 1986). Narrative analyses shows how social actions are performed 'in the telling,' signaling subgroup differences, decision making, change, and so forth (Boje, 1991). It also helps elucidate the means by which ideological control is achieved by reinforcing key values and reifying privileged structures (Mumby, 1987).

Disadvantages: There may be a tendency to downplay or ignore the material over the social, which raises issues of relativism. Narrative analysis "runs the risk of accepting the voice of personal experience as the uncontested and authentic source of understanding and sensemaking" (Gabriel, 2004, p. 73).

Resources: Boje (1991, 2001; Boje et al., 2001), Bruner (1986, 1990), Czarniawska-Joerges (1997, 2004), Fisher (1984), Gabriel (1999, 2004), Weick (1995; Weick, Sutcliffe, & Obstfeld, 2005)

Appendix B: Transcript of Police Rescue

Cy=Conway, Dis=Dispatcher, **1030, 1080, 1240**=Police Supervisors

1 Cy: Help! I need assistance! I'm shot in the (car)!

2   (2.0)

3 Dis: *Where* do you need it?

4 Cy: Help! I need help!

5   (1.5)

6 **1030:** 1238 Elm. I believe, 1030, I believe I heard shots fired there.

7 Cy: [(((Unintelligible screaming)) please!

8 Dis: [-Location?

9   (1.0)

10 Dis: 1212, what's your location?

11   (6.5)

12 **1080:** 1080, we got a location?

13   (1.0)

14 Dis: Negative

15   ((line sounds))

16 Dis: Officer needs assistance, District One, unknown location. 12th 12th and Elm.

17   Officer needs assistance, 12th and Elm. Possibly shots fired.

18   (3.0)

19 **1080:** 1080 35, 12th and Elm, do not *see* them.

20   (2.5)

21 **1240:** 1240. Play the tape back

22   (2.5)

23 Dis: 1212, what's your location?

24 Cy: Distress. I've been involved in a shooting (0.3) on Central Parkway (0.5)

25   north (.) of Liberty. I need some help hhh

26   (0.5)

27	**1080:**	1080, I [copy that. Check on her safety.
28	**Dis:**	[are you hurt?
29		(0.5)
30	**Dis:**	1212, are you hurt?
31		(0.3)
32	**Cy:**	That's affirmative.
33		(0.5)
34	**1080:**	1080, I'll be there in five seconds. Blockin' it off with four cars.
35		((line sounds))
36	**Dis:**	Attention all cars, all departments. An officer has been *in*jured. Possible
37		shooting offense hh at 12th and Central Parkway.=Repeating, Cincinnati
38		officer needs assistance hhh at 12th and Central Parkway, a possible *shoo*ting
39		offense. =The officer reporting she is injured, approach with caution.
40		(0.3)
41	**1080:**	She's at. Correct- correction, she's at *Li*berty (.) and, uh, Elm.
42	**1240:**	1240
43	**Dis:**	[12 . . .
44	**1240:**	[1240, no more cars.
45		((unintelligible sounds))
46	**Dis:**	1240, are you on the scene?
47	**1080:**	Come on you guys=
48	**1240:**	=Assist assist! All emergency traffic. Let me talk.
49	**Dis:**	Go ahead
50	**1240:**	OK. We're about, uh, we're about just about north of uh (.) uh Central
51		Parkway. We're going to need a couple rescue units. We've got an officer in
52		the car shot. ((sirens in the background))
53	**Dis:**	OK, I- you need to go slower.
54	**1080:**	Where are you?
55	**Dis:**	Where are you?
56	**1240:**	1240. We are at the corner of Central Parkway, just north of ((sounds)) No

57		more cars
58	Dis:	OK. Parkway, north of *what*.
59	1240:	North of Liberty. West *Li*berty street
60	Dis:	OK. You got any other cars with [you?
61	1240:	[I - need (.)
62		a rescue unit. I need a rescue unit!
63		(2.5)
64		((line sounds))
65	Dis:	Attention, all cars all departments. *No* additional officers are to respond hh
66		reference the officer shot (0.5) on Central Parkway, just North of Liberty.
67		Repeating
68	1240:	1240=
69	Dis:	=No other units are to respond on the assistance.
70		(1.5)
71	Dis:	1240
72	1240:	Hey!
73	Dis:	1240, go ahead.
74	1240:	Hey. I will take care of it on the scene here. We have the perimeter secure.
75		We need a fire company to *ex*pedite.
76	Dis:	Fire company is responding. (.) Other units
77	1240:	No other units to transmit at this point. I'm also gonna need the uh
78		recall list
79	Dis:	OK. I need, if you can give us a call to know the condition right now also.
80	1240:	I'll give you one in two minutes
81		(1.0)
82		((unintelligible sounds))
83	1240:	We've got the address right. 1627 Central Parkway.
84	Dis:	Copy 1627 Central
85	Dis:	Copy 1627 Central

86		(1.0)
87	**1215:**	Car 15 responding
88		(1.0)
89	**Dis:**	Car 15 copy
90	**1230:**	1230
91		(0.5)
92	**Dis:**	1230 copy
93	**1230:**	12 (.) 1230
94	**Dis:**	Car 1230.
95	**1230:**	Get the air care to stand by. And we have the night chief responding
96		(0.5)
97	**Dis:**	The night chief is responding.
98	**1230:**	Is homicide responding?
99		(2.5)
100	**Dis:**	I'm notifying now.
101	**( ):**	Okay, so do you know who might have done this?

References

Abelson, R. (1981). Psychological status of the script concept. *American Psychologist, 36,* 715–729.

Albert, M., Cagan, L., Chomsky, N., Hahnel, R., King, M., Sargent, L., et al. (1986). *Liberating theory.* Boston: South End Press.

Altman, I., Vinsel, A., & Brown, B. B. (1981). Dialectic conceptions in social psychology: An application to social penetration and privacy regulation. In L. Berkowitz (Ed.), *Advances in experimental and social psychology* (pp. 107–160). New York: Academic Press.

Alvesson, M., & Deetz, S. A. (1996). Critical theory and postmodernism approaches to organizational studies. In S. R. Clegg, C. Hardy, & W. R. Nord (Eds.), *Handbook of organization studies* (pp. 191–217). London: Sage.

Alvesson, M., & Kärreman, D. (2000a). Taking the linguistic turn in organizational research. *Journal of Applied Behavioral Science, 36,* 1125–1149.

Alvesson, M., & Kärreman, D. (2000b). Varieties of discourse: On the study of organizations through discourse analysis. *Human Relations, 53,* 1125–1149.

Alvesson, M., & Skoldberg, K. (2000). *Reflexive methodology: New vistas for qualitative research.* London: Sage.

Alvesson, M., & Sveningsson, S. (2003a). Good visions, bad micro-management and ugly ambiguity: Contradictions of a (non-)leadership in a knowledge-intensive organization. *Organization Studies, 24,* 961–988.

Alvesson, M., & Sveningsson, S. (2003b). The great disappearing act: Difficulties in doing "leadership." *Leadership Quarterly, 14,* 359–381.

Alvesson, M., & Willmott, H. (2002). Identity regulation as organizational control: Producing the appropriate individual. *Journal of Management Studies, 39,* 619–664.

Antaki, C., Condor, S., & Levine, M. (1996). Social identities in talk: Speakers' own orientations. *British Journal of Social Psychology, 35,* 473–492.

Antonakis, J., Cianciolo, A. T., & Sternberg, R. J. (2004). Leadership: Past, present, and future. In J. Antonakis, A. T. Cianciolo, & R. J. Sternberg (Eds.), *The nature of leadership* (pp. 3–15). Thousand Oaks, CA: Sage.

Ashcraft, K. L. (2000). Empowering 'professional' relationships: Organizational communication meets feminist practice. *Management Communication Quarterly, 13,* 347–392.

Ashcraft, K. L., & Mumby, D. K. (2004). *Reworking gender: A feminist communicology of organizations.* Thousand Oaks, CA: Sage.

Ashmore, M. (1989). *The reflexive thesis: Wrighting sociology of scientific knowledge.* Chicago: University of Chicago Press.

Astley, W. G. (1985). Administrative science as socially constructed truth. *Administrative Science Quarterly, 30,* 497–513.

Atkinson, J. M., & Heritage, J. (Eds.). (1984). *Structures of social action: Studies in conversation analysis.* Cambridge, UK: Cambridge University Press.

Austin, J. L. (1962). *How to do things with words.* Cambrdige, MA: Harvard University Press.

Austin, J. L. (1975). *How to do things with words* (2nd ed.). Cambridge, MA: Harvard University Press.

Avolio, B. J., & Gardner, W. L. (2005). Authentic leadership development: Getting to the root of positive forms of leadership. *Leadership Quarterly, 16,* 315–338.

Avolio, B. J., Gardner, W. L., Walumbwa, F. O., Luthans, F., & May, D. R. (2004). Unlocking the mask: A look at the process by which authentic leaders impact follower attitudes and behaviors. *Leadership Quarterly, 15,* 801–823.

Avolio, B. J., & Yammarino, F. J. (Eds.). (2002). *Transformational and charismatic leadership: The road ahead.* Amsterdam: JAI Press.

Bakeman, R., & Gottman, J. M. (1986). *Observing interaction: An introduction to sequential analysis.* Cambridge, UK: Cambridge University Press.

Baker, D., & Ganster, D. C. (1985). Leader communication style: A test of average versus vertical dyad linkage models. *Group and Organizational Studies, 10,* 242–259.

Bakhtin, M. (1981a). *The dialogical imagination.* Austin: University of Texas Press.

Bakhtin, M. (1981b). *Speech genres and other late essays.* Austin: University of Texas Press.

Bales, R. F. (1950). *Interaction process analysis.* Cambridge, MA: Addison-Wesley.

Barge, J. K. (2004). Reflexivity and managerial practice. *Communication Monographs, 71,* 70–96.

Barge, J. K., & Craig, R. T. (in press). Practical theory. In L. Frey & K. Cissna (Eds.), *Handbook of applied communication.* Mahwah, NJ: Erlbaum.

Barge, J. K., & Oliver, C. (2003). Working with appreciation in managerial practice. *Academy of Management Review, 28,* 124–142.

Barge, J. K., & Schleuter, D. W. (1991). Leadership as organizing: A critique of leadership instruments. *Management Communication Quarterly, 4,* 541–570.

Barker, C. (2003). *Cultural studies: Theory and practice* (2nd ed.). London: Sage.

Barker, R. A. (1997). How can we train leaders if we do not know what leadership is? *Human Relations, 50,* 343–362.

Barlow, G. (1989). Deficiencies and the perpetuation of power: Latent functions in management appraisal. *Journal of Management Studies, 26,* 499–518.

Barnard, C. (1938). *The functions of the executive.* Cambridge, MA: Harvard University Press.

Barrett, F. J., Thomas, G. F., & Hocevar, S. P. (1995). The central role of discourse in large-scale change: A social construction perspective. *Journal of Applied Behavioral Science, 31,* 352–372.

Bass, B. M. (1981). *Stogdill's handbook of leadership.* New York: Free Press.

Bass, B. M. (1985). *Leader and performance: Beyond expectations.* New York: Free Press.

Bass, B. M. (1988). Evolving perspectives on charismatic leadership. In J. A. Conger & R. N. Kanungo (Eds.), *Charismatic leadership* (pp. 40–77). San Francisco: Jossey-Bass.

Bass, B. M. (1990). From transactional to transformational leadership: Learning to share the vision. *Organizational Dynamics, 18,* 19–31.

Bass, B. M. (2002). Cognitive, social, and emotional intelligence of transformational leaders. In R. E. Riggio, S. E. Murphy, & F. J. Pirozzolo (Eds.), *Multiple intelligences and leadership,* (pp. 105–118). Mahwah, NJ: Lawrence Erlbaum.

Bass, B. M., Avolio, B. J., & Goodheim, L. (1987). Biography and the assessment of trans-formational leadership at the world-class level. *Journal of Management, 13,* 7–19.

Bateson, G. (1972). *Steps to an ecology of the mind.* New York: Ballentine.

Bauer, T. N., & Green, S. G. (1996). The development of leader–member exchange: A longitudinal test. *Academy of Management Journal, 39,* 1538–1567.

Baxter, L. (1988). A dialectical perspective on communication strategies in relation-ship development. In S. Duck, D. Hay, S. Jobfoll, W. Ickes., & B. Montgomery (Eds.), *Handbook of personal relationships: Theory, research, and interventions* (pp. 257–274). Chichester, UK: Wiley.

Baxter, L. (1990). Dialectical contradictions in relationship development. *Journal of Personal and Social Relationships, 7,* 69–88.

Baxter, L., & Montgomery, B. (1996). *Relating: Dialogue and dialectics.* New York: Guilford.

Bennis, W. G., & Nanus, B. (1985). *Leaders: Strategies for taking charge.* New York: Harper & Row.

Bennis, W. G., & Thomas, R. J. (2002). *Geeks & geezers: How era, values, and defining moments shape leaders.* Boston: Harvard Business School Press.

Berger, P., & Luckman, T. L. (1966). *The social construction of knowledge: A treatise on the sociology of knowledge.* Garden City, NY: Doubleday.

Berglas, S. (2002, June 3). The very real dangers of executive coaching. *Harvard Business Review,* pp. 87–92.

Bevan, S., & Thompson, M. (1991). Performance management at the crossroads. *Personnel Management, 23,* 36–39.

Beyer, J. M. (1999). Taming and promoting charisma to change organizations. *Leadership Quarterly, 10,* 307–330.

Biggart, N. W., & Hamilton, G. G. (1987). An institutional theory of leadership. *Journal of Applied Behavioral Science, 23,* 429–442.

Billig, M. (1985). Prejudice, categorization, and particularization: From a perceptual to a rhetorical approach. *European Journal of Social Psychology, 15,* 79–103.

Blake, R., & Mouton, J. (1964). *The managerial grid.* Houston, TX: Gulf Publishing.

Bligh, M. C., Kohles, J. C., & Meindl, J. R. (2004). Charisma under crisis: Presidential leadership, rhetoric, and media responses before and after the September 11th terrorist attacks. *Leadership Quarterly, 15,* 211–240.

Bochner, A. P. (1985). Perspectives on inquiry: Representation, conversation, and reflec-tion. In M. L. Knapp & G. R. Miller (Eds.), *Handbook of interpersonal communica-tion* (pp. 27–58). Beverly Hills, CA: Sage.

Boden, D. (1990). The world as it happens: Ethnomethodology and conversation analy-sis. In G. Ritzer (Eds.), *Frontiers of social theory: The new synthesis* (pp. 185–213). New York: Columbia University Press.

Boden, D. (1994). *The business of talk: Organizations in action.* Cambridge, UK: Polity.

Boje, D. (1991). The storytelling organization: A study of story performance in an office supply firm. *Administrative Science Quarterly, 36,* 106–126.

Boje, D. (2001). *Narrative methods for organizational and communication research.* London: Sage.

Boje, D., Alvarez, R. C., & Schooling, B. (2001). Reclaiming story in organization: Narratologies and action sciences. In R. Westwood & S. Linstead (Eds.), *The language of organization* (pp. 132–175). London: Sage.

Bowles, M. L., & Coates, G. (1993). Image and substance: The management of perfor-mance as rhetoric or reality? *Personnel Review, 22,* 3–21.

Brady, D. (2006, June 26). Charm offensive: Why America's CEOs are suddenly so eager to be loved. *Business Week,* pp. 76–80.

Brady, F. N. (1997). Finding history for management. *Journal of Management Inquiry, 6,* 160–167.

Brief, A. P., & Weiss, H. M. (2002). Organizational behavior: Affect in the workplace. *Annual Review of Psychology, 53,* 279–307.

Bruner, J. S. (1986). *Actual minds, possible worlds.* Cambridge, MA: Harvard University Press.

Bruner, J. S. (1990). *Acts of meaning.* Cambridge, MA: Harvard University Press.

Bryman, A. (1992). *Charisma and leadership in organizations.* London: Sage.

Bryman, A. (1996). Leadership in organizations. In S. R. Clegg, C. Hardy, & W. R. Nord (Eds.), *Handbook of organization studies* (pp. 276–292). London: Sage.

Bryman, A. (2004). Qualitative research on leadership: A critical but appreciative review. *Leadership Quarterly, 15,* 729–770.

Bryman, A., Bresnen, M., Beardsworth, A., & Keil, T. (1988). Qualitative research and the study of leadership. *Human Relations, 41,* 13–30.

Burke, K. (1954). Fact, inference, and proof in the analysis of literary symbolism. In L. Bryson (Ed.), *Symbols and values: An initial study* (Thirteenth Symposium of the Conference on Science, Philosophy, and Religion) (pp. 283–306). New York: Harper.

Burke, K. (1957). *The philosophy of literary forms.* New York: Vintage.

Burke, K. (1962). *A rhetoric of motives.* Berkeley: University of California Press.

Burns, J. M. (1978). *Leadership.* New York: Harper & Row.

Burrell, G., & Morgan, G. (1979). *Sociological paradigms and organizational analysis.* London: Heinemann.

Buzzanell, P. M. (1994). Gaining a voice: Feminist organizational communication theorizing. *Management Communication Quarterly, 7,* 339–383.

Buzzanell, P. M. (2000). *Rethinking organizational and managerial communication from feminist perspectives.* Thousand Oaks, CA: Sage.

Byrne, J. A. (1998, June 8). Jack: A close-up look at how America's number 1 manager runs GE. *Business Week,* p. 90.

Cahan, B., & Ball, M. (2002, January). GIS at Ground Zero—Spatial technology bolsters World Trade Center response and recovery. *GEO World.* Available: http://www.geoplace.com

Calder, B. J. (1977). An attribution theory of leadership. In B. M. Staw & G. R. Salancik (Eds.), *New directions in organizational behavior* (pp. 179–202). Chicago: St. Clair Press.

Callon, M. (1986a). The sociology of an actor–network: The case of the electric vehicle. In M. Callon, J. Law, & A. Rip (Eds.), *Mapping the dynamics of science and technology* (pp. 19–34). London: Macmillan.

Callon, M. (1986b). Some elements in a sociology of translation: Domestication of the scallops and fishermen of St. Brieuc Bay. In J. Law (Ed.), *Power, action, and belief* (pp. 196–223). London: Routledge/Kegan Paul.

Callon, M., & Latour, B. (1981). Unscrewing the big leviathan: How actors macrostructure reality and how sociologists help them to do so. In A. V. Cicourel & K. Knorr-Centina (Eds.), *Advances in social theory and methodology: Towards an integration of micro- and macro-sociologies* (pp. 277–303). Boston: Routledge/Kegan Paul.

Cannon, M. D., & Witherspoon, R. (2005). Actionable feedback: Unlocking the power of learning and performance improvement. *Academy of Management Executive, 19,* 120–134.

Cantor, N., & Mischel, W. (1977). Traits as prototypes: Effects on recognition memory. *Journal of Personality and Social Psychology, 35,* 38–48.

Cantor, N., & Mischel, W. (1979). Prototypes in person perception. In L. Berkowitz (Eds.), *Advances in experimental social psychology* (Vol. 12). London: Academic Press.

Carlson, S. (1951). *Executive behavior.* Stockholm: Strombergs.

Carroll, S. J., & Gillen, D. J. (1987). Are classical management functions useful in describing managerial work? *Academy of Management Review, 12,* 38–51.

Caruso, D. R., Mayer, J. D., & Salovey, P. (2002). Emotional intelligence and emotional leadership. In R. E. Riggio, S. E. Murphy, & F. J. Pirozzolo (Eds.), *Multiple intelligences and leadership* (pp. 55–74). Mahwah, NJ: Erlbaum.

Casey, C. (1999). "Come, join our family": Discipline and integration in corporate organizational culture. *Human Relations, 52,* 155–178.

Chia, R. (2000). Discourse analysis as organizational analysis. *Organization, 7,* 513–518.

Chouliaraki, L., & Fairclough, N. (1999). *Discourse in late modernity: Rethinking critical discourse analysis.* Edinburgh, Scotland: Edinburgh University Press.

Church, A. H., & Bracken, D. W. (1997). Advancing the state of the art 360-degree feedback. *Group and Organization Management, 22,* 149–161.

Clair, R. P. (1998). *Organizing silence: A world of possibilities.* Albany: State University of New York Press.

Cloud, D. L. (2005). Fighting words: Labor and limits of communication at Staley, 1993 to 1996. *Management Communication Quarterly, 18,* 509–542.

Coleman, J. S. (1970). Social inventions. *Social Forces, 49,* 163–173.

Collinson, D. L. (1988). 'Engineering humor': Masculinity, joking and conflict in shopfloor relations. *Organization Studies, 9,* 181–199.

Collinson, D. L. (1992). *Managing the shop floor: Subjectivity, masculinity, and workplace culture.* New York: Walter de Gruyter.

Collinson, D. L. (2003). Identities and insecurities: Selves at work. *Organization, 10,* 527–547.

Collinson, D. L. (2006). Rethinking followership: A post-structuralist analysis of follower identities. *Leadership Quarterly, 17,* 179–189.

Collinson, D. L., & Hearn, J. (1996a). Breaking the silence: On men, masculinities, and managements. In D. L. Collinson & J. Hearn (Eds.), *Men as managers, managers as men* (pp. 1–24). London: Sage.

Collinson, D. L., & Hearn, J. (1996b). *Men as managers, managers as men: Critical perspectives on men, masculinities, and managements.* London: Sage.

Conger, J. A. (1989). *The charismatic leader.* San Francisco: Jossey-Bass.

Conger, J. A. (1991). Inspiring others: The language of leadership. *The Executive, 5,* 31–45.

Conger, J. A. (1998). Qualitative research as the cornerstone methodology for understanding leadership. *Leadership Quarterly, 9,* 107–121.

Conger, J. A., & Kanungo, R. M. (1987). Toward a behavioral theory of charismatic leadership in organizational settings. *Academy of Management Review, 12,* 637–647.

Conger, J. A., & Kanungo, R. N. (1988). Training charismatic leadership: A risky and critical task. In J. A. Conger & R. N. Kanungo (Eds.), *Charismatic leadership* (pp. 309–323). San Francisco: Jossey-Bass.

Conger, J. A., & Kanungo, R. N. (1998). *Charismatic leadership in organizations.* Thousand Oaks, CA: Sage.

Connelly, S., Gaddis, B., & Helton-Fauth, W. (2002). A closer look at the role of emotions in transformational and charismatic leadership. In B. Avolio & F. J. Yammarino (Eds.), *Transformational and charismatic leadership: The road ahead* (pp. 255–283). Amsterdam: JAI Press.

Conrad, C. (2004). Organizational discourse analysis: Avoiding the determinism–volunteerism trap. *Organization, 11,* 427–439.

Conrad, C., & Haynes, J. (2001). Developing key constructs. In F. M. Jablin & L. L. Putnam (Eds.), *The new handbook of organizational communication* (pp. 47–77). Thousand Oaks, CA: Sage.

Cooley, C. H. (1902). *Human nature and the social order.* New York: Scribner.

Cooperrider, D., Barrett, F., & Srivastva, S. (1995). Social construction and appreciative inquiry: A journey in organizational theory. In D. Hosking, P. Dachler, & K. Gergen (Eds.), *Management and organization: Relational alternatives to individualism* (pp. 157–200). Aldershot, UK: Avebury Press.

Cooren, F. (1999). Applying socio-semiotics to organizational communication: A new approach. *Management Communication Quarterly, 13,* 294–304.

Cooren, F. (2001). *The organizing property of communication.* Amsterdam/Philadelphia: John Benjamins.

Cooren, F. (2004). Textual agency: How texts do things in organizational settings. *Organization, 11,* 373–393.

Cooren, F. (In press). The organizational world as a plenum of agencies. In F. Cooren, J. R. Taylor, & E. J. Van Every (Eds.), *Communication as organizing: Empirical and theoretical explorations in the dynamic of text and conversation.* Mahwah, NJ: Erlbaum.

Cooren, F., & Fairhurst, G. (2002). The leader as a practical narrator: Leadership as the art of translating. In D. Holman & R. Thorpe (Eds.), *The manager as a practical author* (pp. 85–103). London: Sage.

Cooren, F., & Fairhurst, G. (2004). Speech timing and spacing: The phenomenon of organizational closure. *Organization, 11,* 797–828.

Cooren, F., & Fairhurst, G. (in press). Dislocation and stabilization: How to scale up from interactions to organization. In L. L. Putnam & A. Nicotera (Eds.), *Communication as constitutive of organizing.* Thousand Oaks, CA: Sage.

Cooren, F., & Taylor, J. R. (1997). Organization as an effect of mediation: Redefining the link between organization and communication. *Communication Theory, 7,* 219–260.

Cooren, F., & Taylor, J. R. (1998). The procedural and rhetorical modes of the organizing dimension of communication: Discursive analysis of a parliamentary commission. *Communication Review, 3,* 65–101.

Cooren, F., Taylor, J. R., & Van Every, E. J. (Eds.). (2006). *Communication as organizing.* Mahwah, NJ: Lawrence Erlbaum.

Corman, S. R., & Poole, M. S. (Eds.). (2000). *Perspectives on organizational communication: Finding common ground.* New York: Guilford Press.

Corman, S. R., Kuhn, T., McPhee, R. D., & Dooley, K. J. (2002). Studying complex discursive systems. *Human Communication Research, 28,* 157–206.

Coser, R. L. (1960). Laughter among colleagues: A study of the social functions of humor among the staff of a mental hospital. *Psychiatry, 23,* 81–95.

Courtright, J. A., Fairhurst, G. T., & Rogers, L. E. (1989). Interaction patterns in organic and mechanistic systems. *Academy of Management Journal, 32,* 773–802.

Craig, R. T. (1989). Communication as a practical discipline. In B. Dervin, L. Grossberg, B. J. O'Keefe, & E. Wartella (Eds.), *Rethinking communication: Vol. 1: Paradigm issues* (pp. 97–122). Newbury Park, CA: Sage.

Craig, R. T. (1999). Communication theory as a field. *Communication Theory, 9,* 119–161.

Craig, R. T., & Tracy, K. (1995). Grounded practical theory: The case of intellectual discussion. *Communication Theory, 5,* 248–272.

Cronen, V. E. (1995a). Coordinated management of meaning: The consequentiality of communication and the recapturing of experience. In S. J. Sigman (Ed.), *The consequentiality of communication* (pp. 17–65). Hillsdale, NJ: Erlbaum.

Cronen, V. E. (1995b). Practical theory and the tasks ahead for social approaches to communication. In W. Leeds-Hurwitz (Ed.), *Social approaches to communication* (pp. 217–242). New York: Guilford Press.

Cronen, V. E. (2001). Practical theory, practical art, and the pragmatic-systemic account of inquiry. *Communication Theory, 11,* 14–35.

Cunliffe, A. L., Luhman, J. T., & Boje, D. (2004). Narrative temporality: Implications for organizational research. *Organization Studies, 25,* 261–286.

Czarniawska, B. (2004). *Narratives in social science research.* London: Sage.

Czarniawska-Joerges, B. (1997). *Narrating the organization: Dramas of institutional identity.* Chicago: University of Chicago Press.

Dale, K. (2005). Building a social materiality: Spatial and embodied politics in organizational control. *Organization, 12,* 649–678.

Dansereau, F., Alutto, J. A., & Yammarino, F. J. (1984). *Theory testing in organizational behavior: The varient approach.* Englewood Cliffs, NJ: Prentice Hall.

Dansereau, F., Graen, G. B., & Haga, W. J. (1975). A vertical dyad linkage approach to leadership within formal organizations: A longitudinal investigation of the role making process. *Organizational Behavior and Human Decision Processes, 13,* 46–78.

Daudi, G. (1986). *Power in the organization.* Cornwall, UK: TJ Press.

Day, D.V., Gronn, P., & Salas, E. (2006). Leadership in team-based organizations: On the threshold of a new era. *Leadership Quarterly, 17,* 211–216

Deal, T., & Kennedy, A. (1982). *Corporate cultures: The rites and rituals of corporate life.* Reading, MA: Addison-Wesley.

Deetz, S. A. (1992). *Democracy in an age of corporate colonization: Developments in communication and the politics of everyday life.* New York: State University of New York Press.

Deetz, S. A. (1995). *Transforming communication, transforming business: Building responsive and responsible workplaces.* Cresskill, NJ: Hampton Press.

Deetz, S. A. (1996). Describing differences in approaches to organization science: Rethinking Burrell and Morgan and their legacy. *Organization Science, 7,* 190–207.

Deming, W. E. (1982). *Out of crisis.* Cambridge, MA: Cambridge University Press.

Dent, E. B., Higgins, M. E., & Wharff, D. M. (2005). Spirituality and leadership: An empirical review of definitions, distinctions, and embedded assumptions. *Leadership Quarterly, 15,* 625–654.

Derrida, J. (1988). *Limited inc.* Evanston, IL: Northwestern University Press.

DeSanctis, G., & Poole, M. S. (1994). Capturing the complexity in advanced technology use: Adaptive structuration theory. *Organization Science, 5,* 121–147.

Dienesch, R. M., & Liden, R. C. (1986). Leader–member exchange model of leadership: A critique and further development. *Academy of Management Review, 11,* 618–634.

van Dijk, T. A. (1985). *Handbook of discourse analysis*. New York: Academic Press.

van Dijk, T. A. (1991). *Racism and the press*. London: Routledge.

van Dijk, T. A. (1997). The study of discourse. In T. A. van Dijk (Ed.), *Discourse as structure and process* (Vol. 1, pp. 1–34). London: Sage.

Drew, P., & Heritage, J. (Eds.). (1992). *Talk at work: Interaction in institutional settings*. Cambridge, UK: Cambridge University Press.

Dreyfus, H. L., & Rabinow, P. (1983). *Michel Foucault: Beyond structuralism and hermeneutics*. Chicago: University of Chicago Press.

du Gay, P., & Salaman, G. (1996). The conduct of management and the management of conduct: Contemporary managerial discourse and the constitution of the "competent manager." *Journal of Management Studies, 33,* 263–282.

Dumaine, B. (1993, October 18). America's toughest bosses: Seven CEOs who make your top dog look like a pussycat. *Fortune,* pp. 38–50.

Dunn, V. (1999). *Command and control of fire emergencies*. Saddle Brook, NJ: Fire Engineering.

Eagly, A. H. (2005). Achieving relational authenticity in leadership: Does gender matter? *Leadership Quarterly, 16,* 459–474.

Edwards, D. (1994). Script formulations: An analysis of event descriptions in conversation. *Journal of Language and Social Psychology, 13,* 211–247.

Edwards, D. (1997). *Discourse and cognition*. London: Sage.

Edwards, D. (2005). Discursive psychology. In K. L. Fitch & R. E. Sanders (Eds.), *Handbook of language and social interaction* (pp. 257–273). Mawah, NJ: Erlbaum.

Edwards, D., & Potter, J. (1992). *Discursive psychology*. London: Sage.

Eisenberg, E. (1984). Ambiguity as strategy in organizational communication. *Communication Monographs, 51,* 227–242.

Eisenberg, E., & Goodall, H. L. Jr. (2004). *Organizational communication: Balancing creativity and constraint* (4th ed.). Boston: Bedford/St. Martin's.

Ellis, D. G. (1995). Fixing communicative meaning: A coherentist theory. *Communication Research, 22,* 515–544.

Emrich, C. G., Brower, H. H., Feldman, J. M., & Garland, H. (2001). Images in words: Presidential rhetoric, charisma, and greatness. *Administrative Science Quarterly, 46,* 526–557.

Engeström, Y. (1999). Expansive visibilization of work: An activity-theoretical perspective. *Computer Supported Cooperative Work, 8,* 63–93.

Erickson, R. J. (1995). The importance of authenticity for self and society. *Symbolic Interaction, 18,* 121–144.

Fairclough, N. (1992). *Discourse and social change*. Cambridge, UK: Polity.

Fairclough, N. (1993). Critical discourse analysis and the marketization of public discourse: The universities. *Discourse & Society, 4,* 133–168.

Fairclough, N. (1995). *Critical discourse analysis: The critical study of language*. London: Longman.

Fairclough, N. (2003). *Analysing discourse: Textual analysis for social research*. London: Routledge.

Fairclough, N., & Thomas, P. (2004). The discourse of globalization and the globalization of discourse. In D. Grant, C. Hardy, C. Oswick, N. Phillips, & L. Putnam (Eds.), *The Sage handbook of organizational discourse* (pp. 379–396). London: Sage.

Fairclough, N., & Wodak, R. (1997). Critical discourse analysis. In T. A. van Dijk (Ed.), *Discourse as social interaction* (pp. 258–284). London: Sage.

Fairhurst, G. (2001). Dualisms in leadership research. In F. M. Jablin & L. L. Putnam (Eds.), *The new handbook of organizational communication* (pp. 379–439). Thousand Oaks, CA: Sage.

Fairhurst, G. T. (1993a). Echoes of the vision: When the rest of the organization talks Total Quality. *Management Communication Quarterly, 6,* 331–371.

Fairhurst, G. T. (1993b). The leader–member exchange patterns of women leaders in industry: A discourse analysis. *Communication Monographs, 60,* 321–351.

Fairhurst, G. T. (2004). Textuality and agency in interaction analysis. *Organization, 11,* 335–354.

Fairhurst, G. T. (2005). Reframing the art of framing: Problems and prospects for leadership. *Leadership, 1,* 165–185.

Fairhurst, G. T. (2006). Liberating leadership in *Corporation After Mr. Sam*: A response. In F. Cooren (Ed.), *Interacting and organizing: Analyses of a board meeting* (pp. 53–71). Mahwah, NJ: Erlbaum.

Fairhurst, G. T., & Chandler, T. A. (1989). Social structure in leader–member interaction. *Communication Monographs, 56,* 215–239.

Fairhurst, G. T., & Cooren, F. (2004). Organizational language in use: Interaction analysis, conversation analysis, and speech act schematics. In D. Grant, C. Hardy, C. Oswick, N. Phillips, & L. Putnam (Eds.), *The Sage handbook of organizational discourse* (pp. 131–152). London: Sage.

Fairhurst, G. T., Green, S. G., & Courtright, J. A. (1995). Inertial forces and the implementation of a sociotechnical systems approach: A communication study. *Organization Science, 6,* 168–185.

Fairhurst, G. T., & Hamlett, S. R. (2003). The narrative basis of leader–member exchange. In G. B. Graen (Ed.), *Dealing with diversity* (pp. 117–144). Greenwich, CT: Information Age Publishing.

Fairhurst, G. T., & Putnam, L. L. (2004). Organizations as discursive constructions. *Communication Theory, 14,* 5–26.

Fairhurst, G. T., Rogers, L. E., & Sarr, R. (1987). Manager–subordinate control patterns and judgments about the relationship. In M. McLaughlin (Ed.), *Communication yearbook 10* (pp. 395–415). Beverly Hills, CA: Sage.

Fairhurst, G. T., & Sarr, R. A. (1996). *The art of framing: Managing the language of leadership*. San Francisco: Jossey-Bass.

Fayol, H. (1949). *General and industrial management*. London: Pitman.

Feldman, M. S. (2000). Organizational routines as a source of continuous change. *Organization Science, 11,* 611–629.

Fiedler, F. E. (1971). *Leadership*. Morristown, NJ: General Learning Press.

Fiol, C. M., Harris, D., & House, R. J. (1999). Charismatic leadership: Strategies for effecting social change. *Leadership Quarterly, 10,* 449–482.

Firth, A. (Ed.) (1995). *The discourse of negotiation: Studies of language in the workplace.* Oxford, UK: Pergamon.

Fisher, W. R. (1984). Narration as a human communication paradigm: The case of public moral argument. *Communication Monographs, 51,* 1–22.

Fleming, P. (2005). Metaphors of resistance. *Management Communication Quarterly, 19,* 45–66.

Fleming, P., & Spicer, A. (2003). Working at a cynical distance: Implications for power, subjectivity and resistance. *Organization, 10,* 157–179.

Foucault, M. (1972). *The archeology of knowledge and the discourse on language.* London: Tavistock.

Foucault, M. (1973). *The order of things.* New York: Vintage Books.

Foucault, M. (1979). On governmentality. *Ideology and Consciousness, 6,* 5–22.

Foucault, M. (1980). *Power/knowledge: Selected interviews and other writings 1972–1977.* New York: Pantheon.

Foucault, M. (1983). The subject and power. In H. L. Dreyfus & P. Rabinow (Eds.), *Michel Foucault: Beyond structuralism and hermeneutics* (pp. 208–226). Chicago: University of Chicago Press.

Foucault, M. (1990). *The history of sexuality: Volume 1.* New York: Vintage/Random House.

Foucault, M. (1995). *Discipline and punish.* New York: Vintage/Random House.

Fournier, V., & Grey, C. 2000. At the critical moment: Conditions and prospects for critical management studies. *Human Relations, 53,* 7–32.

Frost, P. J. (2003). *Toxic emotions at work.* Boston: Harvard Business School Press.

Funderburg, S. A., & Levy, P. E. (1997). The influence of individual and contextual variables on 360-degree feedback system attitudes. *Group and Organization Management, 22,* 210–235.

Gabriel, Y. (1999). Beyond happy families: A critical reevaluation of the control-resistance-identity triangle. *Human Relations, 52,* 179–203.

Gabriel, Y. (2004). Narratives, stories, and texts. In D. Grant, C. Hardy, C. Oswick, N. Phillips, & L. Putnam (Eds.), *Sage handbook of organizational discourse* (pp. 61–77). London: Sage.

Gardner, W. L., & Avolio, B. J. (1998). The charismatic relationship: A dramaturgical perspective. *Academy of Management Review, 23,* 32–58.

Gardner, W. L., Avolio, B. J., Luthans, F., May, D. R., & Walumbwa, F. (2005). "Can you see the real me?" A self-based model of authentic leader and follower development. *Leadership Quarterly, 16,* 343–372.

Garfinkel, H. (1967). *Studies in ethnomethodology.* Englewood Cliffs, NJ: Prentice Hall.

Gargiulo, T. L. (2005). *The strategic use of stories in organizational communication and learning.* Armonk, NY: M.E. Sharpe.

Geertz, C. (1984). 'From the native's point of view': On the nature of anthropological understanding. In R. Shweder & R. LeVine (Eds.), *Culture theory* (pp. 123–137). New York: Cambridge University Press.

George, J. M. (2000). Emotions and leadership: The role of emotional intelligence. *Human Relations, 53,* 1027–1055.

Gergen, K. (1991). *The saturated self: Dilemmas of identity in contemporary life.* New York: Basic Books.

Gergen, K. (1999). *An invitation to social construction.* London: Sage.

Gergen, K. (2001). *Social construction in context.* London: Sage.

Gergen, K. (2003). Beyond knowing in organizational inquiry. *Organization, 10,* 453–456.

Gersick, C. J. G. (1988). Time and transition in work teams: Toward a new model of group development. *Academy of Management Journal, 31,* 9–41.

Gerstner, C. R., & Day, D. V. (1997). Meta-analytic review of leader–member exchange theory: Correlates and construct issues. *Journal of Applied Psychology, 82,* 827–844.

Gibbs, N. (2001, December 31). Person of the year. *Time,* pp. 34–36.

Gibson, J. J. (1979). *The ecological approach to visual perception.* Mahwah, NJ: Erlbaum.

Giddens, A. (1979). *Central problems in social theory.* Berkeley: University of California Press.

Giddens, A. (1984). *The constitution of society.* Berkeley: University of California Press.

Giddens, A. (1991). *Modernity and self-identity*. Cambridge, UK: Polity.

Gilbert, G. N., & Mulkay, M. (1984). *Opening Pandora's box: A sociological analysis of scientists' discourse*. Cambridge, UK: Cambridge University Press.

Gioia, D. A. (2003). Give it up! Reflections on the interpreted world (A commentary on Meckler and Baillie). *Journal of Management Inquiry, 12*, 285–292.

Gioia, D. A., & Chittipeddi, K. (1991). Sensemaking and sensegiving in strategic change initiation. *Strategic Management Journal, 12*, 433–448.

Gioia, D. A., & Pitre, E. (1990). Multiparadigm perspectives on theory building. *Academy of Management Review, 15*, 584–602.

Gioia, D. A., & Poole, P. P. (1984). Scripts in organizational behavior. *Academy of Management Review, 9*, 449–459.

Gioia, D. A., & Sims, H. P. Jr. (1986). Cognition–behavior connections: Attribution and verbal behavior in leader–subordinate interactions. *Organizational Behavior and Human Decision Processes, 37*, 197–229.

Goffman, E. (1959). *The presentation of self in everyday life*. New York: Doubleday.

Goldman, P. (1994). Searching for history in organizational theory: Comment on Kieser. *Organization Science, 5*, 621–623.

Goleman, D. (1995). *Emotional intelligence*. New York: Bantam.

Goleman, D., Boyatzis, R., & McKee, A. (2002). *Primal leadership: Realizing the power of emotional intelligence*. Boston: Harvard Business School Press.

Gordon, C. (1980). *Power/knowledge: Selected interviews and other writings by Michel Foucault*. New York: Pantheon.

Graen, G. B., Novak, M., & Sommerkamp, P. (1982). The effects of leader–member exchange and job design on productivity and satisfaction: Testing a dual attachment model. *Organizational Behavior and Human Performance, 30*, 109–131.

Graen, G. B., & Scandura, T. A. (1985). *When your boss invests in your career*. Unpublished manuscript, University of Cincinnati.

Graen, G. B., & Scandura, T. A. (1987). Toward a psychology of dyadic organizing. In B. Staw & L. L. Cummings (Eds.), *Research in organizational behavior* (pp. 175–208). Greenwich, CT: JAI Press.

Graen, G. B., & Uhl-Bien, M. (1995). Relationship-based approach to leadership: Development of a leader–member exchange (LMX) theory of leadership over 25 years— Applying a multi-level multi-domain perspective. *Leadership Quarterly, 6*, 219–247.

Graham, J. W. (1991). Servant-leadership in organizations: Inspirational and moral. *Leadership Quarterly, 2*, 105–119.

Gramsci, A. (1971). *Selections from the prison notebooks*. New York: International Publishers.

Grant, D., Keenoy, T., & Oswick, C. (1998). Organizational discourse: Of diversity, dichotomy and multi-disciplinarity. In D. Grant, T. Keenoy, & C. Oswick (Eds.), *Discourse and organization* (pp. 1–13). London: Sage.

Greimas, A. J. (1987). *On meaning: Selected writings in semiotic theory*. London: Frances Pinter.

Greimas, A. J. (1988). *Maupassant. The semiotics of text: Practical exercises*. Amsterdam: John Benjamins.

Greimas, A. J., & Courtes, J. (1982). *Semiotics and language: An analytical dictionary*. Bloomington: Indiana University Press.

Grint, K. (1997). *Leadership: Classical, contemporary, and critical approaches*. Oxford, UK: Oxford University Press.

Grint, K. (2000). *The arts of leadership.* Oxford, UK: Oxford University Press.

Grint, K., & Woolgar, S. (1997). *The machine at work: Technology, work and organization.* Cambridge, UK: Polity.

Gronn, P. (1982). Neo-Taylorism in educational administration? *Education Administration Quarterly, 18,* 17–35.

Gronn, P. (1983). Talk as the work: The accomplishment of school administration. *Administrative Science Quarterly, 28,* 1–21.

Gronn, P. (1993). Psychobiography on the couch: Character, biography, and the comparative study of leaders. *Journal of Applied Behavioral Science, 29,* 343–358.

Gronn, P. (1995). Greatness re-visited: The current obsession with transformational leadership. *Leading and Managing, 1,* 14–27.

Gronn, P. (2000). Distributed properties: A new architecture for leadership. *Educational Management and Administration, 28,* 317–338.

Gronn, P. (2002). Distributed leadership as a unit of analysis. *Leadership Quarterly, 13,* 423–451.

Gronn, P. (2005). Questions about autobiographical leadership. *Leadership, 1,* 481–490.

Gumperz, J. H. (1972). Introduction. In J. J. Gumperz & D. Hymes (Eds.), *Directions in sociolinguistics: The ethnography of communication.* New York: Holt, Rinehart & Winston.

Habermas, J. (1984). *The theory of communicative action, volume 1: Reason and the rationalization of society.* Boston: Beacon Press.

Hacking, I. (1999). *The social construction of what?* Cambridge, MA: Harvard University Press.

Hales, C. P. (1986). What do managers do? A critical review of the evidence. *Journal of Management Studies, 23,* 88–115.

Halkowski, T. (1990). 'Role' as an interactional device. *Social Problems, 37,* 564–577.

Hammersley, M. (2003a). Conversation analysis and discourse analysis: Methods or paradigms? *Discourse & Society, 14,* 751–781.

Hammersley, M. (2003b). The impracticality of scepticism: A further response to Potter. *Discourse & Society, 14,* 803–804.

Hanges, P. J., Lord, R. G., & Dickson, M. W. (2000). An information-processing perspective on leadership and culture: A case for connectionist architecture. *Applied Psychology: An International Review, 49,* 133–161.

Hardy, C., & Clegg, S. R. (1996). Some dare call it power. In S. R. Clegg, C. Hardy, & W. R. Nord (Eds.), *Handbook of organization studies* (pp. 622–641). London: Sage.

Harré, R., & Secord, P. F. (1972). *The explanation of social behavior.* Totowa, NJ: Littlefield, Adams.

Hart, R. (1984). *Verbal style and the presidency.* New York: Academic Press.

Hart, R. (1987). *The sound of leadership: Presidential communication in the modern age.* Chicago: University of Chicago Press.

Haslett, B. J. (1987). *Communication: Strategic action in context.* Hillsdale, NJ: Erlbaum.

Hassard, J. (1988). Overcoming hermeticism in organization theory: An alternative to paradigm incommensurability. *Human Relations, 41,* 247–259.

Hassard, J. (1991). Multiple paradigms and organizational analysis: A case study. *Organization Studies, 12,* 279–299.

Hassard, J., Holliday, R., & Willmott, H. (2000). *Body and organization.* London: Sage.

Hayward, M. L. A., Rindova, V. P., & Pollock, T. G. (2004). Believing one's own press: The causes and consquences of CEO celebrity. *Strategic Management Journal, 25,* 637–655.

Hegde, R. S. (1998). A view from elsewhere: Locating difference and the politics of representation from a transnational feminist perspective. *Communication Theory, 8,* 271–297.

Hegele, C., & Kieser, A. (2001). Control the construction of your legend or someone else will: An analysis of texts on Jack Welch. *Journal of Management Inquiry, 10,* 298–309.

Helmer, J. (1993). Story telling in the creation and maintenance of organizational tension and stratification. *Southern Communication Journal, 59,* 34–44.

Heritage, J. (1997). Conversation analysis and institutional talk. In D. Silverman (Ed.), *Qualitative research: Theory, method, and practice* (pp. 161–182). London: Sage.

Herzberg, F. (1966). *Work and the nature of man.* Cleveland, OH: World Publishing Company.

Herzberg, F. (1968). One more time: How do you motivate employees? *Harvard Business Review, 46,* 53–62.

Hester, S. K., & Eglin, P. (1997). *Culture in action.* Washington, DC: University Press of America.

Hickman, C. R. (1990). *Mind of a manager, soul of a leader.* New York: Wiley.

Hilbert, R. (1981). Toward an understanding of 'role.' *Theory and Society, 10,* 207–226.

Hill, R. P., & Stephens, D. L. (2005). The multiplicity of selves and selves management: A leadership challenge for the 21st century. *Leadership, 1,* 127–140.

Hinde, R. (1979). *Toward understanding relationships.* New York: Academic Press.

Hodge, R., & Kress, G. (1988). *Social semiotics.* Cambridge, UK: Polity.

Hogg, M. (2001). Social identification, group prototypicality, and emergent leadership. In M. Hogg & D. J. Terry (Eds.), *Social identity processes in organizational contexts* (pp. 197–228). Philadelphia: Psychology Press.

Hogg, M., & Terry, D. J. (2000). Social identity and self-categorization processes in organizational contexts. *Academy of Management Review, 25,* 121–140.

Holman, D., & Thorpe, R. (2003). *Management and language: The manager as a practical author.* London: Sage.

Holmer-Nadesan, M. (1996). Organizational identity and space of action. *Organization Studies, 17,* 49–81.

Holmes, M. E., & Rogers, L. E. (1995). *"Let me rephrase that question": Five common criticisms of interaction analysis studies.* Annual conference of the Western States Communication Association, Portland, OR.

Holstein, J. A., & Gubrium, J. F. (2000). *The self we live by: Narrative identity in a postmodern world.* New York: Oxford University Press.

Hoskin, K. (2004). Spacing, timing, and the invention of management. *Organization, 11,* 743–757.

Hosking, D. M. (1988). Organising, leadership and skilful process. *Journal of Management Studies, 25,* 147–166.

Hosking, D. M., & Morley, I. E. (1988). The skills of leadership. In J. G. Hunt, R. Baglia, & C. Schriesheim (Eds.), *Emerging leadership vistas.* Lexington, MA: Arlington Heights.

Hosking, D. M., & Morley, I. E. (1991). *A social psychology of organizing: People, processes, and contexts.* New York: Harvester/Wheatsheaf.

House, R. J. (1977). A 1976 theory of charismatic leadership. In J. G. Hunt & L. L. Larson (Eds.), *Leadership: The cutting edge* (pp. 189–207). Carbondale: Southern Illinois University Press.

House, R. J., & Aditya, R. N. (1997). The social scientific study of leadership: Quo vadis? *Journal of Management, 23,* 409–473.

House, R. J., Spangler, W. D., & Woycke, J. (1991). Personality and charisma in the U.S. presidency: A psychological theory of leader effectiveness. *Administrative Science Quarterly, 36,* 364–396.

Hughes, T. (1988). The seamless web: Technology, science, et cetera, et cetera. In B. Elliott (Ed.), *Technology and social process* (pp. 9–19). Edinburgh, Scotland: Edinburgh University Press.

Hunt, J. G. (1991). *Leadership: A new synthesis.* Newbury Park, CA: Sage.

Hurst, D. (1992). Thoroughly modern—Mary Parker Follett. *Business Quarterly, 56,* 55–59.

Huspek, M. (2000). Oppositional codes: The case of the Penitentiary of New Mexico riot. *Journal of Applied Communication, 28,* 144–163.

Husserl, E. (1962). *Ideas: General introduction to pure phenomenology.* London: Collier MacMillan.

Ilies, R., Morgeson, F. P., & Nahrgang, J. D. (2005). Authentic leadership and eudaemonic well-being: Understanding leader–follower outcomes. *Leadership Quarterly, 16,* 373–394.

Isaacs, W. (1999). *Dialogue: And the art of thinking together.* New York: Currency.

Jackson, N., & Carter, P. (1991). In defense of paradigm incommensurability. *Organization Studies, 12,* 109–127.

Jackson, S. (1986). Building a case for claims about discourse structure. In D. G. Ellis & W. A. Donohue (Eds.), *Contemporary issues in language and discourse processes* (pp. 129–147). Hillsdale, NJ: Erlbaum.

Jacobs, S. (1986). How to make an argument from example in discourse analysis. In D. G. Ellis & W. A. Donohue (Eds.), *Contemporary issues in language and discourse processes* (pp. 149–168). Hillsdale, NJ: Erlbaum.

Jacobs, S. (1988). Evidence and inference in conversation analysis. In J. A. Anderson (Ed.), *Communication Yearbook 11* (pp. 433–443). Newbury Park, CA: Sage.

Jacobs, S. (1990). On the especially nice fit between qualitative analysis and the known properties of conversation. *Communication Monographs, 57,* 243–249.

Jacques, E. (1990, January/February). In praise of hierarchy. *Harvard Business Review,* pp. 127–133.

Jayyusi, L. (1984). *Categorization and the moral order.* Boston: Routledge/Kegan Paul.

Jermier, J. M., Knights, D., & Lord, W. R. (1994). *Resistance and power in organizations.* New York: Routledge.

Jorgenson, J. (2002). Engineering selves: Negotiating gender and identity in technical work. *Management Communication Quarterly, 15,* 350–380.

Juran, J. M. (1964). *Managerial breakthrough.* New York: McGraw-Hill.

Juran, J. M. (1988). *Juran on planning quality.* New York: Free Press.

Kanter, R. M. (1977). *Men and women of the corporation.* New York: Basic Books.

Kanter, R. M. (1983). *The changemasters.* New York: Simon & Schuster.

Karon, L. A. (1976). Presence in the new rhetoric. In R. D. Dearin (Ed.), *The new rhetoric of Chaim Perelman: Statement and response* (pp. 163–178). New York: University Press of America.

Katerberg, R., & Hom, P. (1981). Effects of within-group and between-group variation in leadership. *Journal of Applied Psychology, 66,* 218–223.

Katz, D., & Kahn, D. L. (1978). *The social psychology of organizations* (2nd ed.). New York: Wiley.

Keller, T., & Dansereau, F. (1995). Leadership and empowerment: A social exchange perspective. *Human Relations, 48,* 127–145.

Keltner, D., & Haidt, J. (1999). Social functions of emotions at four levels of analysis. *Cognition and Emotion, 13,* 505–521.

Keltner, D., & Kring, A. M. (1998). Emotion, social function, and psychopathology. *Review of General Psychology, 2,* 320–342.

Kerfoot, D., & Knights, D. (1996). 'The best is yet to come?': The quest for embodiment in managerial work. In D. L. Collinson & J. Hearn (Eds.), *Men as managers, managers as men* (pp. 78–98). London: Sage.

Kernis, M. H. (2003). Toward a conceptualization of optimal self-esteem. *Psychological Inquiry, 14,* 1–26.

Kerr, S., & Jermier, J. M. (1978). Substitutes for leadership: Their meaning and measurement. *Organizational Behavior and Human Performance, 12,* 374–403.

Kets de Vries, M. F. R. (1990a). Leaders on the couch. *Journal of Applied Behavioral Science, 26,* 423–431.

Kets de Vries, M. F. R. (1990b). The organizational fool: Balancing a leader's hubris. *Human Relations, 43,* 751–770.

Kets de Vries, M. F. R. (1991). Whatever happened to the philosopher-king? The leader's addiction to power. *Journal of Management Studies, 28,* 339–351.

Kets de Vries, M. F. R. (2005). Leadership group coaching in action: The Zen of creating high performance teams. *Academy of Management Executive, 19,* 61–76.

Kieser, A. (1994). Why organization theory needs historical analyses—and how this should be performed. *Organization Science, 5,* 608–620.

Kihlstrom, J. F., & Klein, S. B. (1994). The self as a knowledge structure. In J. R. S. Wyer & T. K. Srull (Eds.), *Handbook of social cognition* (2nd ed., pp. 153–208). Hillsdale, NJ: Erlbaum.

Kirtzman, A. (2001). *Rudy Giuliani: Emperor of the city.* New York: Perennial.

Knights, D., & McCabe, D. (2000). 'Ain't misbehavin'? Opportunities for resistance under new forms of 'quality' management. *Sociology, 34,* 421–436.

Knights, D., & McCabe, D. (2001). 'A different world': Shifting masculinities in the transition to call centres. *Organization, 8,* 619–646.

Knights, D., & Morgan, G. (1991). Corporate strategy, organizations, and subjectivity: A critique. *Organization Studies, 12,* 251–273.

Knights, D., & Willmott, H. (1992). Conceptualizing leadership processes: A study of senior managers in a financial services company. *Journal of Management Studies, 29,* 761–782.

Kollock, P., Blumstein, P., & Schwartz, P. (1985). Sex and power in interaction: Conversational privileges and duties. *American Sociological Review, 50,* 24–46.

Komaki, J. L. (1986). Toward effective supervision: An operant analysis and comparison of managers at work. *Journal of Applied Psychology, 71,* 270–279.

Komaki, J. L. (1998). *Leadership from an operant perspective.* London: Routledge.

Komaki, J. L., & Citera, M. (1990). Beyond effective supervision: Identifying key interactions between superior and subordinate. *Leadership Quarterly, 1,* 91–106.

Komaki, J. L., Zlotnick, S., & Jensen, M. (1986). Developing an operant-based taxonomy and observational index of supervisory behavior. *Journal of Applied Psychology, 71,* 260–269.

Kondo, D. K. (1990). *Crafting selves: Power, gender, and discourses of identity in a Japanese workplace.* Chicago: University of Chicago Press.

Kotter, J. P. (1990). *A force for change: How leadership differs from management.* New York: Free Press.

Kouzes, J. M., & Posner, B. Z. (1995). *The leadership challenge: How to keep getting extraordinary things done in organizations.* San Francisco: Jossey-Bass.

Kress, G., & van Leeuwen, T. (1990). *Reading images.* Geelon, Victoria, Australia: Deakin University Press.

Laclau, E. (1990). *New reflections on the revolution of our time.* London: Verso.

Laclau, E., & Mouffe, C. (1985). *Hegemony and socialist strategy.* London: Verso.

Larson, G. L., & Tompkins, P. K. (2005). Ambivalence and resistance: A study of management in a concertive control system. *Communication Monographs, 72,* 1–21.

Latour, B. (1986). The powers of association. In J. Law (Ed.), *Power, action and belief* (pp. 264–280). London: Routledge/Kegan Paul.

Latour, B. (1987). *Science in action.* Milton Keynes, UK: Open University Press.

Latour, B. (1988). *The Prince* for machines as well as machinations. In B. Elliott (Ed.), *Technology and social process* (pp. 20–43). Edinburgh, Scotland: Edinburgh University Press.

Latour, B. (1994). On technical mediation: Philosophy, sociology, genealogy. *Common Knowledge, 3,* 29–64.

Latour, B. (1996). On interobjectivity. *Mind, Culture, and Activity, 3,* 228–245.

Latour, B. (1999). *Pandora's hope: Essays on the reality of science studies.* Cambridge, MA: Harvard University Press.

Latour, B., & Woolgar, S. (1986). *Laboratory life: The construction of scientific facts* (2nd ed.). Princeton, NJ: Princeton University Press.

Law, J. (1987). Technology and heterogeneous engineering: The case of Portuguese expansion. In W. E. Bijker, T. P. Hughes, & T. Pinch (Eds.), *Social construction of technological systems* (pp. 111–134). Cambridge: MIT Press.

Lee, J., & Jablin, F. M. (1995). Maintenance communication in superior–subordinate work relationships. *Human Communication Research, 22,* 220–257.

Liden, R. C., Sparrowe, R. T., & Wayne, S. J. (1997). Leader–member exchange theory: The past and potential for the future. In G. R. Ferris (Ed.) *Research in personnel and human resources management* (pp. 47–119). Greenwich, CT: JAI Press.

Liden, R. C., Wayne, S. J., & Stilwell, D. (1993). A longitudinal study on the early development of leader–member exchange. *Journal of Applied Psychology, 78,* 662–674.

Likert, R. (1961). *New patterns of management.* New York: McGraw-Hill.

Likert, R. (1967). *The human organization.* New York: McGraw-Hill.

London, M., Smither, J. W., & Adsit, D. J. (1997). Accountability: The Achilles' heel of multisource feedback. *Group and Organization Management, 22,* 162–184.

Lord, R. G., & Brown, D. J. (2004). *Leadership processes and follower self-identity.* Mahwah, NJ: Erlbaum.

Lord, R. G., Brown, D. J., & Freiberg, S. J. (1999). Understanding the dynamics of leadership: The role of follower self-concepts in the leader/follower relationship. *Organizational Behavior and Human Decision Processes, 78,* 167–203.

Lord, R. G., & Emrich, C. G. (2001). Thinking outside the box by looking inside the box: Extending the cognitive revolution in leadership research. *Leadership Quarterly, 11,* 551–579.

Lord, R. G., Foti, R. J., & De Vader, C. L. (1984). A test of leadership categorization theory: Internal structure, information processing, and leadership perceptions. *Organizational Behavior and Human Performance, 34,* 343–378.

Lord, R. G., Foti, R. J., & Phillips, J. S. (1982). A theory of leadership categorization. In J. G. Hunt, U. Sekaran, & C. A. Schriesheim (Eds.), *Leadership: Beyond establishment views* (pp. 104–121). Carbondale: Southern Illinois University Press.

Lord, R. G., & Hall, R. (2003). Identity, leader categorization, and leadership schema. In D. van Knippenberg & M. A. Hogg (Eds.), *Leadership and power: Identity processes in groups and organizations* (pp. 48–64). London: Sage.

Lord, R. G., & Maher, K. J. (1991). *Leadership and information processing.* Boston: Unwin Hyman.

Lowe, K. B., & Gardner, W. L. (2000). Ten years of *The Leadership Quarterly:* Contributions and challenges for the future. *Leadership Quarterly, 11,* 459–515.

Ludeman, K., & Erlandson, E. (2004, May). Coaching the alpha male. *Harvard Business Review,* pp. 58–67.

Machiavelli, N. (1984). *The prince.* Oxford, UK: Oxford University Press.

Manz, C. C., & Sims, H. P. Jr. (1987). Leading workers to lead themselves: The external leadership of self-managing work teams. *Administrative Science Quarterly, 32,* 106–128.

Markus, H., & Wurf, E. (1987). The dynamic self-concept: A social psychological perspective. *Annual Review of Psychology, 38,* 299–337.

Martin, J., Feldman, M. S., Hatch, M. J., & Sitkin, S. B. (1983). The uniqueness paradox in organizational stories. *Administrative Science Quarterly, 28,* 438–453.

Martin, J., & Meyerson, D. (1999). Women and power: Conformity, resistance, and disorganized coaction. In R. M. Kramer & M. A. Neale (Eds.), *Power and influence in organizations* (pp. 311–348). Thousand Oaks, CA: Sage.

Martin, J., & Siehl, C. (1983). Organizational culture and counterculture: An uneasy symbiosis. *Organizational Dynamics, 12,* 52–64.

Maslow, A. H. (1954). *Motivation and personality.* New York: Harper & Row.

Maslow, A. H. (1971). *The farther reaches of human nature.* New York: Viking.

Mayo, E. (1945). *Social problems of an industrial civilization.* Boston: Graduate School of Business Administration, Harvard University.

McDermott, R. P., & Roth, D. R. (1978). The social organization of behavior: Interactional approaches. *Annual Review of Anthropology, 7,* 321–345.

McGregor, D. (1960). *Human side of enterprise.* New York: McGraw-Hill.

McPhee, R. D., & Zaug, P. (2000). The communicative constitution of organizations: A framework for explanation. *The Electronic Journal of Communication, 10,* 1–16.

Mead, G. H. (1934). *Mind, self, and society.* Chicago: University of Chicago Press.

Meindl, J. R. (1993). Reinventing leadership: A radical, social psychological approach. In J. K. Munighan (Ed.), *Social psychology in organizations: Advances in theory and research* (pp. 89–118). Englewood Cliffs, NJ: Prentice Hall.

Meindl, J. R. (1995). The romance of leadership as a follower-centric theory: A social constructionist approach. *Leadership Quarterly, 6,* 329–341.

Meindl, J. R., Ehrlich, S. B., & Dukerich, J. M. (1985). The romance of leadership. *Administrative Science Quarterly, 30,* 78–102.

Michael, M. (1996). *Constructing identities.* London: Sage.

Miles, R. (1965). Keeping informed—Human Relations or Human Resources? *Harvard Business Review, 43,* 148–163.

Miller, P., & Rose, N. (1990). Governing economic life. *Economy and Society, 27,* 1–31.

Mills, C. W. (1951). *White collar.* London: Oxford University Press.

Mintzberg, H. (1970). Structured observation as a method to study managerial work. *Journal of Management Studies, 7,* 87–104.

Mintzberg, H. (1973). *The nature of managerial work.* New York: Harper & Row.

Mintzberg, H. (1975, July/August). The manager's job: Folklore and fact. *Harvard Business Review,* pp. 49–61.

Mintzberg, H. (1982). If you're not serving Bill and Barbara, then you're not serving leadership. In J. G. Hunt, U. Sekaran, & C. A. Schriesheim (Eds.), *Leadership: Beyond establishment views* (pp. 239–259). Carbondale: Southern Illinois University Press.

Morrill, C., Zald, M. N., & Hayagreeva, R. (2003). Covert political conflict in organizations: Challenges from below. *Annual Review of Sociology, 29,* 391–415.

Mumby, D. K. (1987). The political function of narrative in organizations. *Communication Monographs, 54,* 13–127.

Mumby, D. K. (1988). *Communication and power in organizations: Discourse, ideology and domination.* Norwood, NJ: Ablex.

Mumby, D. K. (1996). Feminism, postmodernism, and organizational communication: A critical reading. *Management Communication Quarterly, 9,* 259–295.

Mumby, D. K. (1997). The problem of hegemony: Rereading Gramsci for organizational communication studies. *Western Journal of Communication, 61,* 343–375.

Mumby, D. K. (2005). Theorizing resistance in organization studies: A dialectical approach. *Management Communication Quarterly, 19,* 1–26.

Mumby, D. K., & Clair, R. P. (1997). Organizational discourse. In T. A. van Dijk (Ed.), *Discourse as social interaction* (Vol. 2, pp. 181–205). London: Sage.

Murphy, J. M. (1994). Presence, analogy, and earth in the balance. *Argumentation and Advocacy, 31,* 1–16.

Nelson, K. E. (1986). *Event knowledge: Structure and function in development.* Hillsdale, NJ: Erlbaum.

Newton, T. (1998). Theorizing subjectivity in organizations: The failure of Foucauldian studies? *Organization Studies, 19,* 415–447.

Newton, T., & Findlay, P. (1996). Playing God? The performance appraisal. *Human Resource Management Journal, 6,* 42–58.

Nickles, T. (1981). What is a problem that we may solve it? *Synthese, 47,* 85–118.

O'Connor, E. S. (1997). Telling decisions: The role of narrative in organizational decision making. In Z. Shapira (Ed.), *Organizational decision making* (pp. 304–323). New York: Cambridge University Press.

Ochs, E. (1997). Narrative. In T. A. van Dijk (Ed.), *Discourse as structure and process* (Vol. 1, pp. 185–207). London: Sage.

Offe, C. (1976). *Industry and inequality.* London: Edward Arnold.

O'Keefe, B. J., Lambert, B. L., & Lambert, C. A. (1993). *Effects of message design logic on perceived communication effectiveness in supervisory relationships.* Washington, DC: International Communication Association.

Orlikowski, W. J. (1996). Improvising organizational transformation over time: A situated change perspective. *Information Systems Research, 7,* 63–92.

Orr, J. (1990). Sharing knowledge, celebrating identity: Community memory in a service culture. In D. S. Middleton & D. Edwards (Eds.), *Collective remembering: Memory in society* (pp. 169–189). Newbury Park, CA: Sage.

Oswick, C., Keenoy, T., & Grant, D. (1997). Managerial discourses: Words speak louder than actions? *Journal of Applied Management Studies, 6,* 5–12.

Ouchi, W., & Wilkins, A. (1985). Organizational culture. *Annual Review of Sociology, 11,* 457–483.

Parker, I. (1998). *Social constructionism, discourse and realism.* London: Sage.

Parker, K. (2005, July 8). Hillary's whoever she needs to be. *Cincinnati Enquirer,* p. B15.

Parker, M., & McHugh, G. (1991). Five texts in search of an author: A response to John Hasard's 'Multiple paradigms and organizational analysis.' *Organization Studies, 12,* 451–456.

Parry, K. W. (1998). Grounded theory and social process: A new direction for leadership research. *Leadership Quarterly, 9,* 85–105.

Pascale, R. T., & Athos, A. G. (1981). *The art of Japanese management.* New York: Simon & Schuster.

Patriotta, G. (2003). Sensemaking on the shop floor: Narratives of knowledge in organizations. *Journal of Management Studies, 40,* 349–373.

Pearce, W. B. (1995). A sailing guide for social constructionists. In W. Leeds-Hurwitz (Ed.), *Social approaches to communication* (pp. 88–113). New York: Guilford Press.

Perelman, C., & Olbrechts-Tyteca, L. (1969). *The new rhetoric: A treatise on argumentation.* Notre Dame, IN: University of Notre Dame Press.

Peters, T., & Waterman, R. (1982). *In search of excellence: Lessons from America's best-run companies.* New York: Harper & Row.

Pfeffer, J. (1981). Management as symbolic action: The creation and maintenance of organizational paradigms. In L. L. Cummings & B. M. Staw (Eds.), *Research in organizational behavior* (pp. 1–52). Greenwich, CT: JAI Press.

Phillips, L., & Jørgensen, M. W. (2002). *Discourse analysis as theory and method.* London: Sage.

Platow, M. J., Haslam, S. A., Foddy, M., & Grace, D. M. (2003). Leadershp as an outcome of self-categorization processes. In D. van Knippenberg & M. A. Hogg (Eds.), *Leadership and power: Identity processes in groups and organizations* (pp. 34–47). London: Sage.

Pomerantz, A. (1990). Conversation analytic claims. *Communication Monographs, 57,* 231–235.

Pomerantz, A., & Fehr, B. J. (1997). Conversation analysis: An approach to the study of social action as sense making practices. In T. A. van Dijk (Ed.), *Discourse as social interaction* (Vol. 2, pp. 64–91). London: Sage.

Pondy, L. R. (1978). Leadership is a language game. In J. M. W. McCall & M. M. Lombardo (Eds.), *Leadership: Where else can we go?* (pp. 88–99). Durham, NC: Duke University Press.

Poole, M. S., & DeSanctis, G. (1992). Microlevel structuration in computer-supported group decision making. *Human Communication Research, 19,* 5–49.

Potter, J. (1996). *Representing reality: Discourse, rhetoric and social construction.* London: Sage.

Potter, J. (1997). Discourse analysis as a way of analyzing naturally occurring talk. In D. Silverman (Ed.), *Qualitative research: Theory, method and practice* (pp. 144–160). London: Sage.

Potter, J. (2003). Discursive psychology: Between method and paradigm. *Discourse & Society, 14,* 783–794.

Potter, J. (2005). Making psychology relevant. *Discourse & Society, 16,* 739–747.

Potter, J., & Wetherell, M. (1987). *Discourse and social psychology.* London: Sage.

Potter, J., Wetherell, M., Gill, R., & Edwards, D. (1990). Discourse: Noun, verb or social practice? *Philosophical Psychology, 3,* 205–217.

Prasad, P., & Prasad, A. (2000). Stretching the iron cage: The constitution and implications of routine workplace resistance. *Organization Science, 11,* 387–403.

Prebles, E. A. (2002). Sensemaking in narratives and the uniqueness paradox in leader–member exchange. Unpublished master's thesis, University of Cincinnati.

Psathas, G. (1995). *Conversation analysis: The study of talk-in-interaction.* London: Sage.

Psathas, G. (1999). Studying the organization in action: Membership categorization and interaction analysis. *Human Studies, 22,* 139–162.

Putnam, F. M., & Boys, S. (2006). Revisiting metaphors of organizational communication. In S. R. Clegg, C. Hardy, & W. Nord (Eds.), *Handbook of organizational studies* (2nd ed) pp. 541–576. London: Sage.

Putnam, L. L. (1983). Organizational communication: Toward a research agenda. In L. L. Putnam & M. E. Pacanowsky (Eds.), *Communication and organizations: An interpretive approach* (pp. 31–54). Beverly Hills, CA: Sage.

Putnam, L. L., & Fairhurst, G. T. (2001). Discourse analysis in organizations. In F. M. Jablin & L. L. Putnam (Eds.), *The new handbook of organizational communication* (pp. 78–136). Thousand Oaks, CA: Sage.

Putnam, L. L., & Wilson, S. R. (1989). Argumentation and bargaining strategies as discriminators of integrative outcomes. In M. A. Rahim (Ed.), *Managing conflict: An interdisciplinary approach* (pp. 121–141). New York: Praeger.

Rafaeli, A., & Sutton, R. I. (1987). Expression of emotion as part of the work role. *Academy of Management Review, 12,* 23–37.

Ranson, S., Hinnings, B., & Greenwood, R. (1980). The structuring of organizational structures. *Administrative Science Quarterly, 25,* 1–17.

Reardon, K. K. (1995). *They don't get it, do they? Communication in the workplace— Closing the gap between men and women.* Boston: Little, Brown.

Reave, L. (2005). Spiritual value and practices related to leadership effectiveness. *Leadership Quarterly, 16,* 655–688.

Redding, W. C. (1973). *Communication within the organization.* Lafayette, IN: Purdue Research Foundation.

Reed, M. I. (1984). Management as a social practice. *Journal of Management Studies, 21,* 273–285.

Reed, M. I. (2000). The limits of discourse analysis in organization analysis. *Organization, 7,* 524–530.

Reed, M. I. (2001). *The explanatory limits of discourse analysis in organisation analysis— A review.* Washington, DC: Academy of Management.

Reed, M. I. (2004). Getting real about organizational discourse. In C. H. D. Grant, C. Oswick, N. Phillips, & L. Putnam (Eds.), *The Sage handbook of organizational discourse* (pp. 413–420). London: Sage.

Rhoads, C. (2005, September 9). After Katrina, city officials struggled to keep order. *The Wall Street Journal.* Available online at: http://www.post-gazette.com/pg/pp/05252/568686.stm

Rindova, V. P., Pollock, T. G., & Hayward, M. L. A. (2006). Celebrity firms: The social construction of market popularity. *Academy of Management Review, 31,* 50–71.

Roberts, N. C., & Bradley, R. T. (1988). Limits of charisma. In J. A. Conger & R. M. Kanungo (Eds.), *Charismatic leadership: The elusive factor in organizational effectiveness* (pp. 253–275). San Francisco: Jossey-Bass.

Robichaud, D. (2003). Narrative institutions we organize by: The case of a municipal administration. In B. Czarniawska & P. Gagliardi (Eds.), *Narratives we organize by* (pp. 37–53). Amsterdam: John Benjamins.

Robinson, V. M. J. (2001). Embedding leadership in task performance. In K. Wong & C. W. Evers (Eds.), *Leadership for quality schooling* (pp. 90–102). London: Routledge/Falmer.

Rogers, C. R. (1961). *On becoming a person: A therapist's view of psychotherapy*. Boston: Houghton Mifflin.

Rogers, L. E., & Escudero, V. (2004a). *Relational communication: An interactional perspective to the study of process and form*. Mahwah, NJ: Erlbaum.

Rogers, L. E., & Escudero, V. (2004b). Theoretical foundations. In L. E. Rogers & V. Escudero (Eds.), *Relational communication: An interactional perspective to the study of process and form* (pp. 222–239). Mahwah, NJ: Erlbaum.

Rogers, L. E., & Farace, R. V. (1975). Relational communication analysis: New measurement procedures. *Human Communication Research, 1*, 222–239.

Rogers, L. E., Millar, F. E., & Bavelas, J. B. (1985). Methods for analyzing marital conflict discourse. *Family Process, 24*, 175–187.

Roloff, M. E. (1981). *Interpersonal communication: The social exchange approach*. Beverly Hills, CA: Sage.

Rorty, R. (1979). *Philosophy and the mirror of nature*. Princeton, NJ: Princeton University Press.

Rorty, R. (1982). *Consequences of pragmatism (Essays: 1972–1980)*. Minneapolis: University of Minnesota Press.

Rosch, E. (1978). Principles of categorization. In E. Rosch & B. B. Lloyd (Eds.), *Cognition and categorization*. Hillsdale, NJ: Erlbaum.

Rost, J. C. (1991). *Leadership for the twenty-first century*. New York: Praeger.

Rost, J. C. (1993). Leadership development in the new millennium. *The Journal of Leadership Studies, 1*, 92–110.

Roth, I. (1995). Conceptual categories. In I. Roth & V. Bruce (Eds.), *Perception and representation: Current issues*. Buckingham, UK: Open University Press.

Sacks, H. (1966). *No one to turn to*. Unpublished doctoral dissertation, University of California, Berkeley.

Sacks, H. (1972). An initial investigation of the usability of conversational data for doing sociology. In D. Sudnow (Ed.), *Studies in social interaction* (pp. 31–74). New York: Free Press.

Sacks, H. (1992). *Lectures on conversation, vols. 1 and 2*. Oxford, UK: Blackwell.

Sacks, H., Schegloff, E. A., & Jefferson, G. (1974). A simplest systematics for the organization of turn-taking for conversation. *Language, 50*, 696–735.

Sanders, R. E. (1995). A neo-rhetorical perspective: The enactment of role-identities as interactive and strategic. In S. Sigman (Ed.), *The consequentiality of communication* (pp. 67–120). Mahwah, NJ: Erlbaum.

Sanders, R. E. (2006). The effect of interactional competence on group problem-solving. In F. Cooren (Ed.), *Interacting and organizing: Analyses of a board meeting* (pp. 234–262). Mahwah, NJ: Erlbaum.

Sayles, L. R. (1964). *Managerial behavior: Administration in complex enterprises*. New York: McGraw-Hill.

Schank, R., & Abelson, R. (1977). *Scripts, plans, goals, and understanding.* Hillsdale, NJ: Erlbaum.

Schegloff, E. A. (1979). Identification and recognition in telephone conversation openings. In G. Psathas (Ed.), *Everyday language* (pp. 23–78). New York: Irvington.

Schegloff, E. A. (1988). Presequence and indirection: Applying speech act theory to ordinary conversation. *Journal of Pragmatics, 12,* 55–62.

Schegloff, E. A. (1991). Reflections on talk and social structure. In D. Boden & D. Zimmerman (Eds.), *Talk and social structure: Studies in ethnomethodology and conversation analysis* (pp. 44–70). Cambridge, UK: Polity.

Schegloff, E. A. (1997). Whose text? Whose context? *Discourse & Society, 8,* 165–188.

Schegloff, E. A. (1998). Reply to Wetherell. *Discourse & Society, 9,* 413–416.

Schegloff, E. A. (2001). Accounts of conduct in interaction: Interruption, overlap and turn-taking. In J. H. Turner (Ed.), *Handbook of sociological theory* (pp. 287–321). New York: Kluwer Academic.

Schein, E. (1985). *Organizational culture and leadership.* San Francisco: Jossey-Bass.

Scherer, A. (1998). Pluralism and incommensurability in strategic management and organization theory: A problem in search of a solution. *Organization, 5,* 147–168.

Schön, D. A. (1983). *The reflective practitioner: How professionals think in action.* New York: Basic Books.

Schriesheim, C. A., Castro, S. L., & Coglister, C. C. (1999). Leader–member exchange (LMX) research: A comprehensive review of theory, measurement, and data-analytic practices. *Leadership Quarterly, 10,* 63–114.

Schriesheim, C., Coglister, C. C., & Neider, L. L. (1995). 'Is it trustworthy?' A multiple levels-of-analysis reexamination of an Ohio State leadership study with implications for future research. *Leadership Quarterly, 6,* 111–145.

Schriesheim, C., Neider, L. L., Scandura, T. A., & Tepper, B. J. (1992). Development and preliminary validation of a new scale (LMX–6) to measure leader–member exchange in organizations. *Education and Psychological Measurement, 52,* 135–147.

Searle, J. R. (1969). *Speech acts: An essay in the philosophy of language.* London: Cambridge University Press.

Searle, J. R. (1979). *Meaning and expression: Studies in the theory of speech acts.* Cambridge, UK: Cambridge University Press.

Searle, J. R. (1989). How performatives work. *Linguistics and Philosophy, 12,* 535–558.

Searle, J. R. (1995). *The construction of social reality.* New York: Free Press.

Seidler, V. J. (1989). *Rediscovering masculinity: Reason, language and sexuality.* London: Routledge.

Seligman, M. E. P., & Csikszentmihalyi, M. (2000). Positive psychology: An introduction. *American Psychologist, 55,* 5–14.

Senge, P. (1990). *The fifth discipline.* New York: Doubleday.

Shamir, B. (1999). Leadership in boundaryless organizations: Disposable or indispensable. *European Journal of Work and Organizational Psychology, 8,* 49–71.

Shamir, B., Arthur, M. B., & House, R. J. (1994). The rhetoric of charismatic leadership: A theoretical extension, a case study, and implications for research. *Leadership Quarterly, 5,* 25–42.

Shamir, B., & Eilam, G. (2005). 'What's your story?' A life-stories approach to authentic leadership development. *Leadership Quarterly, 16,* 395–417.

Shamir, B., House, R. J., & Arthur, M. B. (1993). The motivational effects of charismatic leadership: A self-concept based theory. *Organization Science, 4,* 577–594.

Shamir, B., & Howell, J. M. (1999). Organizational and contextual influences on the emergence and effectiveness of charismatic leadership. *Leadership Quarterly, 10,* 257–284.

Shapiro, M. (1992). *Reading the postmodern polity.* Minneapolis: University of Minnesota Press.

Sheep, M. L. (2006). *When categories collide: A discursive psychology approach to the elasticity of multiple identities.* Unpublished doctoral dissertation: Department of Management, University of Cincinnatti.

Sherman, S., & Freas, A. (2004). The Wild West of executive coaching. *Harvard Business Review, 82,* 82–93.

Shils, E. (1958). The concentration and dispersion of charisma: Their bearing on economic policy in underdeveloped countries. *World Politics, 11,* 1–19.

Shils, E. (1965). Charisma, order, and status. *American Sociological Review, 30,* 199–213.

Shotter, J. (1993). *Conversational realities: Constructing life through language.* London: Sage.

Shotter, J., & Cunliffe, A. L. (2003). Managers as practical authors: Everyday conversations for action. In D. Holman & R. Thorpe (Eds.), *Management and language* (pp. 1–37). London: Sage.

Sias, P. M. (1996). Constructing perceptions of differential treatment: An analysis of coworker discourse. *Communication Monographs, 63,* 171–187.

Sigman, S. J. (1992). Do social approaches to interpersonal communication constitute a contribution to communication theory? *Communication Theory, 2,* 347–356.

Sinclair, J. M., & Coulthard, M. (1975). *Towards an analysis of discourse: The English used by teachers and pupils.* Oxford, UK: Oxford University Press.

Singleton, V., & Michael, M. (1993). Actor-networks and ambivalence: General practitioners in the UK Cervical Screening Programme. *Social Studies of Science, 23,* 227–264.

Skinner, B. F. (1957). *Verbal behavior.* Englewood Cliffs, NJ: Prentice Hall.

Skinner, B. F. (1974). *About behaviorism.* New York: Vintage.

Smircich, L., & Morgan, G. (1982). Leadership: The management of meaning. *Journal of Applied Behavioral Science, 18,* 257–273.

Smith, G. (1989). Defining managerial problems: A framework for prescriptive theorizing. *Management Science, 35,* 963–981.

Smith-Lovin, L., & Brody, C. (1989). Interruptions in group discussions: The effects of gender and group composition. *American Sociological Review, 54,* 424–435.

Soderberg, A. (2003). Sensegiving and sensemaking in an integration process. In B. Czarniawska & P. Gagliardi (Eds.), *Narratives we organize by* (pp. 3–35). Amsterdam: John Benjamins.

Sparrowe, R. (2005). Authentic leadership and the narrative self. *Leadership Quarterly, 16,* 419–439.

Sparrowe, R., & Liden, R. C. (1997). Process and structure in leader–member exchange. *Academy of Management Review, 22,* 522–552.

Staw, B. M. (1985). Repairs on the road to relevance and rigor: Some unexplored issues in publishing organizational research. In L. L. Cummings & P. J. Frost (Eds.), *Publishing in the organizational sciences* (pp. 96–107). Homewood, IL: Irwin.

Stewart, R. M. (1967). *Managers and their jobs.* London: Macmillan.

Stewart, R. M. (1983). Managerial behaviour: How research has changed the traditional picture. In M. J. Earl (Ed.), *Perspectives on management* (pp. 82–98). London: Oxford University Press.

Stogdill, R. M. (1974). *Handbook of leadership: A survey of the literature.* New York: Free Press.

Stogdill, R. M., & Coons, A. E. (1957). *Leader behavior: Its description and measurement.* Columbus: Ohio State University, Bureau of Business Research.

Stohl, C., & Cheney, G. (2001). Participatory processes/paradoxical practices. *Management Communication Quarterly, 14,* 349–407.

Tajfel, H. (1978). *Differentiation between social groups.* London: Academic Press.

Taylor, F. (1919). *Principles of scientific management.* New York: Harper & Row.

Taylor, J. R., & Cooren, F. (1997). What makes communication 'organizational'? How the many voices of a collectivity become the one voice of an organization. *Journal of Pragmatics, 27,* 409–438.

Taylor, J. R., & Robichaud, D. (2006). Management as meta-conversation: The search for closure. In F. Cooren (Ed.), *Interacting and organizing: Analyses of a board meeting* (pp. 7–41). Mahwah, NJ: Erlbaum.

Taylor, J. R., & Van Every, E. (2000). *The emergent organization: Communication as its site and surface.* Mahwah, NJ: Erlbaum.

Taylor, J. R. (2006). Coorientation: A conceptual framework. In F. Cooren, J. R. Taylor, & E. J. Van Every (Eds.), *Communicating as organizing.* Mahwah, NJ: Erlbaum.

Tergesen, A. (2006, June 14). What price college admission. *Business Week,* pp. 82–83.

Tichy, N. M. (1997). *The leadership engine: How winning companies build leaders at every level.* New York: HarperCollins.

Townley, B. (1989). Selection and appraisal: Reconstituting "social relations." In J. Storey (Ed.), *New perspectives in human resource management* (pp. 92–108). London: Routledge.

Townley, B. (1993a). Foucault, power/knowledge, and its relevance for human resource management. *Academy of Management Review, 18,* 518–545.

Townley, B. (1993b). Performance appraisal and the emergence of management. *Journal of Management Studies, 30,* 27–44.

Tracy, K. (1995). Action-implicative discourse analysis. *Journal of Language and Social Psychology, 14,* 195–215.

Tracy, S. J., & Tretheway, A. (2005). Fracturing the real-self<—>fake-self dichotomy: Moving toward 'crystallized' organizational discourses and identities. *Communication Theory, 15,* 168–195.

Traub, J. (2001, November 4). No-fun city. *New York Times Magazine,* pp. 36–74.

Trent, J. S. (1978). Presidential surfacing: The ritualistic and crucial first act. *Communication Monographs, 45,* 281–292.

Trent, J. S., & Friedenberg, R. V. (2004). *Political campaign communication* (5th ed.). New York: Rowman & Littlefield.

Trice, H. M., & Beyer, J. M. (1986). Charisma and its routinization in two social movement organizations. *Research in Organizational Behavior, 8,* 113–164.

Trist, E. L., Higgin, G., Murray, H., & Pollock, A. (1963). *Organizational choice.* London: Tavistock.

Tronick, E. Z., Bruschweiler-Stern, N., Harrison, A. M., Lyons-Ruth, K., Morgan, A. C., Nahum, J. P., et al. (1998). Dyadically expanded states of consciousness and the process of therapeutic change. *Infant Mental Health Journal, 19,* 290–299.

Tsoukas, H. (2000). False dilemmas in organization theory: Realism or social constructivism. *Organization, 7,* 531–535.

Tsoukas, H., & Chia, R. (2002). On organizational becoming: Rethinking organizational change. *Organization Science, 13,* 567–582.

Tucker, J. (1993). Everyday forms of employee resistance. *Sociological Forum, 8,* 25–45.

Tulving, E. (2002). Episodic memory: From mind to brain. *Annual Review of Psychology, 53,* 1–25.

Uhl-Bien, M., & Graen, G. B. (1992). Self-management and team-making in cross-functional work teams: Discovering the keys to becoming an integrated team. *Journal of High Technology Management, 3,* 225–241.

Vanderveken, D. (1990–1991). *Meaning and speech acts.* Cambridge, UK: Cambridge University Press.

Vecchio, R., & Gobdel, B. (1984). The vertical dyad linkage model. *Organizational Behavior and Human Decision Processes, 34,* 5–20.

Wasielewski, P. L. (1985). The emotional basis of charisma. *Symbolic Interaction, 8,* 207–222.

Watson, R. (1997). Some general reflections on 'categorization' and 'sequence' in the analysis of conversation. In S. Hester & P. Eglin (Eds.), *Culture in action: Studies in membership categorization analysis* (pp. 49–76). Washington, DC: International Institute for Ethnomethodology and Conversation Analysis & University Press of America.

Watson, T. J. (1994). Towards a managerially relevant but non-managerialist organization theory. In J. Hassard & M. Parker (Eds.), *Towards a new theory of organizations* (pp. 209–224). London: Routledge.

Watson, T. J. (2001). Beyond managism: Negotiated narratives and critical management education in practice. *British Journal of Management, 12,* 385–396.

Weaver, G. R., & Gioia, D. A. (1994). Paradigms lost: Incommensurability vs structurationist inquiry. *Organization Studies, 15,* 565–590.

Weber, M. (1968). *Economy and society* (3 vols.). New York: Bedminster. (Originally published 1925)

Weedon, C. (1997). *Feminist practice and poststructuralist theory* (2nd ed.). Cambridge, MA: Blackwell.

Weick, K. (1979). *The social psychology of organizing* (2nd ed.). Reading, MA: Addison-Wesley.

Weick, K. (1995). *Sensemaking in organizations.* Thousand Oaks, CA: Sage.

Weick, K. (1998). Improvisation as a mindset for organizational analysis. *Organization Science, 9,* 543–555.

Weick, K. (2004). A bias for conversation: Acting discursively in organizations. In D. Grant, C. Hardy, C. Oswick, N. Phillips, & L. Putnam (Eds.), *The Sage handbook of organizational discourse* (pp. 405–412). London: Sage.

Weick, K., & Roberts, K. H. (1993). Collective mind in organizations: Heedful interrelating on flight decks. *Administrative Science Quarterly, 38,* 357–381.

Weick, K., Sutcliffe, K. M., & Obstfeld, D. (1999). Organizing for high reliability: Processes of collective mindfulness. In R. I. Sutton & B. M. Staw (Eds.), *Research in organizational behavior* (pp. 81–123). Stamford, CT: JAI Press.

Weick, K. E., Sutcliffe, K. M., & Obstfeld, D. (2005). Organizing and the process of sensemaking. *Organization Science, 16,* 409–421.

Weingart, L. R., Hyder, E. B., & Prietula, M. J. (1996). Knowledge matters: The effect of tactical descriptions on negotiation behavior and outcome. *Journal of Personality and Social Psychology, 35,* 366–393.

Weisinger, H. (1998). *Emotional intelligence at work: The untapped edge for success.* San Francisco: Jossey-Bass.

Westley, F., & Mintzberg, H. (1989). Visionary leadership and strategic management. *Strategic Management Journal, 10,* 17–32.

Wetherell, M. (1998). Positioning and interpretative repertoires: Conversation analysis and post-structuralism in dialogue. *Discourse & Society, 9,* 387–412.

Whalen, J., & Zimmerman, D. H. (1998). Observations on the display and management of emotion in naturally occurring activities: The case of hysteria in calls to 911. *Social Psychology Quarterly, 61,* 141–159.

Wheeler, M. A., Stuss, D. T., & Tulving, E. (1997). Towards a theory of episodic memory: The frontal lobes and autonoetic consciousness. *Psychological Review, 121,* 331–354.

White, H. (1987). *The content of the form.* Baltimore: Johns Hopkins University Press.

Whyte, W. H. J. (1956). *The organization man.* New York: Simon & Schuster.

Wilhelm, A. J., & Fairhurst, G. (1997). I heard it through the grapevine: Dealing with office rumors, politics, and Total Quality Management. In B. Sypher (Ed.), *Case studies in organizational communication* (Vol. 2, pp. 240–248). New York: Guilford Press.

Willmott, H. C. (1984). Images and ideals of managerial work: A critical examination of conceptual and empirical accounts. *Journal of Management Studies, 21,* 349–368.

Wilson, S. R. (2002). *Seeking and resisting compliance: Why people say what they do when trying to influence others.* Thousand Oaks, CA: Sage.

Wittgenstein, L. (1953). *Philosophical investigations.* Oxford, UK: Blackwell.

Wolffe, R., & Bailey, H. (2006, June 9). At last a rosy day. *Newsweek,* pp. 36–38.

Woodilla, J. (1998). Workplace conversations: The text of organizing. In D. Grant, T. Keenoy, & C. Oswick (Eds.), *Discourse and organization* (pp. 31–50). London: Sage.

Yammarino, F. J., Dionne, S. D., Chun, J. U., & Dansereau, F. (2005). Leadership and levels of analysis: A state-of-the-science review. *Leadership Quarterly, 16,* 879–920.

Yukl, G. (1999). An evaluation of conceptual weaknesses in transformational and charismatic leadership theories. *Leadership Quarterly, 10,* 285–305.

Yukl, G. (2002). *Leadership in organizations* (5th ed.). Upper Saddle River, NJ: Prentice Hall.

Zaleznik, A. (1977). Managers and leaders: Are they different? *Harvard Business Review, 55,* 67–78.

Zimmerman, D. H. (1992). The interactional organization of calls for emergency assistance. In P. Drew & J. Heritage (Eds.), *Talk at work: Interaction in institutional settings* (pp. 418–469). Cambridge, UK: Cambridge University Press.

Zoller, H. M., & Fairhurst, G. T. (2006). *Resistance as leadership: A critical, discursive perspective.* Paper presented at the annual conference of the National Communication Association, San Antonio, TX.

Zorn, T. E. (1995). Bosses and buddies: Constructing and performing simultaneously hierarchical and close friendship relationships. In J. T. Wood & S. Duck (Eds.), *Understudied relationships: Off the beaten path* (pp. 122–145). Thousand Oaks, CA: Sage.

Index

Abelson, R., 38, 126
Actants, 34, 144, 146, 147, 156
Action-at-a-distance, 91
Actor-network theory (ANT), 142,
    144–150, 162–163, 172
  analytic impartiality in, 146–147
  author role and, 146–147, 154
  fragility of networks and, 146, 161
  hybrid agency and, 145
  Montreal school and, 147–149,
    161, 162
  revision of, leadership and, 149–150
  spokespersons/macroactors, alliance
    formation and, 146
  translation function and, 145–146
  See also Giuliani leadership case
    example; Neo-charismatic
    leadership theories
Actual dialogue, 9
Adjacency pairs, 29–32
Agency:
  actors' language use and, 14
  constraint/structure and, 14
  hybrid agency, 142, 145, 147,
    148–149, 161–162
  leadership-organizing skills and, 23
  power/influence, conceptions
    of, 11–12
  reflexive agency vs.
    untheorized/exaggerated
    agency, 12–14
  relativism and, 14

  space of action and, 99–100
  symbolic agency, 56, 57–59, 143–144
  thin actors vs. essences and, 9–11
Albert, M., 4
Alpha female, 105–106
Alpha male, 87–90, 102, 105, 107
Alvesson, M., 6, 100, 184
AMC sequence, 39
  effective AMC sequence, 39, 40
  ineffective AMC sequence, 39–40
  inferred behavioral script analysis
    and, 39–41
  Operant Supervisory Taxonomy
    and Index, 40
Analytical units, 8–9
Antaki, C., 54
Appraisal. See Performance appraisal;
    Performance management
    technologies
Appreciative inquiry, 174
Archeological analysis, 77, 92, 196
Articulation points of action, 31–32
Ashcraft, K. L., 105, 106
Authentic leadership, viii, 4, 5, 98, 100,
    102–104, 127
Author role, 146–147, 154, 158, 159–160

Bakhtin, M., 173
Barge, J. K., 167, 173, 174, 183–185
Barlow, G., 83
Barrett, F. J., 44, 114, 169
Bass, B. M., vii, 141

Bateson, G., 13, 15, 184
Bavelas, J. B., 24
Baxter, L., 122
Behavioral scripts, 38–41
Bennis, W. G., 7, 77, 170, 171
Beyer, J. M., 141
Biggart, N. W., 15
Blackboxing, 145, 146, 162, 163
Boas, S., 175–176
Boden, D., 30, 31
Boje, D., 131, 132, 187
Breach formulations, 41–42
Brown, D. J., 97, 98, 116
Bruner, J. S., 120, 147
Bruschweiler-Stern, N., 159
Bryman, A., 13, 23, 56
Buber, M., 173

Cagan, L., 4
Calder, B. J., 188
Callon, M., 144, 146, 155, 156
Carroll, S. J., 1, 2
Category-bound activities, 30, 51
Categorization theory. See Membership
    categorization
Center for Creative Leadership (CCL), 183
Charismatic leaders, 12, 141–142
See also Giuliani leadership case example;
    Neo-charismatic leadership theories
Chia, R., 44, 113
Chomsky, N., 4
Chrobot-Mason, D., 182–183
Clegg, S. R., 5
Cleveland Clinic study, 169–170, 174
Cloud, D. L., 143, 144, 149
Coaching. See Executive coaching
Coding interaction, 26–29
Cognitive categorization approaches,
    49–50, 62
Cognitive scripts, 33, 38
Collective mind, 28
Command presence, 37, 45
Communication model, 17
Communication process, 5

constructionist path vs. essentializing
    theory and, 10
dialogue approaches, 173–174
managerial communication
    skills, 167–168
meaning-centered models of, 17, 190
meaning creation and, 50
minds-in-communication view, 17
primary vs. subsidiary status
    of, 16–17
relationship and, 13–14, 24
speaking subjects and, 80
transmission model of
    communication, 17, 190
See also Discourse; Discursive
    leadership
Complementary holism, 4
Condor, S., 54
Confessional technology, 82–83,
    85–86, 89, 90, 93
Conformity, 81–82
Conger, J. A., 141
Constraint, 32, 67–68, 143–144, 168
Constructionist stance. See Social
    constructionism
Context, 15–16, 57
Context-free/context-sensitive
    action, 30–31
Contingency theory of leadership,
    viii, 9–10, 99
Conversation analysis (CA), 10,
    11, 16, 17, 29–30, 191–192
adjacency pairs and, 31
constructed nature of
    conversation, 168
context-free/context-sensitive
    action and, 30–31
sequential pacing/verbal
    rhythms and, 30, 168
turn taking and, 31–32
Cooperrider, D., 169
Cooren, F., 27, 33, 34, 35, 36, 38,
    147, 149, 187–188
Craig, R. T., 17, 173

Critical discourse analysis (CDA), 144, 197
Critical theory, 5, 7, 173
Cronen, V. E., 8, 9, 16, 17, 133
Crucibles, 171
Csikzentmihalyi, M., 103
Cultural aspects of leadership,
     viii–ix, 78, 92, 112
Czarniawska-Joerges, B., 187

Dale, K., 150
Daudi, G., 99
Deetz, S. A., 11, 102, 174
Democratic processes, 5
Dialogue approaches, 173–174, 190
Disciplinary power, 75–76, 93, 170–171
     confessional technology and, 82–83,
          85–86, 89, 90
     examination technique and, 82, 84, 86
     executive coaching and, 85–89, 90
     expertise and, 91–92
     Foucauldian analyses and, 76–83
     hierarchical observation and,
          81–83, 84
     normalizing judgment and, 81–82, 84
     performance appraisal and,
          83–84, 90, 91
     performance management
          governmentality and, 90–92
     performance management
          technologies and, 83–90
     power/knowledge relations and, 91
     resistance and, 85, 89–90
     self-discipline/self-regulation and, 90
     surveillance, normalizing judgment
          and, 81–82
     technologies of power, 81–83, 90
     360-degree feedback and, 84–85, 86,
          88, 89, 90
     translation function and, 92
Discourse:
     big 'D' Discourse, 7
     definition of, 6–7, 92
     ideas, historic systems for
          formation/articulation of, 7

little 'd' discourse, 6–7
multiple Discourses, 100–104
social practices, talk/text and, 6–7
     See also Discourse analysis; Discursive
          leadership; Foucauldian analyses;
          Interactional processes
Discourse analysis, 6–7, 10, 17
     conversation analysis, 29–32, 44,
          167–168, 191–192
     critical discourse analysis, 144, 197
     discursive psychology, 42–44, 195
     Foucauldian analyses, 76–83, 196
     interaction analysis, 24, 26–29, 44,
          193, 199–202
     materialist critiques of, 143–144
     narrative analyses, 198
     speech act schematics, 33–38, 45, 194
Discursive formation, 9, 76, 78
Discursive grammar, 172–173, 174, 190
Discursive leadership, viii–ix, 8
     communication, primary vs.
          subsidiary status of, 16–17
     complementary holism and, 4
     cross-disciplinary work and, 190
     decentered subjects, thin actors vs.
          essences, 9–11
     discourse vs. mental theater
          and, 8–9
     interpretive orientation and, 5
     leadership psychology and, 3–4,
          174–175
     observational units, discursive
          approaches, 9
     ontological units, discursive
          approaches, 9
     organizational discourse
          approaches and, 3–4
     power/influence, encompassing vs.
          dualistic conceptions
          of, 11–12
     praxis and, 167–174
     reflexive agency vs.
          untheorized/exaggerated
          agency and, 12–14

social construction processes and, 5–6

textual/con-textual vs. variable
analytic tradition and, 14–16

See also Leadership; Leadership
psychology; Self-identities

Discursive psychology (DP), 42–44, 195

Discursive scholars, 183–188

Discursive template, 171

Dislocation, 99–100

Double interact. See Interactional
processes

Downsizing, 85, 113, 126

Dreyfus, H. L., 78, 80

du Gay, P., 77

Dukerich, J. M., 188

Dulac, T., 179

Dunn, V., 37

Eagly, A. H., 106

Edwards, D., 17, 18, 41, 42, 50, 109

Ehrlich, S. B., 188

Eilam, G., 127

Emotional scaffolding, 158, 159–160

Employee performance monitoring, 38–41

See also Performance management
technologies

Encompassing power and influence, 11–12

En passant enactment, 55, 63

Episodic closure, 33, 35, 37, 45

Erlandson, E., 88, 89, 90, 105

Essence of leadership, ix, 9–10

hybrid agency and, 145

variable analytic tradition and, 14–15

Exaggerated agency, 12–14

Examination technique, 82, 84, 86, 93

Executive coaching, 76, 85, 90, 93

alpha males and, 87–90, 107

confessional technology and,
85–86, 89

examination techniques and, 86

expertise and, 91–92

gender and, 105–106

intellectual capital and, 85

masculinity, management and, 88

popularity of, 93–94

psychological discourses, clinical
orientation and, 87

surrogate gaze in, 86, 91

360-degree feedback and,
86, 88, 89, 90

translation function and, 92

trust relationship and, 86

See also Disciplinary power

Expertise, 91–92

Fairclough, N., 7, 144, 149, 197

Fairhurst, G. T., 27, 35, 36, 38, 42, 56,
57, 113, 121, 122, 123, 126,
127, 134, 149, 171

Farace, R. V., 26

Fayol, H., 1

Feedback. See Executive coaching;
Performance management technologies;
360-degree feedback

Feldman, M. S., 126

Female leaders. See Alpha female;
relational authenticity

Fiedler, F. E., viii

Findlay, P., 84

Fleming, P., 108

Foddy, M., 49

Follower self-identity theory, 97–98

Foti, R. J., 49

Foucauldian analyses, 76, 92–93, 196

archeological analysis and, 77

confession ritual and, 82–83, 86

discursive formation and, 76, 78

examination ritual and, 82, 84

genealogical analysis and, 77–78, 79

governmentality and, 81, 90–91

management Discourses and, 77–78

objectification and, 79–80

power/knowledge relations in,
81, 91, 92

relational power and, 81

resistance, power effects and,
78, 89–90

subjects, emergence of, 80

subjects/objects and, 78–83
surveillance, normalizing judgment
    and, 81–82, 84
technologies of power and, 81–83
See also Disciplinary power;
    Performance management
    governmentality; Performance
    management technologies
Foucault, M., ix, 4, 7, 12, 76–83, 86, 89,
    90, 98, 133, 196
Freiberg, S. J., 98
Frost, P. J., 157

Gabriel, Y., 100, 107, 198
Garfinkel, H., 14
Geertz, C., 98
Gender, vii, viii
    identity work and, 104–108
    leadership Discourses and, 106–108
    masculinity Discourses, 105–106, 107
    organizations and, 105–108, 115
    relational authenticity and, 106
Genealogical analysis, 77–78, 79, 92, 196
Gibbs, N., 151
Giddens, A., 14, 23, 100
Gilbert, G. N., 161
Gill, R., 109
Gillen, D. J., 1, 2
Gioia, D. A., 2, 38
Giuliani leadership case example,
    150–151, 163
    background events/texts in, 151–154
    charismatic central/sacred,
        association with, 156–159
    emotional scaffolding,
        authoring/networking activities
        and, 158, 159–160
    hybrid agency/actor networks and,
        155–156, 160–162
    Machiavellian comparison and, 157
    macroactor role and, 154–156
    social/constructed nature of
        leadership and, 160–161, 162
    translation function and, 155, 156

See also Actor-network theory (ANT);
    Neo-charismatic leadership
    theories
Goal-directed action. *See* Speech act
    schematics (SAS)
Goffman, E., 144
Goldman, P., 75
Gordon, C., 81
Governmentality. *See* Performance
    management governmentality
Grace, D. M., 49
Graen, G. B., 171
Graham, J. W., 141
Grammar of practice, 173, 174, 190
Grant, D., 6
Great Man school of thought, vii, 75
Green, S. G., 176–178, 190
Greimas, A. J., 33, 34, 38, 147, 161, 188
Grint, K., 3, 9, 10, 17, 78, 149, 160,
    162, 164, 172
Gronn, P., 8, 9, 13, 23
Grounded practical theory, 173
Gubrium, J. F., 98, 99, 100, 102, 109, 112

Hacking, I., 4, 169, 170
Hahnel, R., 4
Halkowski, T., 54
Hamilton, G. G., 15
Hamlett, S. R., 121, 122, 123, 126, 127
Hammersley, M., 10, 11,
    190, 191, 195
Hardy, C., 5
Harré, R., 33
Harrison, A. M., 159
Haslam, S. A., 49
Hatch, M. J., 126
Henderson, D. J., 179
Hierarchy:
    category-bound activities of, 30
    discipline, normalizing judgment
        and, 81–82
    hierarchical observation, 81–83, 84
    leadership knowledge structures
        and, 49

membership categories, 62–66
360-degree feedback and, 84–85
High-reliability organizations (HROs), 28, 44, 53
Hilbert, R., 54
Hinde, R., 24
Historical analysis, 77, 92
Hocevar, S. P., 44, 114
Holistic social theory, 4
Holman, D., 185
Holstein, J. A., 98, 99, 100, 102, 109, 112
Hosking, D. M., 12, 13, 23, 24, 32, 45
House, R. J., 141
Howell, J. M., 142
Hughes, T., 156
Humanistic psychology, 98
Human relations, 77, 79
Human resources, 77, 79, 83, 84, 85
Hunt, J. G., 180–181
Hybrid agency, 142, 145, 147, 148–149, 161–162, 172

Identity:
    organizational identity/role, 54–55
    plasticity of identity categories, 54–55
    See also Membership categorization;
        Self-identities
Individuals, viii
    charismatic/transformational leaders, 13
    essences vs. thin actors, 10–11
    individual/leader-centrist studies, 8–9
    power, local/relational nature of, 12
    variable analytic tradition and, 14–15
    See also Discursive leadership;
        Interactional processes;
        Leadership psychology;
        Self-identities
Inferred behavioral script analysis, 38–41, 45
Influence processes, 6, 11–12
Institutionalized form of intelligibility, 112–113
Intellectual capital, 85
Interactional consequences, 40–41

Interactional processes, 8–9, 23–25
    act/interact/double interact behaviors, 25–29
    articulation points of action and, 31–32
    breach formulations and, 41, 42
    command presence and, 37
    communication, primary vs. subsidiary status of, 16–17
    communication as relationship and, 13–14, 24
    competence in, 168
    constraint forces and, 32, 67
    description, constructed nature of, 42–44
    inferred leader behavioral script analysis, 38–41, 45
    interactional consequences, 40–41
    interaction analysis and, 24
    leadership, definition of, 15
    leadership-organizing skills and, 23, 44–45
    narrative schemas/episodes and, 32–38
    performance monitoring research and, 38–41, 45
    relational control, leadership behaviors and, 26–29
    rhetorical presence and, 37–38
    script formulations, 41–44, 45
    scripts/knowledge structures and, 38–41
    sequence/temporal form and, 23–24
    text function, pragmatic approach, 15–16
    turn taking/adjacency pairs, conversation analysis and, 29–32
    See also Interaction analysis (IA);
        Leader-member exchange (LMX) theory; Membership categorization

Interaction analysis (IA), 24, 44, 193
  coding scheme in, 26–29
  inferred leader behavioral script
    analysis and, 38–41
  police rescue example, 27–28,
    199–202
  See also Conversation
    analysis (CA); Interactional
    processes
Interactive kind, 169
Interpretive orientation, 5
  cultural practices and, 78
  description, constructed
    nature of, 42–44
Interpretative repertoires, 109–114,
    133–137, 171, 173–174
        interpretative repertoires,
  subject positioning and, 109–114
    leader-member exchange,
        interpretative
        repertoire/Discourse and,
        133–137
    narrating the self and, 100
Interruption behavior, 16
Interview discourse, 9

Jablin, F. M., 122
Jauch, L. R., 181
Jayyusi, L., 56, 60, 61, 65, 68, 112
Jefferson, G., 30

Kant, I., 8
Kanungo, R. N., 141
Kärreman, D., 6
Keenoy, T., 6
Kerfoot, D., 88, 107
Kets de Vries, M. F. R., 87
Kieser, A., 75
King, M., 4
Kirtzman, A., 151, 154, 155, 157,
    158, 159, 160
Knights, D., 5, 76, 88, 107
Knowledge. *See* Power/knowledge
    relations; Self-identities
Komaki, J. L., 2, 38, 39, 40

Laclau, E., 99, 143, 144
Language. *See* Linguistic aspects; Sited
    language games
Latour, B., 91, 144, 145, 146, 147,
    149, 155, 157, 161
Leader categorization theory (LCT), 49–50
Leader-follower dualism, 13
Leader-member exchange (LMX) theory,
    viii, 63, 119–120, 137–138, 171–172
  constructing the exchange,
    talk-in-interaction and, 127–133
  high-quality exchanges, 120,
    126, 128, 133, 137
  leadership-making model, three-stage
    process of, 121–122
  leadership-style research and, 119
  life stories and, 127–128, 136
  low-quality exchanges, 120,
    126, 128, 137
  measurement problems and, 120
  narrative basis of, 121–137
  narrative possibilities in, 120–121
  narrative resources,
    Discourse/interpretative
    repertoire and, 133–137
  relationship development, dialectical
    approaches to, 122
  uniqueness paradox/narrative
    reflection in stories,
    123–127
Leader-member relations, viii, 24, 119
  See also Disciplinary power;
    Interactional processes;
    Leader-member exchange
    (LMX) theory; Membership
    categorization
Leader processes, viii
  managerial roles and, 1–2
  paradoxes of leadership, 3
  See also Discursive leadership;
    Leadership psychology;
    Leadership studies
Leadership, vii, viii
  authentic leadership, 4, 5
  constructionist stance on, 4–5

definition of, 4–6
gender and, vii, viii
meaning management and, 2, 6
practical accomplishment of, 5
text function, pragmatic
    approach, 15–16
See also Discursive leadership;
    Leadership studies;
    Organizational leadership
Leadership-making model, 121–122
Leadership psychologists, 175–183
Leadership psychology, viii, ix
agency and, 12–13
communication, primary vs.
    subsidiary status of, 16–17
complementary holism and, 4
cross-disciplinary work and, 190
discursive leadership approach
    and, 3–4, 174–175
essence of leadership and, 9–10
individual/leader-centrist
    studies and, 8–9
managerial roles and, 1–2
power/influence, dualistic
    conception of, 11–12
variable analytic traditions
    and, 14–15
See also Discursive leadership;
    Executive coaching; Leadership
    studies; Self-identities
Leadership studies:
discursive leadership
    approach, 3–4
empiricist methodology and, 2
interactional processes and, 8–9
management of meaning,
    narrative and, 2
managerial roles and, 1–2
See also Discursive leadership;
    Leadership; Leadership
    psychology
Lee, J., 122
Levine, M., 54
Liden, R. C., 120, 178–179

Linguistic aspects, viii–ix
actors' language use and, 14
coding linguistic/nonlinguistic
    behaviors, 40
observational units, discursive
    approaches, 9
perceptual processing and, 41, 50
performative role of language, 5, 7
reality construction and, 77–78
speaking subjects, 80
variable analytic tradition and, 16
See also Discourse; Discourse analysis;
    Discursive leadership
Linguistic turn, 2–3
Listing activities, 68, 70
Looping effect, 170, 173
Lord, R. G., 49, 97, 98, 116
Ludeman, K., 88, 89, 90, 105
Lyons-Ruth, K., 159

Machiavelli, N., 149, 157
Macroactors, 146, 154–156
Maher, K. J., 49
Management-at-a-distance, 91, 93
Managerial roles, 1–2
management Discourses and, 77–78
management of meaning and, 2, 6
performance appraisal and, 83–84
practical author role, 5
See also Performance management
    governmentality; Performance
    management technologies; Total
    Quality Management (TQM)
Martin, J., 126
Masculinity Discourse, 88, 105–106, 107
Maslow, A., 98
Materialist critique, 143–144, 145
McDermott, R. P., 24
Meaning-centered model of
    communication, 17, 190
Meaning management, 2, 6
categories, performance of, 50
meaning creation,
    communication and, 50

reality, linguistic construction
    of, 77–78
sensemaking, categories and, 56–62
See also Communication processes;
    Sited language game
Mechanism of domination, 5
Meindl, J. R., vii, 188
Membership categorization,
    49–50, 71–72, 169
  category-bound activities and, 51
  characterization of categories
    and, 60–61
  cognitive categorization theories
    and, 50, 62
  definition of, 50–52
  hierarchical membership
    categories, 62–66
  interactive accomplishment of, 55
  interactive kind and, 169
  leader categorization theory
    and, 49
  looping effect and, 170
  meaning management/sensemaking,
    categories and, 56–62
  membership categorization
    devices, 51
  open-ended categories and, 60
  organizational coordination
    and, 52–53
  organizational role/identity
    and, 54–55
  organization conflict, multifunctional
    categories and, 72
  relevance issues and, 62–63, 66
  social identity theory and, 49
  socially situated accomplishment
    of, 51
  social structuring and, 62–66
  task structuring and, 66–71
  type categorization and, 61
  See also Self-identities
Membership categorization devices
    (MCDs), 51
Mental theater, 8, 9

Messages, 2, 6–7, 13, 26–27, 122
Michael, M., 161, 162
Millar, F. E., 24
Miller, P., 84, 92, 102
Mills, C. W., 75
Minds-in-communication view, 17
Mintzberg, H., 1, 2
Modernism, 77
Monitoring employee performance, 38–41
Montreal school, 147–149, 161,
    162, 163–164
Morgan, A. C., 159
Morgan, G., 76, 181
Mouffe, C., 99, 143, 144
Mulkay, M., 161
Multiple Discourses:
  authentic leadership and, 102–104
  leadership and, 100–102
  real-self/fake-self and, 103, 116
  resistance and, 108
Mumby, D. K., 105, 106, 108

Nahum, J. P., 159
Narcissistic alpha males, 107
Narrating the self, 100
Narrative, 2, 5, 6
  ideological control and, 121
  social actions in-the-telling
    and, 121
  storytelling performances and, 121
  See also Narrative analyses (NA)
Narrative analyses (NA), 198
  narrative schemas and,
    32–38, 147, 149
  structural narratology, 33–34
  See also Leader-member exchange
    (LMX) theory
Neo-charismatic leadership
    theories, viii, 6, 77, 78, 79, 141–143
  actor-network theory and, 142,
    144–150, 160–162
  charismatic propensity and, 142
  hybrid agency and, 142, 145, 147,
    148–149

material mediations and,
143–144, 145
Montreal school and,
147–149, 161
narrative schemas and, 147, 149
relational-legal authority and, 142
revised actor-network theory,
leadership and, 149–150
translation function and,
145–146, 147
See also Giuliani leadership case
example
Networks. *See* Actor-network
theory (ANT)
Newton, T., 84
Normalizing judgment, 81–82,
84, 91, 93
Novak, M., 171

Objectification, 79–83, 85, 92, 93
Observational units, 8, 9
Obstfeld, D., 56, 57, 61, 187
Ochs, E., 127
Ohio State Leadership Studies,
viii, 10, 119
Oliver, C., 167, 174
Ontological units, 8, 9
Operant conditioning theory, 38, 40
Operant Supervisory Taxonomy and
Index, 40
Optimal human functioning, 98
Organizational coordination, 52–54
Organizational leadership, vii-viii
change, mastery of, 78,
114, 115, 171
discursive template and, 171
gender in organizations and,
105–108, 115
improvisational abilities, repertoire
diversity and, 115–116
institutionalized form of
intelligibility and, 112–113
language, performative role
of, 5, 77–78

See also Discursive leadership; Leader-
member exchange (LMX)
theory; Leadership; Performance
management technologies;
Team-based organizations
Organizational role/identity, 54–55
Organizing process, 13–14, 23, 44–45
See also Interactional processes
Orlikowski, W. J., 44
Osborn, R. N., 181
Oswick, C., 6

Parker, K., 101
Participative decision-making
model, 169
Perceptions, 41, 49
Performance appraisal, 76, 83–84,
90, 91, 93
Performance management
governmentality, 81, 90–92, 93
Performance management
technologies, 83, 90, 91
executive coaching, 85–90
performance appraisal, 83–84
resistance, power spread and, 89–90
self-discipline/self-regulation and, 90
360-degree feedback, 84–85
See also Disciplinary power;
Performance management
governmentality
Performance monitoring research,
38–41, 45
Phillips, J. S., 49
Platow, M. J., 49
Polyvocality, 173
Poole, P. P., 38
Positive psychology, 98, 103, 174
Postmodernism, 7, 11, 98, 99
Poststructuralism, 11, 14, 99, 106, 107, 174
Potter, J., 11, 42, 109
Power/knowledge relations, 81,
91, 92, 98
Power processes:
constraint forces and, 32

critical discourse analysis and, 197
encompassing vs. dualistic
        conceptions of, 11–12
privilege and, 106
resistance, power effects and, 78
technologies of power, 81–83, 93
See also Agency; Disciplinary power;
        Foucauldian analyses
Practical authorship, 5, 56
Practical discursive grammar,
        172–173, 174
Praxis in discursive leadership, 167–174
Prebles, E. A., 123
Prisoner's Dilemma game, 56–57
Problem setting, 66–67, 68, 70–71, 168
Promotion decisions, 83–84
Psathas, G., 55
Psychology. *See* Executive coaching;
        Leadership psychology;
        Self-identities; Trait theory of
        leadership
Public reality, 78–79
Putnam, L., 185–186

Rabinow, P., 78, 80
Realist conceptions of truth, 1, 2
    agency, conception of, 14
    complementary holism and, 4
    essence of leadership and, 10
    public reality, 78–79
    reality construction processes, 6, 77
    reality-defining activity/sensemaking,
        categories and, 56–62
    relativism and, 14
Real-self/fake-self, 103, 116
Redundant message patterns, 27, 28
Reed, M. I., 143, 144, 149
Reflexive agency, 12–14, 100, 173–174
Relational authenticity, 106
Relational control analyses, 26–29
Relational focus. *See* Communication;
        Interactional processes; Leader-
        member exchange (LMX) theory
Relativism, 14, 143, 144

Relevance issues, 62–63, 66
Repertoires. *See* Interpretative repertoires
Representational theories of knowledge, 2
Research. *See* Leadership psychology;
        Leadership studies
Resistance, 12, 78, 85, 89–90, 93
    agency, space of action and, 99
    gendered identity work and, 107, 108
    leader resistance, 108
Rhetorical presence, 37–38, 45
Roberts, K. H., 28
Robichaud, D., 63, 65, 147
Robinson, V. M. J., 6, 13, 23, 32, 67
Rogers, C., 98
Rogers, L. E., 24, 26
Roles:
    author role, 146–147, 154
    macroactor role, 146, 154–156
    organizational role/identity, 54–55
    See also Managerial roles;
        Membership categorization
Rorty, R., 4, 11, 174
Rosch, E., 49
Rose, N., 84, 92, 102
Roth, D. R., 24

Sacks, H., 30, 50
Salaman, G., 77
Sanders, R. E., 40, 41, 168
Sargent, L., 4
Sarr, R. A., 56, 113, 171
Schank, R., 38, 126
Schegloff, E. A., 13, 16, 30, 51, 55,
        62, 63, 178
Schemas. *See* Narrative analyses;
        Self-identities
Schematic understanding, 41
Schön, D. A., 66, 168
Scripts, 38
    behavioral scripts, 38
    breach formulations and, 41–42
    cognitive scripts, 38
    descriptions, constructed
        nature of, 42–43

inferred leader behavioral script
    analysis and, 38–41
schematic understanding and, 41
script formulations, 41–44, 45
See also AMC sequence; Interactional
    processes
Secord, P. F., 33
Seidler, V. J., 107
Self-discipline/self-regulation, 90
Self-identities, 97, 114–115
    agency, space of action and, 99–100
    authentic leadership and,
        98, 100, 102–104
    contingent identification and, 99
    continuity in self-interpretation
        and, 100
    dislocation and, 99
    follower self-identity theory
        and, 97–98
    gender, identity work and, 104–108
    interpretative repertoires, subject
        positioning and, 109–114
    knowledge, situated selves and, 97
    multiple Discourses and, 100–104
    narrating the self, reflexive
        interpretation and, 100
    real-self/fake-self and, 103, 116
    self-construction and, 98, 99, 102, 109
    sited language games and, 99
    working self-concept and, 97–98
    working subjectivity and, 98–99,
        107, 109, 115
    See also Leadership psychology;
        Organizational leadership
Seligman, M. E. P., 103
Sensemaking, 56–62, 147–148, 173
September 11, 2001. *See* Giuliani
    leadership case example
Sequence. *See* Conversation analysis (CA);
    Interactional processes; Leader-
    member exchange (LMX) theory
Shamir, B., 127, 142
Sheep, M. L., 72
Shils, E., 142, 158

Shotter, J., 5, 56, 57
Sigman, S. J., 5
Sims, H. P., Jr., 2
Singleton, V., 162
Sited language games, 99, 115–116
Sitkin, S. B., 126
Situational theory of leadership, 9–10
Smircich, L., 181
Social constructionism, viii-ix
    discursive approaches and, 5–6
    essence of leadership and, 10
    leadership, definition of, 4–5
    relativism and, 14
    See also Actor-network theory (ANT);
        Montreal school
Social exchange theory. *See* Leader-
    member exchange (LMX) theory
Social identity theory (SIT), 49–50
Social structuring:
    charismatic leadership and, 160
    membership categorization
        and, 62–66
    See also Social constructionism
Sommerkamp, P., 171
Space of action, 99–100, 136
Sparrowe, R., 101
Speech act schematics (SAS),
        33, 45, 147, 148, 194
    command presence and, 37
    narrative schema and, 33–34
    rhetorical presence and, 37–38
    task examples, 34–37
    types of, 33
Spicer, A., 108
Srivastva, S., 169
Staw, B. M., 18
Stories, 33, 121
    See also Leader-member exchange
        (LMX) theory
Structural narratology, 33–34
Subjectivity, 10, 11, 76, 84, 86
    sited language games and, 99
    working subjectivity, 98–99, 100,
        107, 115

See also Foucauldian analyses;
  Self-identities
Subjects, 79–83, 93
  subject positioning, interpretative
    repertoires and, 109–114
  See also Foucauldian analyses;
    Self-identities
Submissive symmetry pattern, 28
Surrogate-driven technologies. *See*
    Executive coaching; 360-degree
    feedback
Surveillance capabilities, 81–82, 91, 93, 108
  See also Disciplinary power;
    Performance management
    technologies
Survey research, 15, 24, 32, 121, 122
Sutcliffe, K. M., 56, 57, 61, 187
Symbolic agency, 56, 57–59, 143–144

Talk-in-interaction, 127–133
Task performance, 13, 23, 32
  employee performance monitoring
    strategy, 38–41
  narrative schemas and, 34–37
  See also Performance management
    technologies; Task structure
Task structure, viii
  categorical contrasts and, 67
  constraint sets and, 67–68
  listing activities of actors
    and, 68, 70
  membership categorization
    and, 66–71
  practical translation problem
    and, 68–70
  problem setting and, 66–67, 68,
    70–71
  structure category in, 67–68
  See also Task performance
Taylorism, 79
Taylor, J. R., 63, 65, 147, 148, 149, 187
Team-based organizations, viii
Technologies of power, 81–83, 93
Temporal form. *See* Interactional processes

Texts, 9
  context and, 15
  forms of, 15–16
  local knowledge and, 15
  textual analysis vs. variable
    analysis, 16
  See also Communication; Discourse;
    Discursive leadership
Thin actors, 10–11
Thomas, G. F., 44, 114
Thomas, R. J., 7, 77, 170, 171
360-degree feedback, 76, 84–85, 86, 88,
    89, 90, 93
Total Quality Management (TQM), 42–44,
    57–60, 77, 79, 110, 113, 114, 171
Townley, B., 81
Tracy, K., 7, 173
Tracy, S. J., 102, 103
Trait theory of leadership, viii, 9–10
  See also Self-identities
Transformational leaders, 12, 76, 78, 141
Translation function, 68–70, 92,
    145–146, 147, 155, 163
Transmission model of
    communication, 17, 190
Tretheway, A., 102, 103
Tronick, E. Z., 159
Truth:
  confession technique and,
    82–83, 86, 93
  politics/power of, 77–78
  real-self/fake-self dichotomy,
    103, 116
  See also Realist conceptions
    of truth
Tsoukas, H., 44, 113
Turn taking, 29–32, 44

Uniqueness paradox, 123–127
Untheorized/exaggerated agency, 12–14

Van Every, E., 147, 148, 187
Variable analytic tradition, 14–15, 16
Vision, 2

Weak leadership approaches, 5
Weber, M., 142
Weick, K. E., 25, 28, 34, 44, 56, 57, 61,
     120, 121, 123, 147, 156, 187
Wetherell, M., 42, 109, 112
White, H., 123
Whyte, W. H. J., 75, 170
Willmott, H., 5, 100
Wittgenstein, L., 78, 94, 99, 113

Woolgar, S., 162
Working self-concept (WSC),
     97–98
Working subjectivity, 98–99, 100,
     107, 109, 115
World Trade Center collapse. *See* Giuliani
     leadership case example

Yukl, G., 141, 142